Lawful Sins

LAWFUL SINS

Abortion Rights and Reproductive Governance in Mexico

Elyse Ona Singer

Stanford University Press
Stanford, California

STANFORD UNIVERSITY PRESS
Stanford, California

This book has been partially underwritten by the Stanford Authors Fund.
We are grateful to the Fund for its support of scholarship by first-time authors.
For more information, please see www.sup.org/authors/authorsfund

Portions of Chapter 2 were originally published in Singer, Elyse O. "Lawful Sinners: Reproductive Governance and Moral Agency around abortion in Mexico." Culture, Medicine & Psychiatry 42 (2018). Reprinted by permission of Springer Nature.

Portions of Chapter 5 were originally published in Singer, Elyse Ona, "Realizing Abortion Rights at the Margins of Legality in Mexico." Medical Anthropology: Cross-Cultural Studies in Health and Illness 38 2 (2019) and Singer, Elyse Ona. "Abortion Exile: Navigating Mexico's Fractured Abortion Landscape." Culture, Health & Sexuality: An International Journal for Research, Intervention and Care 22, no. 8 (2020). Reprinted by permission of Taylor & Francis Ltd, http.//www.tandfonline.com

Printed in the United States of America on acid-free, archival-quality paper

Library of Congress Cataloging-in-Publication Data

Names: Singer, Elyse Ona, author.
Title: Lawful sins : abortion rights and reproductive governance in Mexico
    / Elyse Ona Singer.
Description: Stanford, California : Stanford University Press, 2022. |
    Includes bibliographical references and index. |
Identifiers: LCCN 2021037151 (print) | LCCN 2021037152 (ebook) |
    ISBN 9781503615137 (cloth) | ISBN 9781503631472 (paperback) |
    ISBN 9781503631489 (ebook)
Subjects: LCSH: Abortion—Social aspects—Mexico. | Abortion—Government
    policy—Mexico. | Reproductive rights—Mexico. | Women's rights—Mexico.
    | Women—Mexico—Social conditions.
Classification: LCC HQ767.5.M6 S56 2022 (print) | LCC HQ767.5.M6 (ebook)
    | DDC 362.1988/800972—dc23
LC record available at https://lccn.loc.gov/2021037151
LC ebook record available at https://lccn.loc.gov/2021037152

Cover photo: Protest outside of Santa Marta Clinic. Photograph by author, 2014.
Cover design: Angela Moody

Typeset by Newgen North America in Adobe Garamond Pro 10.5/15

For my parents, whose love is everything.

CONTENTS

ACRONYMS

CPC   Crisis pregnancy center

EVA   Electric vacuum aspiration

ICPD   International Conference on Population and Development

ILE   Interrupción legal del embarazo; legal interruption of pregnancy

IMSS   Instituto Mexicano del Seguro Social; Mexican Social Security Institute

ISSSTE   Instituto de Seguridad y Servicios Sociales de los Trabajadores del Estado; Institute for Social Security and Services for State Workers

IUD   Intrauterine device

MOH   Ministry of Health; Secretaría de Salud

MVA   Manual vacuum aspiration

OV   Obstetric violence

PAN   Partido Acción Nacional; National Action Party

PRD   Partido de la Revolución Democrática; Party of the Democratic Revolution

PRI   Partido Revolucionaro Institucional; Institutional Revolutionary Party

Lawful Sins

INTRODUCTION

AT FIRST, I DIDN'T THINK MUCH about the sonogram images on the screens of Mexico City's public abortion clinics. The scans measured the gestational ages of women's pregnancies to ensure that they qualified for a legal abortion, which in the Mexican capital is available only up to twelve weeks. Since most women arrived early in their pregnancies, the images were blurry and opaque. I could only ever make out a pixelated gray or black blot. Dr. Rios, the medical director of Santa Marta Clinic, told me early on that women sometimes asked to see their scans. "It's morbid," she had said, taking me by surprise, "when they are coming here to *interrupt* the pregnancy." Teresa's scan showed that she was six weeks pregnant when she first visited Santa Marta in the fall of 2014, meaning she qualified for a medical abortion that would be induced pharmacologically. Dr. Rios gave her a dose of mifepristone at the clinic and sent her home with another dose of misoprostol to produce contractions and provoke an abortion.

On the day we met, Teresa had returned to the clinic for a second scan to ensure that the process was complete. No embryonic tissue remained in her uterus but she spoke of a baby that haunted her dreams, tormenting her with hazy visions of blood and flesh. "I worry that come tomorrow I will feel very guilty," she confided to me from a private room in the back of the clinic. Teresa knew that first-trimester abortion was legal and available on demand in the Mexican capital even before she went online to research options after learning she was pregnant. Disputes had captivated the entire country years earlier when proposals to legalize the procedure were introduced to the Mexico City Legislative Assembly. Back then, she recalled, everyone had an opinion on the matter. In her high school classroom she had once defended the issue in a staged debate. "It's ironic," she reflected, "to have ended up here."

As I listened to her talk, it was clear that the classroom exercise hardly captured the complicated moral calculus facing her now. That abstract question suddenly had new weight and consequence, bearing directly on the shape of her future. At twenty-three years old, she had been trying to finish the high school degree she had abandoned after the birth of her son five years earlier. The second pregnancy was an accident. As a single mother she couldn't afford a second child on the wages she earned as a cosmetics clerk in the Zócalo, Mexico City's historic square. Like many Mexican urbanites, Teresa had been raised in a Catholic family, but she rarely went to mass. Though her faith did not conform to religious rules, she had reservations about the abortion. "I did this because I couldn't have another baby at this moment in my life," she told me, "but I still believe that as human beings, what grows inside of us is also human."

I didn't know how to respond, but it felt wrong to sit there silently as my tape recorder memorized her dilemma. So I told her what I thought I would want to hear: that many women had made similar decisions and that abortion was her right. "That's the problem," she replied, resisting my clumsy attempt at comfort. "Like the social workers here at the clinic said, there are many women in Mexico who come for an abortion not once, but two, three times. They use it like a contraceptive method. I think it should be legal, but not for people who are *so irresponsible*."

After that day at Santa Marta I never saw Teresa again. Along with about a dozen other women who had crowded into the small hilltop clinic that morning, she disappeared back into the vast city, anonymous in its multitudes. I was left with a snapshot of her life, like the ultrasound scans, a moment with no before or after. In some ways, reflecting on our conversation later felt like looking at the same hazy images I tried to decipher on the screen; even the details of her face and hair had blurred in my memory. But there was something important there. I had thought that emphasizing the prevalence and legality of abortion might ease her concerns in some small way. Yet abortion, she seemed to suggest, was not a procedure that *should* be ordinary. And its redefinition as a juridical right and a free health service in the Mexican capital, she had implied, was having precisely that effect: women were beginning to devalue their procreative potential. Perhaps that was what Dr. Rios had meant when she questioned her patients' "morbid" desires to *see* the pregnancies they intended to interrupt.

I had not anticipated these kinds of responses when I moved to Mexico City to research abortion politics early in graduate school. As a student of anthropology, I wanted to understand the aftermath of a landmark 2007 reform that legalized voluntary abortion in the national capital, making it the only place in the country where the procedure was permitted on an elective basis. When I arrived for long-term fieldwork, the reform was seven years old. Tens of thousands of women had visited one of the public and private abortion clinics that opened throughout the city as a result. Everyone knew someone—an aunt or sister, a daughter or friend—who had obtained a legal abortion, but many people still talked about it in hushed voices, on the edges of conversations.

When the reform passed, people around the world noticed. Latin America has long been hostile to reproductive rights and is home to some of the world's strictest abortion laws. Across the region the procedure provokes bitter controversy, even though it is widely practiced. The 2007 reform made Mexico City one of just three places in Latin America where voluntary abortion was allowed at the time, in addition to Cuba and Guyana. For the first time in Mexican history women were afforded the right to interrupt their pregnancies up to twelve weeks—for any reason—without legal repercussions. Even more striking, they could now access the procedure for free through a new program provided by the Mexico City Ministry of Health (MOH) called "the ILE program" for its Spanish name *interrupción legal del embarazo* (legal interruption of pregnancy).[1] The reform had resounding implications. Beyond guaranteeing abortion rights, it promised to make the procedure widely accessible, even to the poorest sectors of the population who had long been unable to purchase illegal private abortion care available to wealthier women.[2]

Wherever one stood on the question of abortion, the reform was a watershed. Many Mexicans celebrated a landmark victory for women's rights and citizenship, hailing passage of the law as evidence of a consolidation of democratic processes in the country. At the same time, critics assailed the conferral of abortion rights as a threat to the Mexican family and religious notions of sacred life. The backlash was organized and immediate. Even after the Mexican Supreme Court defended the law against challenges levied by the National Human Rights Commission and the Attorney General's Office, resistance followed.[3] Within two years, sixteen of thirty-two states had modified their constitutions to redefine "life" as beginning from conception to preclude replication of the reform elsewhere across the country.

Despite strident resistance from all directions, women flocked to the ILE program to obtain safe and subsidized abortion care. Most, like Teresa, were residents of Mexico City, but some arrived from far-flung states, desperate for an affordable way to interrupt pregnancies that for a variety of reasons they could not bear to term. Within the first year alone thousands of women had obtained an ILE procedure through one of the public clinics, and demand on the ILE program would only grow in the years to come.

I didn't have such a clear picture of this landscape when I met Teresa at Santa Marta Clinic back in 2014. I had moved to Mexico City to understand how people thought about legal abortion in a country that is home to the second-largest Catholic population in the world. I wanted to know if women and health care providers saw abortion as a right, or in some other way, and how they reconciled its legalization with Catholic proscriptions and their own moral misgivings. Even though I had read everything I could about abortion in preparation for the research, being there—embedded in the whirlwind of clinical life in a country that was not my own—was overwhelming. At first, I could make sense of what I saw only through frameworks I had developed elsewhere.

Much of what I knew about abortion at the time was rooted in the American Midwest, where I had worked part-time as an abortion counselor while developing this study as a graduate student at Washington University in St. Louis. Back then, I spent my time outside class driving my Honda across the Mississippi to a lonely industrial city on the western edge of Illinois. Granite City is home to Hope Clinic, which opened one year after the Supreme Court decision in *Roe v. Wade* legalized first-trimester abortion across the United States in 1973. A few times a week I stayed with the director of counseling well into the evening to learn what things had been like in the aftermath of *Roe*.

At the time, she said, it was impossible not to have a position on abortion. Protesters assembled outside the clinic every week, squeezing their bodies together to block women and staff from entering. She and her coworkers rehearsed drills to prepare for acid spills, arson, kidnapping, and other forms of political violence visited upon abortion clinics across the country. Going to work every day meant exposing oneself to tremendous danger. The most alarming attack came in 1982. The leaves were just starting to dry up that year when a firebomb exploded at the clinic. Only a ghost of the building was left; ash and char dusted the vacant lot. A few months later the clinic owner and his wife were kidnapped at gunpoint by a group that called themselves "the Army of God." The couple spent a week as captives in an army bunker somewhere in the Midwest. "We didn't know if they were going to be found dead or alive," the director of counseling told me, "or whether they would be sent to us in a box piece by piece. We didn't know if we'd be picked off one by one from our homes at night." A decade later police dug up the Army of God manual in the backyard of a woman who had attempted to murder Dr. George Tiller, the celebrated Kansan abortion provider who was eventually assassinated by a different antiabortion protester in 2009.[4]

By the time I started training as a counselor at Hope Clinic in 2012, the violence had died down and the building had been entirely reconstructed with cinder blocks and ballistic windows, like a midcentury fallout shelter. But the attacks haunted it. Old-timers recounted the stories in meticulous detail. Protesters still stalked the entrance each morning, though by then they had abandoned their firebombs and acid. Most waved gory images of dismembered fetuses and heckled women and clinic staff as they entered. For the midwestern providers I came to know, the protesters and their evocative images redoubled their commitments. While I was a newer recruit, they had been at this for years. Most saw themselves on the front lines of an enduring political struggle for women's rights and equality. It didn't take more than a few weeks in their company for me to start referring to the protesters as "the antis." Their terms became mine.

In Mexico's public abortion clinics the lines weren't as clean. At first, I expected the ILE providers and me to share a common vocabulary grounded in "prochoice" politics and a mutual understanding of the boundary between "us" and "the antis." When protesters convened once a week outside the clinic to stage a communal prayer, I assumed the providers would see them as antagonists. But before long it was clear that the Mexican clinicians did not generally think of themselves as a feminist vanguard. To my surprise, much of their work in the clinic entailed discouraging women from seeking subsequent abortions. *Women need to protect themselves*, the clinicians insisted; *they have to take responsibility; abortion is not a game.* Some providers agreed with the protesters that God is the moral arbiter of life and death, even as they facilitated abortions day after day. "I consider it a life," a clinical social worker called Carolina once told me candidly. "But I can't interfere in other people's decisions. I have to be neutral, professional." Unlike my midwestern coworkers, few of the ILE providers had been abortion advocates prior to the Mexico City reform. Even afterwards they rarely spoke about their work in political terms unless I pressed them. Embedding myself in the ILE clinics meant balancing my understandings against the realities of a new and very different context. Intellectually, I struggled to accommodate these differences. Early on in my research the Mexican clinics could seem a world apart from those in the US Midwest.

At the same time, the history of abortion in Mexico is intimately connected to the history of abortion in the United States. Mexico was an indispensable resource for American women seeking abortion services that were largely unavailable at home before *Roe vs. Wade*. In the middle of the twentieth century hundreds of thousands of American women traveled south to procure abortions from underground Mexican providers.[5] After *Roe* the direction of travel reversed and Mexican women who could afford it began to head north for the procedure, evading restrictive laws and avoiding the underground clinics back home.[6] Today, more than four decades after *Roe*, abortion politics have reached a "crisis point" in the United States.[7] In recent years more than half of US states have passed laws to restrict abortion access, and now, with the conservative majority on the Supreme Court, abortion rights are even more precarious. As more and more US clinics succumb to regulatory and funding constraints, women have once again begun flowing into Mexico to obtain abortions. Recent media reports document the passage of Texan women into northern Mexico to acquire the abortifacient drug misoprostol.[8] The drug, whose official use is for gastric ulcers, is regulated in the United States but can be purchased over the counter in Mexico.[9] Circular patterns of abortion travel between the two countries were an indication for me of some of the connections across these apparently disparate spheres.

Lawful Sins is an account of how recent transformations in Mexican reproductive governance bear on the ways that women experience their bodies and their relationship to the Mexican state and its public health institutions. The book follows the experiences of women seeking to interrupt their pregnancies, public health personnel charged with delivering a stigmatized service in the context of overwhelming demand and limited state resources, and the activist networks that have mobilized to expand abortion access beyond existing legal and geographic constraints. The chapters ahead show how a picture of contemporary debates on abortion is incomplete without Mexico, tracing aspects of reproductive politics and care that unsettle prevailing liberal frameworks developed in the Global North.

While this book tells the story of the aftermath of abortion legalization in Mexico City, it gestures to global questions about gender and citizenship, divine versus individual control of the body, and the politics of health care. Teresa's abortion was one of around fifty-six million that are induced across the world each year, making the procedure a common aspect of women's reproductive lives.[10] Although Teresa struggled with ambivalence, research shows that most women do not regret ending their pregnancies.[11] A mixture of feelings ranging from relief and hope to sadness can accompany abortion, depending on the circumstances, and in some parts of the world the procedure is considered unremarkable.[12] At the same time, perhaps because it taps into ethical quandaries about when life begins and ends and who is authorized to draw these boundaries, abortion can raise hard individual and communal questions, such as who has ownership over the body, what makes a person, and who bears responsibility for nascent life.[13] The disavowal of a pregnancy is imagined in many parts of the world to cut against women's biological and cultural imperative to propagate persons and societies, to help us continue anew as humans. Contests over abortion, write anthropologists Elise Andaya and Joanna Mishtal, "trigger wider social debates about gender roles and expectations of the (female) life course, shifting ideas of moral personhood, and contested economic, cultural, and political futures."[14]

Despite its global prevalence, abortion is arguably the single most controversial medical procedure that exists, representing what Joan Caivano and Jane Marcus-Delgado have described as "one of the most loudly contested public struggles in the contemporary global arena."[15] This is especially true in Latin America, where the Catholic Church wields tremendous political and popular power.[16] An astonishing 97 percent of women throughout the region live in countries with restrictive abortion laws, and the procedure is banned entirely in six Latin American countries.[17] It is no secret that criminalization does not stop women from terminating pregnancies they cannot bear to term. Harsh laws push women to obtain illicit and often dangerous procedures, driving up associated morbidity and mortality. In fact, Latin America has the highest rates of abortion in the world, with as many as 6.5 million abortions induced there annually.[18] Even though abortion is remarkably safe when performed in suitable conditions, around 760,000 women across the region suffer entirely preventable abortion-related injuries each year, amounting to what some scholars have called a "clandestine epidemic."[19]

As a Catholic-majority country, Mexico is considered a "strategic point" for global antiabortion activism.[20] The procedure has been banned there since the late nineteenth century, when the first penal codes established after national independence defined it as a crime.[21] Despite the secular values enshrined in the national Constitution of 1917, voluntary abortion remained illegal across the country throughout the twentieth century.[22] Today, rape is the only legal exception for abortion that applies in every state, though many states have additional exemptions, permitting the procedure when necessary to save a woman's life, in the case of fetal anomaly, and, less commonly, for economic reasons.[23] Before a string of reforms loosened constraints on the procedure in the capital beginning in the year 2000, Mexico City's abortion laws had not been revised since 1931.[24] This punitive legal environment has made unsafe abortion the fourth cause of women's death nationally.[25] But the deadly burden is borne most by the poor, racialized, and young. Abortion in Mexico is what Adriana Petryna and Karolina Follis have called "a fault line of survival."[26] This fault cuts across the country in such a way that "the poorest, least educated, and/or indigenous women are nine times more likely to undergo an unsafe abortion" than their wealthier, more educated, and nonindigenous counterparts.[27]

As these figures make plain, there is a good deal at stake in the Mexican abortion debate. Abortion distills long-standing contests over the role of women in society and the place of the Catholic Church in public and political life. Women's bodies have been transformed, in the past few decades, into a "political battlefield" for powerful actors and institutions interested in advancing contrasting moral visions for the future of Mexican society.[28] Feminist activists and women's health advocates place abortion rights at the center of ongoing struggles to secure women's status as citizens afforded equal rights in a secular democracy.[29] The Catholic hierarchy and its political allies in Mexico's right-wing National Action Party (PAN) see abortion as the destruction of "innocent human life." The extension of abortion rights, for these groups, represents an assault on religious visions of family, femininity, and the nation itself. The contested cultural values wrapped up in this simple medical procedure amount to a contemporary "culture war."[30] At the heart of this fierce dispute is the very definition of Mexico and what it means to be Mexican today.

Societal clashes came to a head in April of 2007 with the transformation of voluntary first-trimester abortion from a punishable crime to a protected right of women in Mexico City and a new element of public health care services available there. The reform represented the culmination of over four decades of feminist activism to strengthen gender equity as part of a broader national movement for democratic governance. Advocates declared the law change a historic victory for women's health and equality, and an important step in the ongoing struggle to strengthen democratic processes more generally.[31] For supporters, passage of the law reconfigured women's relationship to the Mexican state, signaling a new era for the production of women's citizenship.[32] Yet little is known about how women make sense of their new reproductive freedoms or how configurations of care across the public ILE clinics shape the materialization of abortion rights.[33] What happened after the law was implemented? And what might be lost in the gap between abortion rights and experience?

For Teresa, a resident of one of Mexico City's working-class boroughs, seeking an abortion raised serious questions about her social and moral responsibilities as a woman, a mother, a person raised in the Catholic faith, and a member of Mexican society. Even after the procedure became legal in the capital, the idea that abortion existed as a transcendent right did not hold up for her, though she herself had sought the procedure. Nor did the legal status of abortion resolve the moral qualms she had about parting with her pregnancy. She knew she could not make ends meet with another child, but she did not know how to face her existing son, or herself, after disavowing her second pregnancy. How, she wondered that day at the clinic, would she answer to God after rejecting a child he had sent? What separated her from the "irresponsible" women whose abortion decisions she, and the ILE clinicians, condemned? For the public health workers staffing the ILE clinics too, the introduction of abortion services posed a number of thorny questions. How many abortions can a woman seek? What happens if she does not arrive in time to meet the twelve-week gestational limit on ILE care? When is the interruption of a pregnancy justified, and when is it indefensible? And what obligations, if any, do women who avail themselves of a publicly funded abortion acquire upon accessing these services?

The extension of abortion rights in the Mexican capital has afforded new reproductive possibilities for hundreds of thousands of women and averted immeasurable suffering. It is hard to overstate the significance of these outcomes. At the same time, the transformation of abortion into a juridical right and a new aspect of public health care services has instigated a process of moral negotiation that women, health workers, and ordinary people must navigate with little scaffolding. This book works to reorient prevailing scholarly and advocacy perspectives that approach abortion rights as a central pillar of women's citizenship in liberal societies. The following chapters cohere around one central claim: while women in Mexico today have new reproductive options not available to them just over a decade ago, they are also subject to the expanded reach of the Mexican state and the Catholic Church over their bodies and reproductive lives. In the pages to come, I place law, religion, and biomedicine as moral orders within the same analytic frame to consider how people grapple with the moral and practical dimensions of pregnancy disruption in ways that rights concepts may not fully resolve.

The panorama of Mexican abortion law has continued to transform since I finished the research behind this book. The southern state of Oaxaca became the second place to legalize elective first-trimester abortion in the fall of 2019, followed by the states of Hidalgo and Veracruz in the summer of 2021. While I was putting the final touches on this manuscript, moreover, the Mexican Supreme Court determined in a watershed vote that the imposition of criminal penalties for abortion is unconstitutional, a historic move that will undoubtedly transform the legal landscape in the years to come. At the time that Teresa sought the procedure, Mexico City was the only place in the country where voluntary abortion was permitted. She is one of roughly 235,000 women from across the country who has accessed an abortion through the public sector ILE program at the time of this writing. Her experience, and the broader story I tell here, capture the aftermath of a historic reform that has transformed the national landscape with reverberations across the region and around the world.

REPRODUCTIVE GOVERNANCE

Teresa's journey through the ILE program, and the questions this experience occasioned for her, are entangled in processes that anthropologists Lynn Morgan and Elizabeth Roberts have labeled "reproductive governance."[34] The concept calls attention to the ways in which a variety of actors—such as states, religious and biomedical institutions, financial organizations, and international agencies—seek to manage reproductive behavior and population dynamics using law, moral arguments, economic incentives, and coercive means. From an anthropological perspective, reproduction is a dynamic field encompassing the biological dimensions of procreation, as well as the "intimate intergenerational material and affective labour that is generative of citizens, and that serve[s] to reproduce membership of, and belonging to, states, nations, societies and thus of 'citizenship' itself."[35] As the process that folds individual bodies into the body politic, reproduction is a key site to trace the deployment of biopower, the collection of techniques for managing populations. Scholars in the Foucauldian tradition contend that reproduction connects the human body to the vitality of the species. Across the world, it thus becomes a problematical field in which different actors and institutions seek to intercede, a space that mediates connections between "the individual and the collective, the technological and the political, the legal and the ethical."[36]

Throughout the twentieth century, governments around the globe intervened in reproductive practices to regulate national birthrates and/or enhance population "quality."[37] Draconian measures such as China's one-child policy and Romania's categorical abortion ban, designed to curtail and stimulate population growth respectively, exemplify some of the more extreme means by which states have interceded in the reproduction of individual and political bodies. But reproductive governance unfurls in subtler ways as well; as Mounia El Kotni and I have argued elsewhere, it is "enfolded in clinical care, public discourse, and media messaging."[38] Efforts to regulate reproduction are rarely enacted consistently across the population. Reproductive subjectivities are stratified along axes of class, race, ethnicity, and gender in such a way that the reproduction of certain groups is accorded value while that of others is disparaged.[39] These processes unfold in accordance with state objectives for crafting the body politic. In Italy, to take one contemporary example, against intense governmental panic about the country's "demographic winter," scholars have pointed to contradictions in how Italian women have been enjoined to boost fertility even as immigrant women's "excessive" fertility comes under heightened scrutiny and control.[40] Hailed in such governing processes are subjects whose differential reproductive behavior is simultaneously construed as "irrational, irresponsible, and even immoral."[41] Reproductive governance captures the idea that ostensibly personal reproductive decisions carried out in the intimate domain of family life are inexorably bound up with wider political agendas and economic processes.[42]

The legalization of abortion in Mexico City reflects dramatic changes in reproductive governance sweeping across Latin America in recent years. Biopolitical regimes shifted considerably throughout the region during the twentieth century. By the Cold War era, concerns about "overpopulation" had come to supplant turn-of-the-century eugenic obsessions with improving the racial stock.[43] More recently, vertical measures of population control that dominated Latin American reproductive policy in the closing decades of the twentieth century have given way to a focus on the protection of reproductive rights and health. This shift mirrors global transformations wrought by two major world conferences on population and development in the 1990s—the International Conference on Population and Development (ICPD) in Cairo and the Fourth World United Nations Conference on Women in Beijing. The conferences defined reproductive and sexual rights as *human rights* for the first time in an international agreement, marking them as a priority in international development agendas.[44] Endorsed by nearly two hundred countries—including Mexico—conference documents ushered in a global paradigm shift in moral regimes of reproduction, replacing Cold War agendas of population control and neo-Malthusian demographic targets with a commitment to safeguard the reproductive health and rights of individuals and couples.[45]

Though Mexican feminists had been pushing for abortion reform for at least two decades by the time the Cairo and Beijing programs of action were published, conference agreements afforded a new discursive strategy to frame their advocacy work. A network of nongovernmental organizations in the capital collaborated throughout the 1990s to transform public discourse on abortion in terms of liberal notions of women's human rights and democratic citizenship, building on a longer national history of feminist activism for "voluntary motherhood."[46] Activists repositioned abortion from a religious or moral question—Are you for or against abortion?—to a pressing public health and social justice issue, calling on the Mexican government to abide by its international obligations.[47] Their campaign was to make abortion safe, legal, and rare, a position sometimes critiqued by US feminists for stigmatizing abortion. In a national context of extreme political and religious opposition, this framing was a strategic move to appease antiabortion factions.[48]

Struggles for abortion reform in the national capital tapped into wider popular demands for democratic governance at the tail end of a seventy-year stretch of single-party authoritarian rule by the Institutional Revolutionary Party (PRI), broken only in the year 2000. A national debt crisis in the 1980s had left many families in economic peril. As the state reduced social services to cut costs, women were burdened with more care work, and access to safe, legal abortion became more necessary than ever. Appeals for abortion reform gained traction as well in the context of growing popular skepticism toward the Catholic hierarchy. The exposure of clerical sexual abuse scandals throughout the 1990s left many Mexicans dubious about the church and its rigid stance on reproductive matters. Deploying the human rights framework was an effective way to wrest abortion from the moral jurisdiction of the Catholic Church and reposition it as a basic component of citizenship in a budding secular democracy.[49]

The strategy proved effective. Abortion laws in Mexico City were relaxed through a series of incremental legislative reforms enacted in 2000 and 2004 that expanded the circumstances in which abortion was admissible, paving the way for the full legalization of voluntary first-trimester abortion in 2007. Rather than simply expanding the conditions that escaped criminal punishment, the 2007 reform prioritized a woman's right to decide on the course of a pregnancy, regardless of the circumstances.[50] On a practical level, the reform accomplished a number of important changes.[51] Key among them, it redefined what abortion *is* by renaming the procedure "legal interruption of pregnancy" (ILE) when performed within the first twelve weeks of gestation. The law also required that first-trimester abortion services be offered on demand and without cost to Mexico City residents and for a small fee based on economic need to nonresidents, establishing the legal directive for construction of the ILE program within the local MOH. On a political level, the 2007 reform catapulted Mexico's capital to the vanguard of struggles for reproductive rights in the region, offering a model for other contexts to follow.

While advocacy narratives celebrate the 2007 reform for transforming women's relationship to the Mexican state, a closer look inside the ILE clinics reveals a morally charged setting in which the ethics of abortion and the terms of women's citizenship are contested in everyday encounters between public health providers and the poor and working-class women who rely on state care. To begin with, a range of institutional entailments circumscribe access to the ILE program, preventing many women from obtaining the care they seek. Women who cannot arrive at an ILE clinic in time to meet the twelve-week gestational limit, moreover, are regularly turned away and left to resolve their pregnancies alone. Inside the ILE clinics, several conditions attach to abortion rights as health workers encourage their patients to embody responsibility in their reproductive lives by avoiding recourse to subsequent abortions.

Although activists anticipated that the 2007 reform would trigger a broader liberalization of abortion laws across the country, outside the capital the abortion situation has become more dire in the aftermath of the Mexico City reform. Opponents have adopted the rights framework to advance their own moral vision of abortion as a mortal sin and an assault on fetal life, constricting reproductive freedoms across twenty states. Many women outside the capital do not know which legal exceptions for abortion apply to them, and even if they do, accessing the procedure can be tremendously difficult.[52] The onslaught of constitutional "life amendments" across several states has generated widespread uncertainty among women and health personnel. Some health care workers are reluctant to provide abortions, even when they are legal, for fear of backlash from medical colleagues or because doing so conflicts with their religious or moral commitments. Research conducted in the states shows that women who present at hospitals in situations of miscarriage are increasingly subject to harassment, interrogation, and prosecution by hospital personnel who suspect them of illegally inducing abortions.[53]

A variety of nongovernmental organizations and feminist accompaniment networks have mobilized, in this patchwork of legal regimes, to compensate for the inequities in obtaining an abortion that so many women still face. Some groups, like the organization I call Conéctame, offer a combination of financial and logistical support to assist women in arriving at the capital from other states to access ILE services. Another organization in the conservative state of Guanajuato, which I call Las Fuertes, openly challenges stringent abortion laws by providing abortion accompaniment services in a context of near-total criminalization. Increasingly, women across the country purchase misoprostol over the counter to induce medical abortions on their own, yet information on safe and appropriate use is not always accessible. While misoprostol has been available in Mexican pharmacies since 1985, many pharmacists either do not know how to use it for abortifacient purposes or are reluctant to offer this information to women for fear of breaking the law.[54] While alternatives to the ILE program therefore exist, since 2007 conditions of unequal abortion access have pushed women from every Mexican state to the capital to interrupt their pregnancies. Yet not everyone can make the journey.

Women's ability to shape the course of their reproductive lives depends entirely on where they live and whether they are able to navigate the labyrinthine legal, temporal, and geographic constraints that define abortion in Mexico today. It is poor women who shoulder the health costs of this restrictive legal landscape, as they are less able than their wealthier counterparts to hire private doctors to perform the procedure clandestinely or travel to the US or other countries for legal abortion care.[55] This contrast conveys the discrepancy between public policy and everyday reality that has long characterized the abortion situation in Mexico, favoring the well-resourced who float above the law. The extension of abortion rights in the national capital, then, would seem to be an entirely positive move creating safer outcomes and freer citizens. Yet rights, as Teresa's story suggests, can take women only so far.

THE TROUBLE WITH RIGHTS

Even though resolutions at the ICPD in Cairo established reproductive rights as *human rights*, the question of abortion was left unsettled. A controversy arose at the conference over how abortion fit within new global agendas and whether it constituted a human right. Conference resolutions ultimately pressed states to avert abortion-related morbidity and mortality through enhanced access to family planning and the provision of postabortion care in contexts where abortion was criminalized, and to make abortion safe and accessible in places where it was legal. Yet the final program of action fell short of defining abortion as a universal human right. "The great contradiction contained in [the ICPD] document," observes Marge Berer, "and the reason why in the short run it was such a let-down on the subject of abortion, is that although it urged on page after page that reproductive health and fertility regulation were to be considered as reproductive rights, the safety and legalization of one of the most commonly used methods of fertility regulation—and a major cause of avoidable mortality and morbidity in women—was eschewed."[56] Nevertheless, the human right to abortion has enjoyed an active, if vexed, "social life" in the ensuing years, as advocates around the world continue to mobilize on its behalf.[57]

The strategy of abortion rights advocates in Mexico and across Latin America reflects the recent ascent of *human rights* as a global metanarrative. Scholars disagree on the precise moment when human rights rose to dominance, but since the 1990s the framework has become what Mark Goodale calls "the most (necessarily) axiomatic of (neo)liberalism's global discourses."[58] Despite the positive associations conjured by human rights, anthropologists have been circumspect.[59] For local communities and grassroots activists, the framework affords a universally legible "idiom" to articulate local concerns and a global set of standards to hold their governments accountable.[60] At the same time, ethnographic research shows that the implementation of human rights standards may undermine local practices and efface kinship arrangements. Some communities feel cynical about the failures of a profitable and ever-expanding industry of elite human rights NGOs to eliminate the systems of power that oppress them. Analysts critique the entanglement of human rights with neoliberal governance and the tendency in human rights activism to supplant broad-based social change with a narrow focus on law reform. At their worst, scholars contend, human rights may "normalize and legitimize unequal structures of power and authority" by channeling popular aspirations for political change through unjust legal systems.[61] Projects for women's human rights, in particular, often cast rights as a "heroic weapon that frees women from an oppressive 'traditional' culture into a world of freedom and choice," erroneously pitting rights against, or outside of, culture.[62]

Until recently, prevailing perspectives in medical and feminist anthropology have approached reproductive rights such as abortion as a cornerstone of women's citizenship in liberal societies.[63] Indeed, anthropological interest in reproduction flourished throughout the 1970s as academics participated in the political struggle for safe, legal abortion, tying their own reproductive concerns to their scholarly agendas.[64] More recently, anthropologists and feminist studies scholars have begun to question the rights paradigm around reproduction, urging analytical distance rather than predetermined support.[65] There is good reason to be cautious about rights-based approaches to reproductive equity.

To begin with, frameworks of reproductive rights generally approach reproduction as a matter of individual choice, but we know that decisions about childbearing are seldom made alone.[66] Even in high-tech arrangements that obviate heteronormative couplings, reproduction entails multiple forms of assistance and generates new relational dependencies.[67] Questions of reproductive assistance figure centrally in parts of Latin America, standing in contrast to the Euro-American emphasis on reproductive autonomy.[68] Decisions not to reproduce, likewise, unfold intersubjectively, as women and parents weigh the viability of bringing about new life against existing responsibilities to care for others. When held up to close ethnographic scrutiny, even abortion decisions—so often positioned in advocacy discourse as a matter of women's "freedom" and "choice"—can reflect quests for *belonging* to family, community, and nation.[69] In many cases, moreover, reproduction does not occur in the context of a "choice" at all, but instead happens in the absence of agentive or willful action. Rights, as they figure in public discourse, can thus misconstrue the intersubjective and circumstantial nature of reproductive life.

While the extension of rights would seem to necessarily increase individual freedoms, in some cases rights can function as a mechanism of reproductive control. Rights-based approaches are predicated on the assumption that those in power can grant, and therefore also retract, the ability to assert agency over one's reproductive life. Activists in some contexts have incorporated this critique, calling for "bodily autonomy" rather than "abortion rights."[70] In other cases, the conferral of reproductive rights can expand processes of reproductive surveillance. In Senegal, where abortion is entirely illegal, a postabortion care program was implemented in the late 1990s to reduce abortion-related mortality in keeping with ICPD mandates. In this setting, sociologist Siri Suh has explored how the same medical professionals who work to save women from potentially deadly injuries according to their global commitments sometimes feel obliged to report them to local authorities for obtaining illegal abortions.[71] When national and global frames of reproductive governance stand in conflict, in other words, the extension of some rights may undermine others.

If the conferral of reproductive rights can work paradoxically to limit reproductive freedom, equally troublesome is what anthropologist Richard Wilson calls the "doctrinal ambiguity" of rights—the idea that ideological opponents can seize rights concepts for their own ends.[72] We see this when prochoice activists make claims for a woman's right to abortion even as self-proclaimed "prolife" activists argue for the right to life of the fetus. "The proliferation of rights-talk can be treacherous," write Lynn Morgan and Elizabeth Roberts, "because it increasingly allows the claims of rights-bearing citizens to be pitted against one another . . . [leading] activists on opposite sides of an issue to insert preferential language into a proliferation of dueling laws and international accords."[73] Such has been the case throughout Latin America, where since the 1990s actors from across the political spectrum have marshalled the rights framework to advance their respective agendas around sexuality and reproduction. The result has been a simultaneous expansion and contraction of reproductive freedoms in the region. The abortion backlash across Mexico in response to the 2007 reform is a case in point.

Corrective models have emerged to address the shortcomings of the rights framework. Beginning in the 1990s, black women activists in the United States collaborated to establish a framework of "reproductive justice," arguing that rights-based approaches prioritize the interests of privileged groups of women at the expense of others.[74] We know, for instance, that the technology necessary to facilitate the reproductive rights of white women in the first world has historically relied on experimentation on the bodies of brown and black women in the developing world.[75] Reproductive justice offers a more capacious and inclusionary framework that invalidates the established binary of "prochoice" versus "prolife" to encompass the right *not to have* children, and also the *right to have* and *to parent* children in environments free from harm.[76] The ability to terminate a pregnancy does little, it is hard to disagree, when dismal economic circumstances and systemic racism prevent some women from bearing desired pregnancies to term and sustaining their communities in dignified conditions.[77] Reproductive justice is a broad appeal for governmental provision of structural supports to enable parenting—such as affordable child care, employment opportunities, fair wages, environmental safety, and access to contraception and abortion—as well as freedom from unjustified state intrusions into women's reproductive lives, such as sterilization abuse, population control, and the criminalization of women of color.[78] As so many scholars have cogently argued, it is a call for the state not simply to step away from "private" reproductive decisions, but to step in and assume responsibility for the care of citizens.

There is no denying that rights concepts have proven advantageous in transforming reproductive policy in Mexico and around the world, often in ways that directly benefit women. Yet for all their utility in the political realm, rights frameworks can strip away nuance and uncertainty, eclipsing the local circumstances and considerations that bear on reproductive life. From an analytical perspective, rights may obscure more than they reveal. I began this project with a stable political commitment to abortion as a legitimate option for women that should be protected in the law; I defined myself as "prochoice." While that underlying commitment has not changed, this research turned everything I thought I knew about abortion inside out, prompting me to reconsider the frameworks that have circumscribed conversations on abortion in my home country. My approach to abortion rights in this book responds to recent scholarly calls for *ambivalence* as an anthropological heuristic.[79] Such a position appreciates the practical potential of rights agendas to expand women's reproductive options, while also considering their adverse effects, potential for co-optation, and possible discord with lay understandings. In her recent account of moral quandaries in assisted dying, anthropologist Mara Buchbinder helpfully differentiates between ambivalence and neutrality.[80] "Where neutrality might mean withholding judgement," she writes, "ambivalence is a more engaged stance, one that entails tracking the moral and affective pulls that orient us to a field of study, even if they lead in confusing or conflicting directions." Ambivalence, as I see it, is not a refusal to take a political stand but rather a studied or deliberate refusal to cling too readily to any one framework. It involves a commitment to stay alive to the multiplicity of viewpoints that anthropological research affords, especially when they unsettle the convictions we value most.

Ultimately, my work in Mexico has led me to think harder about pathways to reproductive justice that do not depend on the law, timely lessons for a US readership facing direct and mounting threats to *Roe v. Wade*. This work, moreover, has pushed me to listen better, and with more empathy, to those whose positions on abortion diverge from my own. The perspectives of providers and patients in Mexico City's public abortion clinics prompted me to abandon many of the neat intellectual frameworks I had brought with me to the field. My hope is that this book will have the same unsettling effect on its readers, prompting you to revisit what you thought you knew about abortion.

While some readers may crave "answers" to the abortion debate, that is not my project here. Rather, I set out to understand the terms by which people in Mexico frame this conflict and how they reconcile the moral quandaries that pregnancy disruption can present in a context where state law has come to contradict other normative frameworks for moral reckoning. As much as this book is about other people, though, it is also about waking up to my own relationship as an interpreter to these questions and the time that has elapsed since I first began to ponder them. In a context where multiple perspectives vie for control over this perennially disputed issue, I did not always have a clear sense of what I was looking at. Abortion in Mexico is marked by competing moral schema defined by the Catholic Church, the state, feminist actors, and the medical sphere.[81] Researching abortion in this setting entailed ambivalences of all kinds.

IN AND BEYOND THE CLINIC

Mexico City is so overwhelming that you can only ever see it from one angle. People who grow up there say there is no way to experience it completely, that it is knowable only in fragments. That's how I remember the city now: street vendors with wheelbarrows of candy and loose cigarettes. Laundry dancing on rooftop lines to dry. The charming stucco facades, their impossibly saturated blues and magentas. An infinite skyline and clouds so heavy they dump rain over the whole city every afternoon in spring. Then there were the tastes, as Lucia Berlin once wrote of her time there: "Everything in Mexico tasted. Vivid garlic, cilantro, lime."[82]

There are less picturesque parts in my memory too, like endless people and pollution. Noise from every direction, a chorus of car horns and pedestrian chatter. It is hard to forget the children who scooted along the metro floor shining shoes for spare change, how they'd look up at you with wide eyes and tangled hair. Or the journalist I knew who always sat with his back to the wall after receiving death threats; I remember the terror that overcame him for months. But these images, frames of spectacular beauty and pain, rob the city of its perpetual movement.

It is not a coincidence, I don't think, that a number of authors have tried to describe Mexico City from a bird's-eye view. "When viewed from the Observation Deck on the 44th floor of the Latin American Tower," writes John Ross, "this monster of a city appears inert, a gargantuan stone mass spreading to the four cardinal directions as far as the eye can see—which is not all that far, given the dismal air quality."[83] But the city is too vast to capture even from an airplane. "On a clear day, from an airplane window, the city is almost comprehensible—a simpler representation of itself, to the scale of the human imagination," Valeria Luiselli writes in *Sidewalks*.[84] I found that sometimes, when the plane floated low enough in the sky, I could glimpse it for a second. But when we touched down the city always eluded me, moving at a pace faster than I could track. *Horizontal Vertigo* is how Juan Villoro titled his recent book about Mexico City.[85] I don't disagree with him that capturing some semblance of this bewildering place with words is "a challenge as elusive as describing vertigo."[86] Even if the city stood still long enough for the human eye to absorb, there is simply nowhere to grab on, no combination of adjectives and verbs that might hang together to represent the mosaic of discordant images that make up this place. Maybe it was the high altitude, the molecular changes in my body that eventually allowed it to operate with less oxygen, but I have never felt more alive than in Mexico City. Nowadays, in my small-town life in Norman, Oklahoma, I yearn for the city—its vitality, its pulse.

I was a teenager the first time I set foot there. At the time I was passing through as part of a college service trip to the Sierra Norte of Puebla, a couple hours southeast. The verdant mountain village where I would spend the summer building ecological stoves with a group of international volunteers felt worlds away from the capital, where millions of demonstrators had set up camp that July in the Zócalo to protest the 2006 presidential elections. Makeshift tents and tarps blanketed the historic square. Everything was swathed in fabric, like a Christo installation. When the right-wing PAN candidate Felipe Calderón was announced the winner by a fraction of a percentage point, Andrés Manuel López Obrador, the center-left Party of the Democratic Revolution (PRD) runner-up, demanded a recount.[87] Reports surfaced that ballots had been discarded in the trash. For many Mexicans the situation was all too familiar. Fearful of a return to the flagrant corruption of the PRI era from which the country had recently emerged, the protesters refused to pack up their tents for several weeks.

For me this was a crash course in Mexican politics, but I had no idea when I paged through some of the protest literature laid out on blue tarps that this controversial election would lay the groundwork for the 2007 abortion reform. Despite its center-left politics, the PRD had not outwardly supported abortion reform during the presidential race for fear of alienating its Catholic base. After the election the party was free of campaign considerations and still in control in the Mexico City legislature and mayoral office. Offering support for the abortion reform was a way for the PRD to publicly mark its political differences from the PAN.[88] The time was right to press for the reform, which passed in a historic vote not a year later.

Anthropological fieldwork, like time, unfolds in cycles, and the cycles behind this book are numerous. It must have been that same year I first visited

Mexico City in college when I got interested in reproductive politics. Back then, most of what I knew about reproduction was divorced from my own life. I had grown up in New England in the 1990s in a context of legal and relatively accessible abortion. I can remember debating the readings from a feminist anthropology class with my mother. When one author argued that attention to the fetus belied feminist agendas, my mother disagreed, describing the affective bond she had felt with her own fetuses during each of her pregnancies. Attention to the fetus may threaten feminist agendas, she conceded, but ignoring its moral weight risked erasing the experiences of many women for whom the fetus is very much a person, or at least person-like. There was "life" there, she had seemed to say. I dismissed her comments with all the haughtiness of a nineteen-year-old. Never mind that she identified as a feminist and had participated in the struggle for safe, legal abortion. When I was a mother, she had countered to put the debate to rest, I would understand.

Perhaps in search of another kind of understanding, I left everything behind to return to Mexico City in 2014. The stories women shared with me about their motivations for seeking an abortion resonated deeply, even though our lives, in many cases, looked considerably different. At the time, having a family was the last thing on my mind. This project has carried me back and forth between the United States and Mexico and through many life stages in the past decade. As another anthropologist once wrote, "This ethnographic project and I have grown up together."[89] One of the hardest parts about working on this book has been watching from afar as several of my closest friends in both countries became mothers. The women whose lives animate these pages have continued to unfold in the intervening years as well, and some, I imagine, have become pregnant again and have opted to bear those pregnancies to term.

My mother didn't remember our debate about fetal personhood when I raised it after completing the first draft of this book. But her admonition—that I would understand once I was a mother—has troubled me in the final stages of this project. A couple decades of feminist scholarship in anthropology have made a similar point: lived experience offers a powerful medium for intellectual insights about reproduction and about gendered experience more broadly.[90] I am not a mother, and I have never been in the situation of considering whether to end a pregnancy. But this research, and the weight of a decade of life since it began, have led me to appreciate the expansiveness of reproduction beyond narrow definitions of procreation or abortion. My longing for a baby at this stage in my life has made it painful, at times, to return to the page each day to write about abortion. It has been challenging to quell my anxieties about the discord between biological and academic rhythms. With the passage of time I have come to appreciate reproductive concerns at the other end of the life cycle as well, as my parents age and their physical and emotional needs grow. These insights have led me to see reproduction not as a singular, bounded event—as in abortion or birth—but as a diachronic process that unfolds over time and assumes new meanings at different moments. There is thus a kind of "chronicity" to reproduction, in that it takes place across the life cycle.[91]

I did not have as much perspective when I began this study. Nor did my classroom training tell me how or where to begin. So much about abortion happens outside the actual procedure—in negotiations with romantic partners and other kin, with medical bureaucracies, and sometimes with God. But since most women do not anticipate an abortion, I had no place to go and could find no women to meet before they needed the procedure. This book moves within and beyond clinical spaces, but the bulk of the research is drawn from a public ILE clinic that I call Santa Marta, and, to a lesser extent, another public ILE clinic that I call Reina María.[92] I carried out sixteen months of fieldwork in and outside these clinics between 2014 and 2015, and on several follow-up trips to Mexico in subsequent years.[93]

Each morning I circulated the clinical waiting room to introduce my study and recruit women for interviews.[94] During these conversations I asked women about the process of seeking an abortion, their reflections on the care provided at the ILE clinic, their position on national abortion laws, and other dynamics. On days when no one volunteered to participate I spoke casually with them about these and other topics. I encountered hundreds of abortion patients while conducting the research for this book. Women came and left the clinic in the span of a few hours, and in most cases I never saw them again. While pouring over my interview transcripts later, I sometimes felt as if I was staring at a photo album: dozens of vivid but fleeting snapshots in time.

If reproduction is an enduring process, abortion is not a chronic condition that keeps women in the hospital for months on end, allowing enough time for the thick relationships that are generally central to ethnographic research. At times I wondered how to place women's abortion experiences in the wider context of their lives when I knew them only in ephemeral glimpses. Dr. Rios once made a comment that still resonates: "I can't remember them all, their names or faces, but their stories stay with me." Ethnographic research in a crowded public clinic could feel as impersonal as the care provided there.

One of the early challenges I faced was the question of when to conduct the interviews. I didn't want these conversations to alter women's experience of abortion, so it seemed logical to interview them after the procedure. Yet for women undergoing medical abortion the process unfolded in stages over the course of days, as they swallowed mifepristone at the clinic and then ingested misoprostol twenty-four hours later at home. Even though all women were instructed to return to the clinic for a follow-up sonogram two weeks later, there was no guarantee that they would make it or that I would be in the clinic on the day they returned. If I interviewed them at their first visit after they took the mifepristone but before they took the misoprostol, would I interrupt the process? When does a medical abortion begin and end?

I eventually resolved that there was no way for me to conduct this research *without* altering women's experiences of abortion; my presence in the clinic inevitably shifted the dynamic. Sometimes, when they did not meet the legal criteria for an ILE procedure, women asked me how to induce a medical abortion on their own using misoprostol purchased over the counter. Though I had reconciled my presence in their lives during such intimate moments, this was a line I felt ethically remiss in crossing, since a medical emergency might arise. In those cases, I directed women to a local abortion advocacy group that could provide instructions that the ILE personnel were unable to offer.

Early on in the research I tried to follow up with women after the procedure to position their experiences in a longer arc of time, but my attempts were largely futile. Women inhabited all corners of the massive city and were overcommitted with child care, school, and work. More often than not it was these factors that had led them to the clinic in the first place. I was left with a cascade of passing encounters, freeze-frames of women's lives during one intense moment. In some ways, though, this is the only way to experience Mexico City: anonymous glances in the wide hallways of the metro or along the city's impossibly crowded streets. Sometimes a month went by before I could visit with friends who lived just a few miles away. The traffic and crowds seemed to curtail everyone's mobility, shaping sociality in profound ways.

Though the temporality of abortion posed certain logistical challenges, it also afforded novel insights about the centrality of time to reproductive experience. Questions of timing dictated whether a woman could access an abortion through the ILE program, as the twelve-week gestational cutoff loomed large. Clinical temporalities collided with the rhythms of pregnancy, bearing down on women and couples as they scrambled to arrive at the clinic "in time." The redefinition of first-trimester abortion as "legal interruption of pregnancy," moreover, demanded a kind of temporal reckoning. Unlike the word *termination* used more frequently in the US context, *interruption* suggests a momentary disruption, a deviation from the expected march of time.[95] The term hearkens backward and forward all at once. In the ILE clinics *interruption* was not just a legal abstraction, as almost everyone I met pointed to the dismal social conditions in Mexico that interrupted their quality of life and shaped their deliberations about childbearing. For those who were already mothers, moreover, the procedure offered a means to prevent the interruption of care they had already committed to existing children.

The finitude of an aspiration abortion, which was performed in one sitting at the clinic, made it slightly different than medical abortion. Early on, I thought that watching aspiration procedures might help me understand what interviews eclipsed. One of the Santa Marta doctors draped a medical coat over my shoulders and the doctor positioned me beside her, directing my gaze toward the woman's cervix. After a few minutes the social workers, Carolina and Roberta, scrambled to place a cotton swab soaked in rubbing alcohol under my nose to revive me when I fainted. But even after I knew what to expect, watching generated more questions than answers. In her research on obstetric fistula in Ethiopia, anthropologist Anita Hannig considers how peering deep inside of a woman whose legs were wedged apart on an operating table felt like a questionable violation of her privacy.[96] I too had to consider, as I glimpsed the most intimate recesses of women's bodies—parts of themselves they could not access—the improbable odds that our positions could be reversed. As I queried women about intimate health information during interviews, our relationships were already inescapably asymmetrical. Standing before a woman whose nude body was subject to my inspective gaze seemed to give full expression to the most unsavory aspects of anthropological research.

Yet there were times throughout this project when women asked *me* if I had ever had an abortion. The question was simple and obvious given my purpose in the clinic. But embedded there, I think, was a more profound query that was harder to answer: Had I ever been in their position? A few months into the research, I decided to undergo a routine Pap smear at Reina María Clinic once all the patients had left. The clinicians insisted that a quick screening procedure would not unduly disrupt daily routines, and I thought it might be an instructive research opportunity. When a nursing student named Tony whom I had come to know asked me if he could observe as part of his training, I declined. I hid my discomfort, anxious not to threaten the rapport we had developed. The experience prompted me to appreciate how my own presence in the operating theater, and in the clinic generally, might have felt similarly intrusive for patients. At some point after my Pap smear I largely avoided observing aspiration procedures unless a woman asked me to hold her hand during the process. Because most women arrived at the ILE clinic early in their pregnancies, the vast majority of patients, in any case, underwent medical abortions, inducing the process at home after obtaining abortifacient pills at the clinic.

Ultimately, I found that the lasting connection I had hoped for with patients was more possible with ILE providers, whose steady or "chronic" presence in the clinic allowed for our relationships to deepen as patients flowed in and out of view. Once the clinicians realized I was there to stay, they put me to work entering patient data into the computer system and assigned me other mundane tasks around the clinic. On many days I found myself washing dishes in the clinic's small bathroom sink or stapling informational packets on birth control in the counseling office. When I wasn't interacting with patients, I simply existed alongside the providers, sharing chilled hibiscus tea and bitter Nescafé during downtime, observing their work, and peppering them with all manner of questions. Thinking back, it was during this unstructured time—moments that I experienced as breaks from the "real research" of interviews—that I first began to see how dynamics of care in the ILE clinics were central to the instantiation of abortion rights there.

Over the months the ILE personnel kept careful watch over me, monitoring fluctuations in my weight and developments in my personal life and chiding me affectionately the same way they did their patients. Whenever I left for the States they put in orders for a range of goods, requesting clothing, perfumes, and candies that were unavailable in Mexico. When my language skills faltered they delighted at my grammatical mistakes, always seizing opportunities for playful teasing. I was grateful when that happened, as it seemed to offset, if only for a moment, some of the imbalances that structured our lives. Even though all the personnel held coveted jobs as medical professionals, many of the "midlevel" providers, including nurses and social workers, had to supplement their modest MOH incomes with work in private clinics to make ends meet. Others sold Tupperware and makeup through catalogs, which they advertised to each other during breaks in the counseling office.

Whatever differences separated the midlevel clinicians from the higher-ranking doctors and program administrators, the chasm between my life and theirs felt more dramatic. I sensed it every time I opted to leave the clinic early because I had grown tired, and especially when I flew in and out of the country at will. Like almost everyone I came to know in Mexico, the clinicians reminded me often of the burdened relationship between their country and mine. I can remember hailing a cab off the street on a recent visit to Mexico City. The driver wove capably through unrelenting traffic without losing track of our conversation. I don't remember discussing Donald Trump, who was a few years into his presidency at the time, but when I handed over the fare, he quipped: "Thanks, I'll put it towards the border wall." Comments like these were sobering reminders that no matter how comfortable I came to feel with people in Mexico, there were walls between us that we were both powerless to remove. Though jokes about the United States were a common means to address the anger that foreign policy imposed, people sometimes engaged me more earnestly about their inability to travel in and out of my country as I could do so readily in theirs. I have found that no amount of reflection offers easy or satisfying answers to these uncomfortable questions, which trouble so much anthropological work.

Despite the barriers that separated our lives, with time I came to think of Carolina, Roberta, and other ILE personnel as true friends. Yet even these relationships posed limits to my understanding. The providers clearly recognized my purpose in the clinic. During my first week of research, I had to intercede when they began to incorporate a pitch on my behalf in their discussions with patients: "Elyse has come here all the way from the US, and it is very important that you participate in her study." When the horizons of my study widened to consider their role in the clinic, the providers responded differently. Even as they sat enthusiastically for interviews, they seemed self-conscious at times, careful to present the clinic and the ILE program in the best possible light. They were prudent when discussing sensitive aspects of their work, like how they handled patients whose pregnancies exceeded the gestational limit on ILE services. Their livelihood depended on discretion, as the ILE program was vulnerable to tremendous opposition. Letting the wrong information slip could threaten the program as well as their job security.

It didn't take me long to realize that second-trimester abortion was available through private clinics for women who could afford to pay. Some of the same ob-gyns who performed abortions within the ILE program were said to offer the procedure in their private practices, which were not subject the same legal oversight as the MOH. I observed several instances in which women who had been denied ILE care because of gestational restrictions later purchased abortions through the private sector. Sometimes I accompanied them. The boundaries between legal and illegal, public and private abortion care, were hazy. Yet whenever I asked the ILE personnel how they counseled women who had fallen outside of program limits they defaulted to perfunctory responses. "If their pregnancies are too far along," Carolina once told me mechanically, "we tell them they have to go to their nearest health center for prenatal care and take plenty of folic acid."

Eventually I moved outside the ILE program in search of answers. The feminist abortion accompaniment networks picked up where the ILE program left off, offering a rounder picture of the ILE program—the women it failed to serve and what became of their pregnancies—and a set of alternative models for realizing abortion rights outside the medical system and independent of the law.[97] I underwent training to serve as an accompanier for Conéctame, whose volunteers assist women in traveling to the capital from other states to obtain abortion care. While I did not interview any of the women seeking abortion through the organization, serving in this role brought me more perspective on the limits of the ILE program. My research also took me to Guanajuato, a state five hours northwest of Mexico City that is home to some of the country's most restrictive abortion laws. When I met the founding director of Las Fuertes at a panel on abortion in Mexico City, she insisted I consider her work. I returned to Mexico in 2016 to spend the summer months at her organization, which provides an alternative model of accompaniment to facilitate at-home abortions in a context of near-complete criminalization.

Central to my research in and outside the capital was learning what I was not supposed to know, and what, if I did glimpse it, had to remain unspoken. As elsewhere in Latin America, people in Mexico often call abortion *un secreto a voces* (an open secret)—a practice that everyone is aware of but only rarely names.[98] Legalization of the procedure in the capital brought local law in line with the reality of widespread abortion practice, pulling abortion from the realm of secrecy into public view. Nonetheless, there remained aspects of abortion that could not be named directly without putting health care workers and women at legal risk. Abortion researchers working in other contexts have emphasized the importance of "[reading] between the lines [to] provide insight into the 'shadowy' spaces where new forms of abortion restriction and the reality of women's sexuality and reproduction collide."[99] I found that these "shadowy spaces" were hard to see and harder to talk about. I managed to avoid exposing any secrets during my resident fieldwork, but writing raised a host of new concerns.

Teresa, whose story opens this book, is not a real name. With the exception of Mexico City and Guanajuato, I use pseudonyms for all places, people, clinics, and organizations in Mexico. Although I cannot conceal them entirely, I have tried to be intentionally vague about clinic locations to protect the privacy of clinicians. In many cases I have taken the added step of altering distinguishable details about medical personnel and patients to conceal their identities without compromising the integrity of their stories. A topic as fraught as abortion demands other considerations about language as well. I have settled on the terms *abortion rights advocate* or *activist* when describing those working to expand access to abortion in any capacity. Since not all of those working in this vein embrace terms more familiar to a US audience, like *feminist* or *prochoice*, I use these labels only when they apply. When describing those whose commitments run in the other direction, at times I use the term *prolife*, not to evince my own stance on these questions, but to preserve the anthropological convention of using the labels that people adopt for themselves.

While I have taken steps to conceal the identities of the people you will soon meet, other elements of Mexican abortion are missing from this account entirely. There are some things I am still working to understand. I could not always see clearly, for instance, what happened to women who fell outside ILE program limits, even though I watched carefully as patients passed through the small ultrasound room each day. Sometimes, it seemed, the sonogram only confirmed what providers already knew. I remember one young woman in particular, how her swollen abdomen had forced the buttons off her jeans, the small scars where her skin had stretched. As the doctor drew the wand along her middle, faint shapes crowded the screen. I couldn't decipher the images before me, but she sobbed in the waiting room when the providers told her that she had not arrived in time.

Making sense of abortion in Mexico meant growing comfortable with images that never quite resolved. The picture offered in the chapters that follow is another rendering of these blurred moments in time, though occasionally, perhaps, a clear image comes through.

CHAPTER ONE

THE PAST IS NEVER DEAD . . .

Reproductive Governance in Modern Mexico

THERE WAS NOTHING about the outside of Santa Marta Clinic to in-dicate the kind of work performed inside. The boxy cement structure looked a lot like the houses nearby. The same iron bars covered the windows and front doorway, and the red paint blistered and peeled like a bad sunburn. A simple sign stamped with the Ministry of Health (MOH) logo read: "Santa Marta Comprehensive Sexual and Reproductive Health Clinic." It was the activity outside the clinic that signaled its purpose, and the controversy it represented for some in this remote neighborhood of Tacalco, one of Mexico City's poorest and most populated boroughs hugging the southern edge of the sprawling capital.[1]

By the time I started visiting Santa Marta, a prolife group had built a cri-sis pregnancy center (CPC) next door in protest. Its staff was adept at luring women into the office for an ultrasound scan—in this case to facilitate bonding with the fetus and dissuade them from going through with the abortion—before most realized they were in the wrong place.[2] Others in the neighborhood also made a living by attaching themselves to the economy of the clinic and the throng of people it drew each day. Taxi drivers lurked at the entrance in the hopes of carting a patient and her family members back to the nearest metro station about twenty minutes away, and vendors rose early to arrange fold-ing tables outside. They peddled a variety of goods to early morning patients: colorful gelatin molds, strawberry tamales, and other sugary snacks. An older woman in the group sold hot *atole* (a syrupy corn drink) on cool mornings. On the days when protesters visited the clinic to recite a communal prayer, she always paused, bowing to join them. In her prayers, she once told me, she con-sidered not only the unborn who were sacrificed daily behind clinic doors but also their mothers, on whom she took pity. I didn't notice until later that the rosary beads she wore around her neck encased tiny plastic fetuses—a gesture of atonement, perhaps, for her complicity in the profane work of the clinic.

Since the Santa Marta ILE clinic opened its doors a few years after the 2007 reform it has served women from all over the capital and nearby states. Most patients, like the clinic personnel, are Tacalco residents. Nearly half of Tacalco's two million inhabitants live in poverty, and many have lim-ited access to basic infrastructure. People there sometimes called the tap water *agua de tamarindo* (tamarind water) because of its brown color. As I moved about the borough it was hard to miss the young men who crowded the traffic intersections throughout the day, rushing in on idling cars to polish windshields for spare change, their clothes stained with car grease and sweat rings. Or the homeless youth who subsisted on inhalants called *activo*— cheap chemicals like solvents and glues that suppress the appetite and dull emotion. They sleepwalked the neighborhood, emaciated under baggy clothes, their skin and hair luminous with chemical traces. A crude joke circulated in the borough about pregnant women addicted to the sub-stance: "El bebé es muy activo" (The baby is very active). Others in Tacalco had better luck. Some scraped out a modest living at one of the local me-chanic shops or commuted to a wealthier zone of the city for better employ-ment opportunities. Many studied in the local university to expand their horizons. Regardless of their fates, people in Tacalco were quick to defend their humble borough. When I arrived, residents didn't hesitate to name the stark divides carved onto the capital, patterns of segregation that made my presence in the borough as a white visitor from the United States unlikely. One woman who lived a block from Santa Marta told me that she was not used to visits from "gente de baro" (people who come from money). Some

Tacalcans asked me directly why I wanted to spend time in "un lugar tan feo" (such an ugly part of town).

Despite its economic deficiencies, Tacalco teemed with vitality. It was all movement and color, a microcosm of the vibrant capital. One main road cut through the borough and past an endless stretch of ragtag mechanic shops where tires and other automobile parts were strewn about in every direction. Off that main artery I used to watch from the backseat window as a taxi driver wound us up a maze of steep streets to arrive at the abortion clinic. There, in one small corner of the capital, we would pass a butcher shop and an improvised bakery with hand-stenciled lettering. Bright cinder block houses bordered either side of the narrow road to the clinic, many half-finished. A fringe of iron rods sprouted from their rooftops like a strange species of wiry plant. In this packed neighborhood there was nowhere to build except up. As they saved money, families slowly added more cinder blocks to those iron frames, which I came to think of as an unlikely symbol of hope.[3] I remember how women observed the daily bustle from their second-floor balconies, standing watch over the neighborhood, and how down below a man used to wheel his cart from house to house selling "GAS!" to replenish home boilers for hot showers.

Amid all of the uneasy scenes I witnessed at Santa Marta, there is one image that I have never been able to shake from my memory. I first glimpsed it on a Wednesday as the regular congregation of protesters formed a slow procession toward the clinic from a nearby church. Once a week a group of elderly women and a local priest made this journey, shuffling down a wide pavement path to arrive by opening time. After a while, whenever I heard them coming I rushed out of the counseling office to observe from the clinic's front stoop. Against Santa Marta's red and cream walls they leaned a large crucifix and assembled a provisional shrine to the Virgin of Guadalupe, Mexico's patron saint, before arranging their bodies in a tight circle and bowing in prayer. For several minutes each week the rhythmic hum of Ave Marías reverberated throughout the neighborhood, softening the sound of car horns and chirping chickens: "Dios te salve, María, llena eres de gracia, el Señor es contigo. Bendita Tú eres entre todas las mujeres, y bendito es el fruto de tu vientre, Jesús. Santa María, Madre de Dios, ruega por nosotros, pecadores, ahora y en la hora de nuestra muerte. Amén." (Hail Mary, full of grace, the

Lord is with thee. Blessed art thou among women, and blessed is the fruit of thy womb, Jesus. Holy Mary, Mother of God, pray for us sinners, now and in the hour of our death. Amen.)[4]

By the time I first witnessed the protesters at work I was accustomed to images of the Virgin of Guadalupe. They are ubiquitous in Mexico, where she graces taxicabs, taco stands, and storefronts and is etched under the skin of many people in tattoo form. Yet the rendition they toted with them each week was unlike any I had seen. It obsessed me in the months to come, forcing its way to the center of my thoughts. Maybe it was all of the vivid colors, the cobalt blue of her cloak and the golden hue behind her head, a mirror for the colorful city. But even more mesmerizing were the three lifeless infants Guadalupe cradled—one deep brown, one creamy white, and one the color of cinnamon. The limp babies appeared as symbolic "victims" of abortion, one with its head cocked back and arms flung to the side. Yet they were different from the images I was used to north of the border, where dismembered fetuses have long been an "iconographic biopolitical tool" of antiabortion activism.[5] These were full-term babies, and they were intact and peaceful, resting in a protective maternal embrace. Below this scene a phrase read: "para evitar que se cometan más abortos en esta clínica" (to ensure that no more abortions are committed in this clinic).

"Guadalupe suffers for every abortion," the Santa Marta social worker named Carolina remarked when I showed her a photograph that I had snapped of the activity outside. "It's a grave sin to take a child's life away." Later on, I couldn't stop looking at that photo of the Virgin pinned to a public clinic. When I took that picture I had not yet learned that religious symbols had been forbidden inside public buildings since the Revolution of 1910, when the postrevolutionary regime sought to limit the power and influence of the Catholic Church. But condensed in the image, I sensed, was a complicated story about gender, religion, and Mexican nationalism. All of its vibrant color and nervousness continued to work on me, and I kept discovering new layers. No meaning seemed beyond La Guadalupe: protection, sin, redemption, latency, maternity, sacrifice, pain, nation. Here was the moral guardian of something understood to be imperiled. Guadalupe, it seemed, might lead me to understand something deeper about abortion, something I was missing. She became a guiding symbol as I sifted through the historical literatures collected in this chapter to make sense of the threat that abortion presented for those who assembled outside Santa Marta and the other ILE clinics every week.[6]

THE INDIAN VIRGIN

"There is a saying here," people in Mexico often told me. "Los hijos que Dios te mande" (One is obligated to have the babies God sends). Sometimes people invoked the proverb as shorthand to explain the Catholic Church's categorical ban on abortion. Other times they used the phrase playfully, at once critiquing and acquiescing to the gendered burdens of childbearing. The maxim has a thick significance given the layered connotation of the Spanish verb *mandar*, which means both "to send" and "to command." God does not just send babies; He commands that they be received and cared for. Embedded in the idiom is the Marian vision of abortion as a selfish pursuit of individual desires at the expense of the family and a flagrant disavowal of God's will. As Elizabeth Maier has observed, "Christian dogma establishes that women's vocation and mission as mothers, their role as wives in binding heterosexual unions, and an embodied sacrificial altruism, sensibility, intuition, and intense loyalty to family and community are not only ideal female virtues but also inherent gender traits."[7] While there are multiple and conflicting gender ideologies in contemporary Mexico, the hegemonic framework of *marianismo*, the veneration of the Virgin Mary, treats abortion as a negation of the source of women's superior moral status and "a condensed symbol for the devaluation of motherhood."[8] Rejecting a baby, God's gift to women, amounts to a profane denial of feminine virtue.

If the abortion debate in the United States is focused overwhelmingly on the ontological status of the fetus—is it a person or not?—in Mexico the contours of the debate are slightly different. Here concerns over the destruction of "fetal life" combine with profound anxieties about the social roles of women and the threat that abortion authorizes against Catholic definitions of sacrificial femininity. For the Catholic hierarchy and its political allies, pregnancy is divinely ordained and abortion constitutes a mortal sin and an assault on feminine duties. A manifestation of the Virgin Mary known as "the Indian Virgin," Guadalupe encompasses all of these layered meanings.

FIGURE I. Protest outside Santa Marta Clinic. Photograph by author, 2014.

The Virgin of Guadalupe embodies a syncretic mixture of European and native ideas of the mother of God and was strategically invoked by the Spanish crown in its project of colonial evangelism.[9] Legend holds that she first appeared to an Indian peasant named Juan Diego in 1531, a decade after the Spanish invaded the Aztec capital of Tenochtitlán.[10] The spectral encounter occurred on the Hill of Tepeyac, at the time the sacred home of the indigenous goddess of fertility, Tonantzin. After summoning him up the hill Guadalupe spoke to Juan Diego in Nahuatl, urging him to make the bishop aware of her apparition.[11] The bishop was unconvinced. Days later the Virgin reappeared, instructing Juan Diego to pick a bundle of flowers from arid soil and deliver them to the bishop as proof of her apparition. He obliged, and when he unfurled his *tilma* (cloak) colorful flowers spilled forth. Struck by the miraculous image of Guadalupe radiating before him, the bishop called for the construction of a shrine devoted to the Virgin on Tepeyac Hill. "Mexico was born at Tepayac," one often hears in reference to this story.

By the seventeenth century the cult of Guadalupe had gained a widespread following in Mexico. Churches and shrines sacralizing the Virgin proliferated throughout the country as indigenous peoples adapted elements of Catholicism.[12] Guadalupe offered hope of salvation to Indians in colonial Mexico, redeeming their humanity and promising spiritual protection at a time when Spanish colonial administrators regarded them as culturally and biologically inferior. For anthropologist Eric Wolf, Guadalupe "validate[d] the Indian's right to legal defense, orderly government, to citizenship; to supernatural salvation, but also to salvation from random oppression."[13]

Long a symbol of redemption, hope, and safety for the defenseless, Guadalupe would find a place in future political struggles as well. During the War of Mexican Independence in 1810 she emerged as a symbol of nationalist struggle when Miguel Hidalgo waved a banner featuring her image while making his way to the national capital.[14] Later on, the first Mexican president is said to have changed his birth name to Guadalupe Victoria as an homage to the patron saint. When a century later rebels Emiliano Zapata and Pancho Villa incited a new revolutionary struggle, remembered today as the Mexican Revolution, they too brandished her image.[15] In the contemporary moment activists in Mexico and in the diaspora sometimes invoke Guadalupe as a symbol of radical feminism, rewriting religious gender frameworks.

In the words of Eric Wolf, Guadalupe "links together family, politics and religion; colonial past and independent present; Indian and Mexican . . . [She] is, ultimately, a way of talking about Mexico: a 'collective representation' of Mexican society."[16] Today the *tilma* featuring the Virgin hangs over the altar in the Basilica of Guadalupe in the northern strip of Mexico City, in the same place where she is said to have appeared to Juan Diego centuries ago. Millions of Catholic faithful from around the world make a pilgrimage to visit her each year. Many carry large statues of the venerated Virgin, and others arrive on their knees in exuberant displays of devotion. In the *tilma* image Guadalupe wears a sash high on her waist suggesting that she is pregnant, the symbolic mother of Mexico.

Though I did not fully understand it when I first observed the collective prayer outside Santa Marta, that scene of protest was charged with historical significance. The national contest over abortion has deep roots, embodying conflicts over the role of the Catholic Church in the modern state that can be traced to the middle of the nineteenth century. Mexico's secular foundations were laid in the 1857 Constitution and reestablished in the 1917 Constitution, both of which curbed the political power of the church that marked the colonial era. While colonial law determined that abortion could be punished with death, the historical record indicates that women interrupted their pregnancies with the help of midwives throughout the colonial period (1521–1821) much as they had before the conquest, and they rarely faced prosecution.[17] As elsewhere in Latin America, abortion became illegal in post-Independence Mexico late in the nineteenth century.[18] The first national penal code established in 1871 permitted the procedure only when necessary to save a woman's life or if accidentally induced.[19] Once abortion was defined as a crime, women were charged more frequently for interrupting their pregnancies, yet even by the close of the nineteenth century they were rarely convicted.[20]

The anticlerical measures first enacted after the Wars of Independence from Spain only intensified after the Revolution of 1910. During his presidency from 1924 to 1928, Plutarco Elías Calles prohibited the church from owning property, eradicated religious education, and banned religious celebrations throughout the country. Many Catholic leaders and lay people resisted the constrictions on religious power. Opposition to the secular regime came to a head in the Cristero Revolt of 1926, a violent multiyear insurrection led by Catholic peasants across Mexico's Central West "Rosary Belt."[21] While the movement ultimately failed to reverse the anticlerical reforms, it was effective in affording the church a stronger platform from which to negotiate with the state. Even as several European countries legalized abortion throughout the 1930s and '40s, Mexican heads of state upheld criminalization to mollify religious leaders. "Abortion rights remained subject to the vagaries of politically expedient gentlemen's agreements between Church and state," explains Adriana Ortiz-Ortega.[22]

Over the course of the last century, state leaders advanced divergent understandings of the relationship between femininity, reproduction, and nationalism. "Despite 'solving' this religious question—or the place of the Church in a Catholic-majority country after a markedly anticlerical revolution," observes historian Madeleine Olson, "the issue frequently came into public discussion throughout the 20th century."[23] Entrenched struggles over "the religious question" have cohered in recent years around women's reproductive rights.[24] Abortion in particular has become a central arena to contest the secular character of the state and a platform to challenge feminist notions of reproduction as a voluntary act.[25] Although opponents of abortion rights have adopted La Guadalupe as a timeless cultural symbol of Mexican maternity to dispute the legal status of abortion in the capital, a brief tour of the historical literature reveals that the meanings of motherhood in modern Mexico are unstable.

EUGENIC PRONATALISM AND POSTREVOLUTIONARY NATIONALISM

In postrevolutionary Mexico bountiful reproduction was defined as a national obligation of women.[26] The nation had emerged from a decade of warfare (1910–20) in a state of disarray, with a depleted population plagued by poverty and illness.[27] In demographic terms, the events took a calamitous toll. While many people died in battle, others succumbed to disease outbreaks such as the Spanish flu epidemic of 1918. Hundreds of thousands more emigrated to the United States to escape the violence or to search for better economic opportunities. And national fertility rates suffered as couples were torn apart during the war.[28] Historians disagree on the exact demographic toll of the political turmoil, but some place the count at over two million.[29]

Faced with a diminished populace, political leaders sought to resupply the cadre of Mexican workers and repatriate the nation, extolling large families as a badge of national pride.[30] Because of their reproductive capacities women figured as key players in the project of postrevolutionary state formation. Historian Nichole Sanders explains that "manipulating the symbol of the Mexican mother was an important way to bolster a particular interpretation of the revolution."[31] Whereas men in postrevolutionary Mexico were charged with embodying a hypermasculine nationalist bravado, women were tasked with producing the next generation with revolutionary zeal. Pronatalist state policies and maternalist Catholic doxa resonated with the social conditions of the era, as rural couples benefited from having more children to help with agricultural work and to confer economic security later in life.[32]

Yet state efforts to boost fertility were selective. In the postrevolutionary moment not all citizens were considered ideal reproducers. Leaders sought to cultivate the population in particular ways according to the nationalist project that was taking shape. They hoped to expand the population but also to enhance its "quality" by monitoring its racial composition. If Mexico was to forge ahead and create for itself a cohesive national identity, leaders reasoned, then its population had to reflect this revolutionary spirit. As in other parts of Latin America, growing faith in the power of science to solve social problems provided an ideal ideological climate for the crystallization of eugenic ideas in postrevolutionary Mexico.[33] Eugenic science offered a glimmer of hope in answering the enduring question of how to integrate "the Indian" into the national populace and how to improve life for the poor.[34]

Eugenic ideals coalesced around the figure of "el mestizo," an embodiment of the racial and cultural integration wrought by the Spanish conquest. According to national lore the original mestizo was the son of La Malinche, the indigenous Nahua interpreter given over to Spanish conquistador Hernán Cortés upon his arrival in Mexico early in the sixteenth century. Her union with the European invader yielded a mestizo son, "the first Mexican"—progeny of violent conqueror and sexually defeated woman, mixture of Spanish and indigenous blood. In "the mestizo" anthropologists and other intellectuals of the era found a national identity that captured Mexico's unique history of cultural and biological mixture. The celebration of *mestizaje* (racial mixture) could unite the fractured nation, bringing Mexico ahead as an integrated whole.

Whereas colonial and Porfirian leaders had denigrated indigenous peoples and cultures as obstacles to national progress, stubborn remnants of a bygone era, the postrevolutionary regime instrumentalized the unique national history of racial mixture as a tool of state formation. Political leaders and intellectual elites exalted mestizaje as an ideology for national renewal.[35] In his capacity as secretary of education between the years of 1920 and 1924, José Vasconcelos promoted his prophetic vision of a "cosmic race," a transcendent mixture of races born from integration. He set out to reeducate the masses according to a romantic interpretation of Mexican history that emphasized the superior cultural mixture born of the conquest, binding the nation together with the myth of racial homogeneity.[36] Vasconcelos hired celebrated artists such as Diego Rivera, José Clemente Orozco, and David Alfaro Siqueiros to manifest his vision through muralism. The public murals painted throughout the country would be an educational tool, visually arresting in their scale and accessible even to the poor and illiterate. The muralism movement sought to define a cohesive national purpose, one that might, for art historian Robin Adèle Greeley, "link in common cause all the nation's inhabitants from the most rustic farmer to the most powerful military and political leaders."[37] Although women figure in the incredible murals that adorn major buildings across Mexico to this day—featured variously as revolutionary soldiers, teachers, and artists—anthropologist Liza Bakewell contends that their centrality in these visual representations contradicts the reality of the era in which they were produced.[38] Compared to their male counterparts, Bakewell writes, "[Women] were anonymous participants in the forward march of Mexican society," useful to the postrevolutionary government primarily for their reproductive potential rather than their artistic talents or political acumen.[39] Indeed, despite the progressive tenor of the revolutionary project, women in Mexico would not gain the right to vote until 1953.

If Diego Rivera has achieved international celebrity for his impressive murals and frescos, Frida Kahlo, his third wife, who is better known for her intimate portraits of the anguish of their tortured romance, offers more clues about reproduction and feminine experience in the postrevolutionary period. While Kahlo's art ostensibly dwells in the intimate, the art historian Eva Zetterman has suggested that her pieces might be better understood as "representations of a critical subject position addressing political issues in contemporary Mexican society."[40] Early in Kahlo's life a trolley accident rendered her infertile, and many of her works depict with raw emotionality the torment she experienced as a result. Early in the twentieth century Kahlo produced a handful of haunting self-portraits featuring vaginal bleeding, sex organs, and lost fetuses. She never titled her 1932 lithograph, which has come to be known variously as *Frida and the Abortion* or *Frida and the Miscarriage*. Drawn in the style of an ex-voto, an artistic tradition that depicts a tragic accident averted by divine intercession, Frida appears upright in the piece, tears streaming from her cheeks and blood dripping from her vagina, a fetus with closed eyes floating outside her body. That same year, in 1932, while accompanying Rivera on a mural commission in Detroit, Kahlo painted *Henry Ford Hospital*, also known as *Lost Desire*. In this piece she lies feebly in a bloodied hospital bed, a fetus, a crushed pelvis, and other symbols suspended from umbilical strings around her.

Kahlo produced these works at a time when femininity was virtually syn-onymous with maternity, and, as Eva Zetterman has intimated, it is possible that her apparent despair over "failed motherhood" was largely performative.[41] While prevailing historiography treats these pieces as depictions of spontaneous miscarriages or therapeutic abortions, Zetterman points to archival records in-dicating that Kahlo may have ingested quinine to induce the abortions with the help of a doctor because she did not want to become a mother. The ambiguity in the historical record and in the works themselves reflects the moral controversy around abortion in the maternalist environment of postrevolutionary Mexico, and also in the United States, where *Henry Ford Hospital* is set. While there is not space here for a thorough account of these artists or the political influence of their work, even cursory consideration of Rivera's murals and Kahlo's por-traits suggests that we are wise to collapse the presumed separation between the public staging of postrevolutionary nationalism and the "private" reproductive concerns of women early in the twentieth century.[42] Kahlo and Rivera never did bear a child together, but their art, replete with imagery of racial and cul-tural mixture, was central to the symbolic production of the mestizo nation.

Early in the twentieth century mestizaje offered a way for the postrev-olutionary state to legitimate itself by forging a sense of national cohesion grounded in a collective history. For Mexican sociologist Roger Bartra, it was *this* nationalist story that allowed the Institutional Revolutionary Party (PRI) to enjoy political stability throughout the twentieth century without ever ac-complishing true and representative democracy.[43] For all its inspirational ap-peal, mestizaje entailed egregious erasures and must not be taken as category that smoothed out difference in an emancipatory way. When politicians and intellectuals deployed mestizaje as an ideology of Mexican nationalism, they implicitly defined indigenous peoples as culturally and biologically "backward," redeemable only through mingling with "superior races."[44] Proponents anticipated that the emergence of the mestizo body politic would absorb and efface the unseemly characteristics of indigenous peoples that were thought to be holding Mexico back. The goal, ultimately, was to exceed the Indian past, understood to be out of time and place, to arrive at a utopic imagined future.

Pronatalism endured as the leading population policy as the postrevolutionary regime consolidated in the first half of the twentieth century. As physicians and social reformers moved ahead with their eugenic mission, women's reproductive lives came under intensive scrutiny. Medical and educational institutions introduced the concept of "responsible motherhood," charging women with nurturing the future cadre of Mexican citizens.[45] As the cultural and biological reproducers of the nation, women were tasked with managing the Mexican family, a key node of revolutionary nationalism. "Mexican women were not simply homemakers and mothers," observes anthropologist Rebecca Lester; "in their wombs and in their homes, they nurtured and shaped the future of the Mexican nation. They would literally bring forth the 'new' Mexican nation from their bodies and suckle it at their breasts."[46]

Even earlier, by the second half of the nineteenth century, Mexican obstetricians had become obsessed by the size and structure of Mexican women's pelves.[47] In the female pelvis physicians searched for clues about the success of the national project of racial and state formation that was under way. "This part of a Mexican woman's body was imbued with multiple meanings: it was the prime suspect in theories of racial degeneration and, at the same time, due to its form and function, bore the stamp of the 'mestizo race'; by extension, it signified the problems of a nation in the process of becoming," write Laura Cházaro and Paul Kersey.[48] Women's reproductive organs thus embodied the imprint of an incomplete project of racial formation and represented the medium through which this promissory vision might be realized.

In the postrevolutionary moment women did not elude state scrutiny even after the birth of their children. Through their child-rearing techniques they were encouraged to impart to their young the proper temperaments and values for the new nation.[49] Women were subject to instruction from cadres of child hygienists on how to properly clean and bathe their offspring according to the biopolitical mandates of the moment. Historian Alexandra Stern explains, "Under the broad banner of reconstituting 'La Gran Familia Mexicana,' eugenicists and child hygienists were entrusted with rescripting the behavior of mothers on behalf of the post-revolutionary state."[50]

Ultimately, the pronatalist policies proved effective in cultivating the population. By the 1960s fertility levels had soared to an all-time high, averaging 7.3 children per woman. While these counts suggest that women took up the revolutionary call to action, it is also possible that women who may have wanted fewer children had limited means to curtail their fertility in the absence of accessible birth control technologies.[51] Manifesting the revolutionary ethos of pronatalism, the national population tallied fifty million by 1970.[52] But change was on the horizon.

REMAKING MODERN MOTHERHOOD

Despite the association in postrevolutionary Mexico of abundant fertility with femininity, the latter part of the century was marked by national panic about the dangers of "overpopulation."[53] National alarm about the size of the population surfaced after a period of sustained economic growth remembered as "the Mexican miracle." At the time, rising rates of rural to urban migration and high birth rates were absorbed by the prosperous economy, substantiating prevailing theories that associated high fertility with economic development. But by the 1960s the population of dispossessed peasants had grown dramatically.[54] Without work, peasants migrated to urban centers such as Mexico City, contributing to the appearance of visible population growth. As unemployment levels soared it became clear that the Mexican economy could no longer absorb population growth, and international warnings about the risks of overpopulation were domesticated.

On the global scale, the threat of overpopulation had come to preoccupy world leaders, emerging as a foremost concern for the future of humanity. It was 1968 when biologist Paul Ehrlich published his manifesto *The Population Bomb*, in which he argued that global fertility rates threatened to deplete the world's natural resources, generate social unrest, and devitalize the human race.[55] Ehrlich advocated for drastic measures, framing population growth as an existential threat to humanity. "The pain will be intense," he wrote, "but the disease is so far advanced that only with radical surgery does the patient have any chance of survival."[56] The sensational warnings gained traction among medical professionals, corporate leaders, politicians, and heads of state. Eager to stem the tide of high fertility, a constellation of nongovernmental organizations, including the Population Council, the Ford Foundation, and the International Planned Parenthood Federation (IPPF) collaborated to implement population control programs in poor countries throughout the developing world.[57] Propaganda circulated through media and grassroots campaigns linking the dangers of high fertility to the rise of social protest movements such as the American civil rights movement and the women's movement, well under way by this time, as well as social ills such as drug addiction and crime.

In the United States fears about overpopulation fused with xenophobic anxieties around immigration from Mexico.[58] Mexican immigrants emerged in popular and political discourse as calculating criminals conniving to leech off welfare and other social programs or to steal "American jobs." Environmentalists and others committed to broadening the reach of family planning fueled panic about the influx of Mexican immigrants and the havoc they would wreak on American society. But even though Mexicans were framed in US political discourse as a source of overpopulation, it was a Mexican chemist who developed the technology to produce the birth control pill in the 1950s using a species of Mexican yam.[59] While birth control would remain largely unavailable in Mexico until decades later, historian Gabriela Soto Laveaga writes that "by 1960 more than 2 million women in the United States were using the Pill, and more than 100,000 Mexican peasants were gathering the raw material used in its production."[60]

The United Nations named 1974 "World Population Year," pledging to play a role in curbing the tide of overpopulation.[61] That same year, under the presidency of Richard Nixon, the US government produced "The Kissinger Report," formally called "National Security Memorandum: Implications of Worldwide Population Growth for U.S. Security and Overseas Interests."[62] The classified document, not released until 1989, described overpopulation in the developing world as an imminent threat to US national security, explaining that the consequences of overpopulation in countries with the highest fertility rates could threaten the United States' position as the leading geopolitical power. Political instability threatened to discourage foreign investment, jeopardizing the US economy and the country's role on the global stage.

Reacting to international pressure and domestic evidence of social ills related to the fast-growing population, Mexican politicians began to take action to address national fertility rates. Contraception was legalized in 1973, and although the Catholic Church officially condemned its use, the alacrity with which women throughout Mexico adopted contraceptive technologies suggests that at least some local priests defied religious prohibitions, absolving their parishioners.[63] Whereas just years earlier Mexican president Luis Echeverría had proudly proclaimed the pronatalist sentiments of the era, declaring that "to govern is to populate," in the mid-1970s he established the first National Population Council (CONAPO) to address the issue of overpopulation and to improve maternal and infant health.[64] At the inauguration of CONAPO politicians cited overpopulation as the determining factor in high rates of poverty, migration to urban centers, illiteracy, malnutrition, and disease. The president advocated contraception as the foremost solution, implicating women in the social crisis and its resolution.

With the future of the Mexican nation in mind, in 1974 Echeverría established a new population law designed to rapidly curb growth. The constitution was amended to read: "Every person has the right to decide in a free, responsible and informed manner on the number and spacing of their children."[65] Massive family planning campaigns encouraged women to adopt modern contraceptive technologies, which were made available free of cost through public clinics, first in urban centers like Mexico City and later in rural areas across the country. The promotion of reproductive responsibility, defined by the use of modern birth control to reduce fertility and space children, was a centerpiece of the campaigns. While just decades earlier (wealthier and whiter) women had been encouraged to increase fertility to repopulate the nation, by the 1970s they were enjoined to create small, modern families.[66] The reigning slogan of the campaigns—"La familia pequeña vive mejor" (The small family lives better)—communicated the idea that having fewer children would cut expenses to enhance quality of life for the national body.

Later that decade a public family planning program called "Promotora de Planificcación Familiar" (PROFAM) was established to offer birth control pills, suppositories, spermicides, and condoms to the public. PROFAM rolled out an extensive campaign to inform the populace about the benefits of modern family planning. The Population Council and other organizations carried out research on "cultural barriers" to the adoption of contraceptive technologies so that more Mexicans might begin to limit their fertility.[67] Certain segments of the population were more heavily targeted for contraceptive uptake. As in earlier eras, the reproduction of rural and indigenous people as well as poor urbanites was considered a particularly problematic barrier to national progress.[68]

Although modifying the constitution to reflect the government's new position on population was accomplished rather swiftly, shifting public attitudes on family size would be a longer and more involved task. The newly inaugurated CONAPO launched a series of social marketing campaigns to establish smaller families as the "*new*" Mexican ideal. "By the 1970s," writes Gabriela Soto Laveaga, "expected parental roles were altered to reflect the needs of a more urban, mobile, and industrialized Mexico."[69] The campaigns sought to eradicate "cultural traits" that might hinder fertility management and stall social progress. If social marketing campaigns could dislodge cultural barriers, large sectors of the population might adopt contraception. Among the characteristics deemed to weaken the social fabric and run counter to development projects were feminine "passivity" and male "machismo," those same gendered traits that had been central to postrevolutionary national propaganda. Through billboards, telenovelas, and TV commercials, Mexican women learned that "modern womanhood" entailed confidence and assertiveness toward one's husband, a willingness to take a stand and demand that their opinions around family formation and other matters were recognized. Women were enjoined to communicate their desires around fertility rather than succumbing to the imagined carnal instincts of men.

Fifty years after the Mexican state directed women to boost their fertility to bring the nation ahead, women were called on again to transform their reproductive lives, now by limiting their fertility.[70] In redefining the new national ideal for motherhood, the campaigns reworked postrevolutionary efforts to regulate women's reproductive bodies as a means to national success. By 1987 the fertility the rate had fallen to 3.7 children per woman, and it would dip to a low of 3.3 by the 1990s.[71] As in much of the developing world, that number continued to plunge toward replacement levels and eventually stabilized early in the twenty-first century.[72] Yet even as fertility control arose as a biopolitical obligation in Cold War–era Mexico, abortion remained illegal. In the closing decades of the twentieth century, however, a feminist movement was taking shape, and the right to abortion had emerged as one of its central demands.

ABORTION RIGHTS AND THE CONSTRUCTION OF VOLUNTARY MOTHERHOOD

The pronatalist polices and economic growth that characterized the early decades of PRI rule generated demographic and social transformations that would ultimately undermine the regime's authority as the century drew to a close.[73] Urbanization and the development of transportation technologies facilitated the rise of broad-based social movements, as Mexicans across the country came in closer contact than ever before. Although rural peasants had predominated when the PRI took power, by the turn of the twentieth century the population was much more educated, urban, and middle class. More and more people were troubled by the corrupt tactics of the ruling party. For decades the PRI had systematically squelched or co-opted popular mobilization. But by the 1960s a student movement for democratic governance had emerged with enough popular support to challenge the regime. Prolonged conflict between protesters and the PRI culminated on the eve of the 1968 Olympics in Mexico City. Military police massacred hundreds of peaceful student protesters and civilians in the Plaza de las Tres Culturas, thrusting the ruling regime into a prolonged "legitimacy crisis."[74] The climate of popular uprising provided a breeding ground for politicization.

At the tail end of the student movement, a second wave of Mexican feminism was gaining force. At the time, the movement was dominated by middle-class university-educated women.[75] Influenced by feminist conversations unfolding in the US and Europe, activists critiqued gendered divisions of labor that relegated women to the domestic sphere. Protected, to a degree, by their economic privilege, they called for revolutionary change and openly critiqued the corruption of the PRI regime. Movement energy coalesced under the banner of "voluntary motherhood," a broad concept including four specific demands for legal rights to sexual education, accessible contraception, freedom from sterilization, and abortion.[76] As part of a broader critique of government repression, activists sought to expose what Adriana Ortiz-Ortega has called the "doble discurso" (double discourse) on abortion, drawing attention to the discrepancy between restrictive abortion law and the presence of private abortion clinics that served the wealthy.[77] The private clinics existed as a tacit secret and largely escaped state harassment, save for the occasional police raids, which served, one assumes, to legitimate state authority in the face of overt insubordination. Feminists emphasized contradictions in the national abortion situation, documenting the health consequences of restrictive laws for women who were unable to afford private abortion services and the legal consequences for the medical providers who put themselves at risk to help them.

Appeals for "voluntary motherhood" were tied to the broader popular struggle for democratic change and the creation of a government that was obliged to protecting citizen rights. Cautious about the PRI strategy of co-opting or repressing dissenters, activists focused their energies on critique and denunciation of the regime rather than collaboration with the political apparatus. Yet, in the face of avid opposition on behalf of the Catholic hierarchy, their appeals went unanswered. Even after a commission of demographers, social scientists, economists, and religious leaders appointed by the National Population Council recommended, in 1976, that abortion be included in public health services, political leaders refused to legalize the procedure in light of fervent opposition from the church.[78]

Irreconcilable tensions splintered the feminist movement in the last two decades of the twentieth century. Disagreements centered on organizing tactics, as some activists had grown weary of revolutionary idealism, calling for concrete reform of the political system.[79] By the 1980s "popular feminism"—a movement of and for the working class—had come to replace the more elite brand of "radical feminism." Though they embraced many of the same demands of their more radical counterparts, popular feminists stood out for prioritizing the unique concerns of working women.[80] Abandoning the antistate politics of preceding years, activists established an array of nonprofit organizations dedicated to political lobbying and advocacy.[81]

Beyond feminist activity, the 1980s were a time of widespread popular disillusionment with the PRI regime.[82] An economic crisis had devastated the national economy and prevented the PRI from buying off dissenters. When an earthquake struck the capital in 1985, the government's failure to respond to the emergency deepened popular disenchantment with the regime. Cynicism peaked again after the fraudulent 1988 presidential election of PRI candidate Carlos Salinas de Gortari, who had allegedly beat out his PRD competitor Cuauhtémoc Cárdenas. Mexicans were outraged by the barefaced resort to fraud in manipulating election results, and the vulnerability of the ruling regime was laid bare.[83]

Against the backdrop of widespread dissent, feminist activists attempted to challenge restrictive abortion laws through legislative channels. In 1980 they made limited headway by convincing the Mexican Communist Party to put forth a bill on "voluntary motherhood" in the Mexican Congress, but the bill was soon shelved. In 1983 the attorney general, the Department of Justice of Mexico City, and the National Institute of Criminology put forward another bill to decriminalize abortion. It was met with a forceful reaction by conservative forces including the church, the PAN, and ProVida, Mexico's largest prolife organization, and eventually this bill too was abandoned. A few years later Mexican police stormed a private abortion clinic, arresting patients, nurses, and the doctor. According to some accounts, police harassed the detained.[84] Activists publicized the incident in the national press to garner popular support for their movement, but efforts for abortion reform did not come to pass.

Advocates of abortion rights encountered yet another barrier when state relations with the Vatican were reestablished in 1992, expanding the church's public presence and threatening hard-won feminist gains. As the church worked to erode the limited reproductive rights that were in place, several NGOs dedicated to securing reproductive rights incorporated throughout Mexico City. International feminist NGOs flooded the capital as well, collaborating with local organizations to secure funding and participate in the movement for women's sexual and reproductive rights. GIRE, the Information Group for Reproductive Choice, founded in 1992 and still in existence today, advocated for reproductive rights including abortion, raised public awareness of sexual and reproductive rights violations in the Mexican media, and used litigation to press for reform of laws that violated women's rights.[85] In 1997 the left-leaning Party of the Democratic Revolution (PRD) gained office in Mexico City, reinvigorating feminist efforts and providing the political conditions for abortion reform.

By the close of the decade the feminist movement had undergone a dramatic transformation. Many participants had come to embrace direct engagement with state politics.[86] Some joined the center-left PRD to struggle for change from within the political system. Radical feminists remained skeptical of the reformist character of newer styles of feminist activity, and tensions peaked between the old school of revolutionary activism and the newer tendency of what Marta Lamas has called "state feminism."[87] Throughout the 1990s, feminism gained a central place in public and political life. As the movement for democratization surged on, voices outside the PRI were taken seriously for the first time. Increasingly, the mainstream feminist movement began to work toward a democratic transition. Activists were eager to shape the course of Mexican politics and have a voice in matters of public policy. As the movement reworked its political strategy, leaders articulated three demands: an end to gender-based violence, equal representation of women in the political sphere, and legal abortion.[88]

When health officials at a hospital in the Mexican state of Baja California obstructed Paulina del Carmen Ramírez Jacinto, a thirteen-year-old rape victim, from accessing her legal right to an abortion in 1999, a team of nongovernmental organizations including the Center for Reproductive Rights (CRR), Alaíde Foppa, and GIRE presented her case to the Inter-American Commission on Human Rights (IACHR) to demand justice.[89] Paulina's case was deeply troubling, both for the horrific details of the assault and the egregious abuses of the medical system. Some disturbing details are useful in conveying the depth of the violence she suffered. A burglar broke into the family's home while they slept, stabbing Paulina with a knife before raping her in front of her family members.[90] When Paulina learned that she was pregnant, she decided to exercise her right to an abortion according to the legal rape exception in place in every Mexican state. The Baja California Attorney General Office ordered the Mexicali General Hospital to perform the procedure, but local prolife actors, political leaders, and hospital personnel conspired to prevent her from obtaining an abortion through harassment and misinformation. Nine months later, Paulina gave birth to a boy. Feminists published the case in the media to garner public support for transforming Mexico's punishing abortion laws. A year after the rape, celebrated Mexican journalist and novelist Elena Poniatowska published an account of Paulina's case to bring her story to the public. In 2006, as part of a so-called friendly agreement, Paulina was paid reparations, and the Mexican state agreed to implement effective mechanisms to ensure the accessibility of abortion after rape, thereby acknowledging, however tacitly, that abortion is a human right of women.[91]

The Paulina case has since become a national flash point for the Mexican abortion debate. It was on the heels of this highly public case that Mexico City began to relax its stringent abortion laws. For many activists, decades of struggle reached fruition with the incremental expansion of legal exceptions for abortion in the capital, beginning with the Ley Robles (enacted in 2000) and resulting in the full legalization of voluntary abortion in 2007. Yet resistance to legal abortion was powerful. It was not a coincidence, for instance, when shortly before the 2007 reform the Virgin of Guadalupe appeared on the winning dress design for the Miss Mexico contest that would be paraded before an international audience that spring in the Miss Universe competition in Mexico City. The judges' decision generated intense controversy. The dress showed the Virgin surrounded by scenes of the Cristero Rebellion, including hanged rebels, towering crosses, and a firing squad. Adding to the dramatic imagery on the dress itself, a loaded ammunition belt hung from the waistline. For critics, the dress was a deliberate attempt by conservative forces to frame the extension of abortion rights in the Mexican capital as the newest instantiation of century-old attacks on religious freedoms in the country.[92] Before the reform was ratified, moreover, members of the Catholic hierarchy threatened legislators who supported the bill with excommunication.[93]

The resistance did not stop there. Religious protesters quickly became a regular fixture outside the ILE clinics that opened throughout the capital. One protester at Reina María Clinic told me that her antiabortion activism had begun years earlier when she traveled to Chicago, Illinois, to obtain a legal abortion in the aftermath of *Roe v. Wade*. Later on, she had struggled to become pregnant, suffering eight miscarriages and a stillbirth—penance, she said, for killing one of God's children. She told me that she wished someone had been there to orient her to the risks of abortion. Today she tries to be that person for other women, waking up before dawn once a week to distribute pamphlets outside the clinic. I'm not sure how she measured her efforts, for the steady stream of patients that flowed into the ILE clinics never seemed to abate.

ABORTION AS STATE SERVICE

If opposition to abortion was discernable outside clinic walls, resistance was also manifest within the ILE program, particularly in the early years of its existence. As soon as the 2007 law passed, the MOH incorporated ILE services into fourteen existing hospitals throughout the capital. Individual medical personnel were afforded the right to conscientious objection (CO), but MOH institutions were required to keep nonobjecting personnel on hand and to provide abortion services to all women requesting the procedure who met the legal criteria for ILE. With backing from PAN allies, members of the Catholic hierarchy rallied medical professionals within the MOH to abstain from performing abortions. Many clinicians took up the call. Within the first few months as many as 85 percent of health care professionals across the participating hospitals refused to partake in the provision of abortion care.[94] "While conservatives in Mexico City lost the battle over [abortion] in both the Legislature and the Supreme Court, they still hoped to win a battle through CO," observes philosopher and bioethicist Gustavo Ortiz-Millán.[95]

Because no new personnel were hired to staff the clinics at the outset, existing clinicians were trained to integrate abortion into their daily workloads.[96] As clinicians defected workloads increased for the personnel who remained. Few had anticipated the extreme demand that would overcome the program. In the early years, women requesting abortions inundated the hospitals by the thousands. Seven thousand procedures were performed in the first year alone. With fewer and fewer staff members, program administrators struggled to manage patient demand. "We tried to raise awareness, to inform health workers that abortion was now legal in Mexico City, that our hospitals had to attend to the women seeking interruptions," María Puerto, the assistant director of the ILE program, once recalled to me about the stress of those years. "There were like fourteen hospitals back then, and in many of them the directors had to attend to the women themselves because there weren't enough doctors. Little by little health workers started leaving the ILE program." The MOH eventually established clear guidelines, determining that only ob-gyns and general surgeons were allowed to conscientiously object because of their direct role in performing abortion procedures. In 2009 the Mexico City General Health

Law established that clinicians could not invoke their right to CO in instances when an abortion was necessary to save a woman's life.[97]

To address personnel shortages and simplify the provision of ILE services, the MOH later established four ambulatory clinics dedicated specifically to ILE within existing MOH hospitals and demarcated with separate entrances. Program administrators recruited new personnel from within the MOH and other institutions to staff the ambulatory clinics according to their willingness to participate in the provision of ILE care. These specialized ILE clinics were strategically located in marginal zones of the city with high population density, economic vulnerability, and high rates of adolescent pregnancy, like Tacalco. At the time of my research ILE services were available through nine MOH hospitals (fewer than the original fourteen) as well as the four ambulatory clinics, which together constituted the ILE program. I often heard whisperings that a fifth specialized ILE clinic might open to accommodate fast-growing demand, but it never did.

Two kinds of abortion procedures were available through the ILE program—medical abortion and aspiration abortion—the latter of which includes both manual vacuum aspiration (MVA) and electric vacuum aspiration (EVA). However, to date the vast majority of procedures performed through the program have been induced pharmacologically.[98] At the time of my research medical abortions were induced using a combined regimen of the drugs mifepristone and misoprostol, reflecting the international gold standard for first-trimester abortion care. Patients undergoing a medical abortion took one pill (200 mg of mifepristone) in the clinic and were sent home with another set of pills (800 mg of misoprostol) to be taken twenty-four hours later in two doses.[99] Because these medicines continually ran out, clinicians occasionally used misoprostol on its own, which is 84–96 percent effective in inducing first-trimester abortion when used correctly, and is approved by the World Health Organization for this purpose.[100] When both the misoprostol and mifepristone ran out, which happened more than once during my research, clinical capacities were reduced to postabortion follow-up and aspiration procedures. Occasionally a local nongovernmental organization donated the drugs before the MOH could replenish the stock, allowing the clinic to resume the full panoply of abortion services.

Though protocols varied between individual ILE clinics and hospitals, at Santa Marta medical abortion was generally offered to women with pregnancies up to 10.5 weeks gestation and aspiration abortion was used for women whose pregnancies measured between 10.6 and 12 weeks. Women arriving from states outside the capital were typically scheduled for aspiration abortions, which are known to be more effective, regardless of the gestational age of their pregnancies. This way, in the event of a failed medical abortion a woman would not have to make the trip to the capital again. It was not until after I concluded my research that the MOH clarified the "twelve-week" gestational limit on abortion to include the last six days of the twelfth week—a space of discursive ambiguity that I consider in a later chapter. At the time of my study, clinicians were left to make determinations about how to define the twelve-week threshold on a case-by-case basis.

Roughly 235,000 ILE procedures have been carried out through the public sector ILE program at the time of this writing, and around 29,000 of those procedures were induced at Santa Marta Clinic.[101] The vast majority of women who have accessed ILE services were residents of Mexico City (over 160,000) and neighboring Mexico State (over 60,000), though women have visited the ILE clinics from every Mexican state since the inauguration of the program in 2007. Almost half of these women were between the ages of eighteen and twenty-four, 54 percent were unmarried, and 80 percent held no more than a high school degree. More than one-third did not work in the formal economy (37 percent), and one-quarter were students.[102] Since ILE is not offered through the federal social security institutions that serve the health needs of employed middle-class Mexicans, and since the procedure can be prohibitively costly in private clinics, middle-class women who might otherwise avoid the MOH do sometimes visit the ILE program to obtain free abortion services. "They come from all socioeconomic levels," Dr. Rios told me about the patients she saw at Santa Marta. "We see the poorest women and the lawyer who arrives in a flashy automobile, illiterate women, and women with PhDs all come here." María Puerto agreed with this assessment. "You see everything," she said. "There are women with a very high cultural, economic, and educational profile, and there are women without this kind of educational and economic profile." Such observations that the

ILE program serves a diverse slice of the Mexican population are apt, even if most ILE patients are not wealthy.

Although the MOH does not collect data on race and ethnicity among ILE patients, these dynamics are central to any discussion of classed distinctions in Mexico, where social class maps closely onto skin color in such a way that light-skinned people generally enjoy higher-paying jobs, preferential treatment, and greater opportunities than their dark-skinned counterparts.[103] Most ILE patients, like the general population, can be considered "mestizo"—that slippery political construct best described as a mythical racial ideology promoted by postrevolutionary leaders and intellectuals bent on producing the fantasy of an integrated nation.[104] Yet if ever I asked patients about their racial or ethnic background, most simply told me they were "Mexican." Politically motivated racial constructs held little relevance for individuals.

Explicit discussions of the racial and class backgrounds of patients were also rare among the ILE personnel. Occasionally a clinic worker sympathized with the situation of a low-income patient or remarked on the audacity of wealthier patients, whom they perceived to be quicker to challenge their medical authority. More often these dynamics were subdued and implicit, hanging in the background. Generally, when I asked clinicians about the racial/ethnic composition of the ILE clientele they offered oblique responses. "Most patients do not speak *dialecto* (dialect, which here refers to an indigenous language)," Carolina once said to me.

Despite the national myth of racial homogeneity, race and ethnicity in Mexico are more complex at the level of lived experience. Anthropologist Laura Braff aptly describes race in Mexico as a "flexible social spectrum of skin color, class, power, and region [whereby] elites tend to be light-skinned, wealthy, powerful, and urban; indigenous people tend to be darker-skinned, poorer, disempowered, and rural; and mestizos (persons of mixed indigenous and Spanish heritage who constitute the majority) occupy variable positions between these two poles."[105] In other words, there is malleability in Mexican racial schemas such that the acquisition of certain forms of cultural and economic capital can serve to symbolically "whiten" regardless of phenotype. Living in the cosmopolitan capital and having a well-remunerated job, for instance, afford a degree of power and prestige regularly allotted to those with light skin. "Whiteness" here does not refer to skin color alone. The term *güero* (white person) connotes all manner of prestige, beauty, money, education, and social status, in addition to light shades of skin. This can also work in reverse. The pejorative term *naco* is generally used to indicate that someone is low class, poor, or culturally "backward" but almost always implies darker shades of skin or indigeneity.

Regardless of the racial and economic diversity of the ILE clientele, the fact that public ILE services are available only through the MOH means, in the words of Ana Amuchástegui and Edith Flores, that "the underprivileged status of the poorest women without social security is transferred to all women seeking abortion [through the ILE program]."[106] Women availing themselves of ILE services are cared for in the lowest tier of the public health system, which typically serves the poor and unemployed. They must contend with long waits, bureaucratic hurdles, and other dynamics of ILE care that wealthier patients can more readily avoid in expensive private clinics. In the process, as we will see in the chapters ahead, even wealthier patients come to occupy the same subject positions as the poor and working women who typically depend on the MOH for health care needs.

The introduction of the specialized ILE clinics, in sum, largely resolved the issue of objecting personnel, offering women across social strata an option for legal and accessible abortion care. Yet moral uncertainties over abortion permeated the clinics and the neighborhoods in which they were built, reflecting a long legacy of conflict over the place of the church in the Mexican state that today is played out on women's bodies.

*   *   *

It has taken me a long time to grasp why the Tacalco priest and his parishioners pinned Guadalupe's image to the wall of Santa Marta Clinic during the weekly protest with which I began this chapter. That image, laced with dense connotations of gender, piety, race, and nationalism, bore the weight of centuries of history. While peeling back these layers I was reminded of William Faulkner's famous words in *Requiem for a Nun*: "The past is never dead; it's not even past."[107] I still look at that photograph of the Virgin from time to time.

It is stored away in a folder on my computer along with other stills I captured from my time in Mexico City: the unbelievable yellow of a home I used to pass, a bonsai tree tucked behind the caged bars covering the window; shabby taxis stationed outside Santa Marta with their red and gold paint that cracked and peeled like the outer walls of the clinic.

In that photograph of the Virgin, Guadalupe cradles three multicolored infants—one indigenous, one European, and one mestizo—synecdoches for a violent colonial history of forced racial and cultural integration. Her gaze is lifted, fixed on a future yet to come. From her post outside the clinic, Guadalupe entreats the women who enter to embrace their unborn, Mexico's prospective citizens. Abortion, she seems to call out, represents an affront to national identity, a violent assault on the motherland. By cradling the "three Mexicos," Guadalupe stands in as the country's iconic mother—a potent symbol collapsing maternity, religion, race, and nation.

The Mexico where the Tacalco priest and his parishioners find themselves today is fast-changing, to be sure. Abortion has been legalized in the capital. Gender and romantic norms are shifting to accommodate companionate couplings that prioritize gender equality.[108] Many women are postponing marriage or deciding not to marry at all, preferring instead to prioritize educational and career goals above family life and to experiment with alternative romantic lifestyles. Atheism is on the rise, and scores of people are deserting the Catholic Church. In the capital, where many urbanites identify as atheists and openly critique the church and its definitions of sacrificial femininity, these changes are unmistakable. Guadalupe embodies a moral vision of Mexico that the protesters hoped to preserve amid sweeping social changes that are reconfiguring everyday life before their eyes.[109]

When I caught the priest's attention one morning after the collective prayer outside Santa Marta, he spoke to these layered meanings. "Abortion came here from the United Sates, from globalization," he said. "Feminists here think they are doing all of this [gesticulating toward the clinic] for the liberation of women, but abortion is murder." Though historians date the practice of abortion to the pre-Columbian era, casting it as a product of more recent US economic and cultural penetration of Mexico is another way of saying that abortion is fundamentally un-Mexican, an embodiment of the harsh and egotistic femininity associated with the United States. For the priest, abortion was an act of spiritual and national betrayal, and its provision through the state health system was evidence that the moral fabric of Mexico had been torn apart. If La Guadalupe is the embodiment of *mexicanidad*, abortion, for those who gathered outside the ILE clinic in protest each week, represents its collapse.[110]

CHAPTER TWO

THE RIGHT TO SIN

Abortion Rights in the Shadow of the Church

WHILE RELIGIOUS IMAGERY was relegated to the space outside Santa Marta Clinic, I found that the meanings condensed in Guadalupe's image animated moral negotiations inside its walls. One afternoon I told the Santa Marta personnel about my friend Luciana, who at the time had just learned she was pregnant. Luciana and her partner had invested vast amounts of money and energy in private fertility treatments. She was thirty-nine when she got the news that three of the embryos that had been implanted in her uterus had taken. Luciana had plans to fly from her home in Mexico City to Houston, Texas, the following week, I told the staff, to see a specialist for a "selective reduction" to remove one of the embryos.[1] As a practicing psychoanalyst and university lecturer, Luciana was wealthier than many of the patients who visited Santa Marta. Her ability to pay for costly private fertility treatment and international private abortion care set her apart. At the same time, however, she and her partner worried about how they would manage the care of three infants at once. And they were concerned about the medical risks of Luciana gestating triplets at her age. Luciana felt confident, I related to the personnel, that the selective reduction was the best path.

"She should have all three babies," a nurse named Lourdes interjected. When I emphasized the medical dangers, she grew insistent. "She should keep them. There is a reason why she is pregnant with triplets" (referencing fate). As a nurse working in an abortion clinic, I considered, surely she was aware of the risks of a multifetal pregnancy such as Luciana's. Yet no one else flinched at Lourdes's protest. "You see, Elyse, *nosotras Mexicanas aguantamos* [we Mexican women put up with struggle]," Lourdes continued, lowering her gaze to catch mine. Endurance in the face of struggle is a core feature of Marian femininity, which entails resignation to the suffering and sacrifice involved in pregnancy and childbirth. Lourdes's comment reflects the idea, documented elsewhere in Mexico, that feminine sacrifice is considered part of a "larger trajectory of the difficult," an expected component of "women's lot in life, part of their biological (even theological) destiny."[2] The staff's insistence that Luciana bring her triple pregnancy to term might be interpreted as a response to her middle-class status and the desired character of her pregnancy, dynamics that distinguished her from the majority of ILE patients. At the same time, for Lourdes and the other ILE personnel, bearing triplets to term at age thirty-nine, however medically risky, represented the properly feminine and properly "Mexican" response to a divinely proffered pregnancy. As they saw it, Luciana should accept rather than cast away "los hijos que Dios le mandó" (the children God sent her).

While the 2007 reform redefined women in the capital as political subjects of abortion rights, the law itself is situated in a country that is marked by the cultural legacy of three centuries of Catholic influence and whose population is predominantly Catholic. Configurations of religiosity are changing across the country as many people embrace Evangelical Protestant denominations and others leave behind organized religion entirely. Religious frameworks of femininity are changing too, and some Catholic thinkers have defended abortion. One Mexico City NGO called Catholics for the Right to Decide has introduced a Catholic feminist perspective that sanctions abortion and other reproductive options, as well as diverse family formations, as possibilities within Catholic faith. All of these changes are particularly apparent in metropolitan centers like the Mexico City, where occupational and educational opportunities are concentrated, activists have for decades contested the conflation of femininity with maternity, and elective first-trimester abortion is now legal and available on demand. Yet Catholicism is still tremendously important for people in Mexico, roughly 81 percent of whom identify as Catholic.[3] How do urbanites seeking to interrupt their pregnancies reconcile legal abortion in light of religious prohibitions?

Regardless of their religious affiliation or faith, women in urban Mexico must navigate competing norms and expectations around gender, reproduction, and maternity when deciding on the course of an untenable pregnancy. To understand how they do so, it is important to consider the local religious landscape.

CATHOLIC EDICTS IN THE BREACH

According to the Catholic catechism, abortion involves the destruction of innocent human life, constituting a mortal sin. Considered a serious breach of God's law, mortal sins are actions that imperil the violator's soul. For an action to be deemed a mortal sin, it must be intrinsically evil, violators must know that what they are doing is immoral, and they must freely choose to commit the behavior. For the Roman Catholic Church and its representatives, seeking an abortion meets all of these conditions.[4] According to canon law, obtaining an abortion results in automatic excommunication.[5] Before Pope Francis issued a papal edict in 2016 granting priests the indefinite power to pardon the sin of abortion, only bishops held the authority to absolve women who confessed.[6] Although more merciful on the issue of abortion than his predecessors, Pope Francis has been unambiguous in his position that life begins at conception and that abortion is a grave sin. Weeks before his home country of Argentina legalized elective abortion up to fourteen weeks in a milestone vote in December 2020, the pope likened the act of procuring an abortion to hiring a hit man to resolve a problem.[7]

I wanted to understand how women seeking legal pregnancy terminations through the ILE program reconciled abortion in light of Catholic proscriptions, and I thought that recruiting a subsample of Catholic abortion patients would be instructive. Early on in my research I made a point to recruit women who fit this criterion. This was a group presumably defined by the church as sinful. How did they resolve abortion decisions that stood in violation of religious edicts without compromising their religious commitments?

My attempts to recruit "Catholic women" in the waiting rooms of the ILE clinics initially proved troublesome. "It's hard to find Catholics here because even if we think we're Catholic, if we don't go to mass or that kind of thing, [the church] tells us we aren't. It's better to ask about *creyentes* [believers]," one patient told me toward the beginning of my fieldwork. Women's objections to my recruitment approach revealed the elusiveness of "Catholic" as a category, underlining the divergences between institutional Catholicism and popular styles of Catholic religiosity.[8] *Creyente* was a more common way for people to describe their faith, which in many cases did not align with formal religious rules. Overall, in the sample of sixty women whom I formally interviewed for this study, thirty-seven described themselves as Catholic *creyentes*, meaning that they had been raised in the Catholic faith but did not always follow religious doctrine in their everyday lives. An additional sixteen women said they had "no religion," four described themselves Christians, and three described themselves as "other." Elizabeth Maier has described the divergence between Catholic directives and sexual behavior among people in Mexico today, pointing to "the increasing tendency toward selective filtering of church doctrine in the creation of diversified contemporary lifestyles."[9] A recent study by the Pew Research Center of national attitudes among Catholics in Mexico confirms this point.[10] Most of those surveyed did not oppose sex before marriage (55 percent), divorce (68 percent), or contraception use (72 percent) despite church categorization of these practices as sinful, even if most of those polled did express opposition to abortion (71 percent).

"Selective filtering" of religious edicts was apparent in the account given by an ILE patient named Monserrat, a twenty-eight-year-old college graduate who lived in Tacalco. She captured wider patterns of popular Catholicism when she told me,

> I'm Catholic because I was born into a family that believes in God. We went to mass. When we were little I had my first communion, all of these religious rituals. But I think it's one thing to be Catholic and it's another thing to be immersed in [institutionalized] religion. What Catholic leaders think should not affect the decisions people make. Because, as they say, if God exists, and you are his child and he loves you above all else, then I don't think it's wrong to get an abortion. My friends and I, my boyfriend, we grew up in this religious sect, yet what the church says with respect to many issues doesn't affect us at all.

Other patients echoed Monserrat's assessment about the discrepancy between religious doctrine and popular forms of Catholic faith. Bianca, a university student from Mexico State, told me, "I believe in religion, I believe in the church, but more than anything because my parents indoctrinated me. I am not devout—I'm like 50 percent devout. I'm a believer but not in an exaggerated way, like I don't go to church every Sunday." When I asked a patient named Isa about her religious affiliation, she responded, "I'd say I'm *creyente*, not Catholic. I'm not very attached [*apegada*] to the church. I just believe, and every once in a while I visit a church." Paloma, who was about to enter college, told me in the same language that she was raised Catholic "but not *apegada*." Her parents by contrast were "very Catholic," and for this reason she had not told them about her decision to pursue an abortion. "I consider myself a Catholic," she clarified, "but only in a certain sense, because I don't agree with certain norms that the church dictates. I respect, I believe, but up to a point." Comments like these were pervasive among the ILE patients, many of whom defended their status as Catholics despite their regular breaches of religious edict. As a woman named Elsa told me, "Many people say that if you don't go to mass every Sunday, you aren't Catholic. But I consider myself Catholic because I believe in God, because I was baptized in the Catholic religion, my children are baptized in the same religion, I pray, and when I'm having a hard time, I seek advice from a priest. No, I don't go every Sunday to mass, but, for example, if I have time in the afternoon I might get my kids and go to church even if there is no mass."

Some people took these ideas further: they were Catholic, yes, but not "fanatics." When I asked Dr. Rios about her faith, she responded like this: "I don't know if I'm Catholic. I don't profess any religion ardently. I'm not a 'Dama de la Vela Perpetua.'" The Ladies of the Perpetual Vela is an association that arose in nineteenth-century Mexico, whose membership commits itself to sustaining an eternal vigil over the Blessed Sacrament.[11] I took Dr. Rios's comment to mean that she was a believer but not a follower of institutionalized Catholicism, and certainly not a "Catholic extremist." The Vela, as Dr Rios's quip suggests, is shorthand for a form of fanatical, overzealous Catholicism, the kind that might motivate a bloody insurrection like the Cristero Rebellion of the late 1920s. Mexicanist historian Margaret Chowning has observed that invocation of the Vela offers a convenient way to critique conservative

Catholicism, "since it conjures up in one fell swoop extremism (an all-day vigil, every day), futility (there is no socially productive outcome of the vigil) and pious intolerance, all bound up with a helpfully derogatory image of feminized Catholicism."[12] Dr. Rios, like Monserrat, Isa, and Paloma, was a believer but not a "fanatic."

It is tempting to read the comments I heard across the ILE clinics as evidence of the waning importance of Catholic faith for Mexican urbanites, particularly younger generations who form the majority of abortion patients. However, anticlerical sentiment is not a new phenomenon in Mexico or elsewhere in Latin America.[13] Nor does it preclude religiosity. Mexican sociologist Roberto Blancarte attributes the prevalence of anticlericalism in Latin America to "an endemic lack of priests, which directly affect[ed] the ecclesiastical capability to cover the whole territory, [and produced] a doctrinally weak religion with strong popular traits,"[14] thereby facilitating the growth of a heavily personalized style of Catholicism from its initial foray into New Spain in the sixteenth century. Recent historiography of Mexico, moreover, contests the conflation of anticlericalism with disenchantment to account for styles of Catholic faith that flout religious dogma.[15] Styles of religious expression in urban Mexico privilege personal exchanges with God above Catholic doctrine and, to a lesser extent, the intercession of priests.

For the ILE patients I encountered, the majority of whom were raised Catholic, an individual relationship with God proved more important than the edicts of the Catholic hierarchy. As one woman told me, "God exists everywhere, not necessarily in the church." When I asked a different patient how often she prayed ("¿Con que frequencia rezas?"), she insisted I clarify my question, noting the difference between the Spanish verbs *rezar*—to recite a formalized prayer in church, and *orar*—to communicate directly with God, as in private petitions for forgiveness. While *oración* (direct communication with God) was a regular part of her life, she rarely recited formalized prayers (*rezar*) because she hardly went to church. Faith, for many of these urbanites, is not bound by the physical or moral strictures of the church. As one ILE patient told me, "I carry out the custom of going to mass every week, but I'm not 100 percent devout. I would say I'm a believer, I've had that foundation ever since I was a child. I believe in God but not in the image that the church paints."

If most abortion patients were not especially worried about church con-demnation of abortion, many were concerned about God's forgiveness. Unlike church officials who echoed Catholic doctrine, God, for many of the women I spoke with, was merciful and understanding. Women conveyed that while God did not approve of abortion, he could appreciate the broader panorama in which they made the decision to terminate their pregnancies. "Before I knew for sure that I was pregnant," one patient told me, "I told God I might be, because I had sexual relations, and I asked [for forgiveness] in a prayer. [I told God,] I don't know how you view that, but right now I am not ready to have a child and you know my circumstances."

While certain women feared divine castigation, most spoke of a merciful God who would be sympathetic to their abortion decisions, which, as they often explained, were carried out by force of circumstance. "I think that [those who oppose abortion] must think that we are selfish about it, [but] caring for yourself and for someone else involves an enormous amount of responsibility if you are not up for it," Monserrat told me. "I don't think God will judge; rather, I think he would applaud that decision because in order to make this kind of decision you need to have sufficient bravery." Women communicated that God could see that it would be far more egregious to bring a child into the world to suffer in scarcity than to interrupt a pregnancy he had sent. That women in my study turned directly to God for forgiveness from actions that defied institutionalized Catholicism signals the importance, in this context, of a personalized relationship with God above religious edicts. Regardless of their professed faith or religious backgrounds, women voiced powerful critiques of the Catholic hierarchy and its position on abortion.

ACCUSATIONS AGAINST THE CHURCH

I had been recruiting women for interviews in the waiting room of Santa Marta Clinic on a weekday morning when an animated conversation took shape among the patients. "I know abortion is considered a sin," one woman announced to the group, "but I'm clear about what I'm doing." She proceeded to narrate a story about a friend of hers who had sought the solace of a Catho-lic priest after the death of a loved one. Before long, the priest and the griev-ing woman became romantically involved and the woman learned she was pregnant. The priest took her to the doctor to acquire prenatal vitamins. Soon after she swallowed the vitamins, the young woman was overcome with powerful contractions and suffered a miscarriage. It took a minute for those of us in the waiting room that day to realize that the alleged vitamins were in fact abortifacient pills. The priest, our narrator clarified, had arranged for his lover to undergo a medical abortion without her knowledge. Objections erupted around the waiting room: He lied to her? How could he?

This was not the first time I had heard a version of this tale, which finds many incarnations in Mexico and other parts of Latin America.[16] In 2002, Mexican director Carlos Carrera presented one version of the story to the public in his film *El Crimen de Padre Amaro* (The Crime of Father Amaro). Adapted from a Portuguese novel, the film relates the story of Father Amaro, a newly ordained Mexican priest whose mentor sends him to Los Reyes, a small town in a fictitious state, to work with an older priest named Father Benito. Young and bright-eyed, Amaro has ambitions to move up in the church. If he can prove himself to Benito, he may one day assume Benito's role. Amaro's professional aspirations are quickly muddled by his fascination with Amelia, a youthful and pretty catechism teacher in town. Before long, his idealism is shattered when he learns that Benito is embroiled in illegal activity, guilty of diverting church funds, and engaged in a romantic affair with a local woman. Amelia, the viewer imagines, is the product of their illegitimate union. The romance between Amaro and Amelia develops quickly, and before long Amaro is guilty of his own religious transgressions. In one scene he drapes a blue cloak resembling that of the Virgin of Guadalupe over a nude Amelia to regale in her celestial beauty. When shortly thereafter Amelia announces that she is pregnant, Amaro does not hang up his robes as she had hoped. At Amaro's urging, Amelia eventually agrees to undergo an abortion that he has arranged in an illegal clinic in town. During the procedure she suffers a hemorrhage. In a dramatic scene he begs for forgiveness while slumped over her limp body, both of them bathed in her blood. The crime for which the film takes its name is open to interpretation. Film critic Roger Ebert has pointed out that Amaro's most egregious offense was not that he succumbed to carnal temptations and thus violated his vow to celibacy, or even that he paid for an illegal abortion.[17] It was, rather, the public cover-up he orchestrated to abdicate responsibility for Amelia's death and secure his own future within the church.

The film would become a box office hit, although it ignited tremendous controversy upon its release in 2002. The date is noteworthy, as it was just two years after Mexico City expanded the limited circumstances under which women could legally terminate their pregnancies. The country was thus embroiled in an intense moment in the epic clash over abortion. Conservative groups like ProVida, as well as several prominent figures within the Catholic Church, registered their criticism, calling for cancellation of the film.[18] One prelate is quoted in an article that ran in *La Jornada*, an important left newspaper, accusing director Carlos Carrera of slander against the church. Even though Carrera stated in response to the vociferous criticism that the film was not intended as an attack on the Catholic Church, the movie made an unmistakable intervention in the national abortion dispute, forcing long-standing questions about clerical hypocrisy to the center of public debate.

As we have seen, the story of the irreverent priest who arranges for an illegal abortion to hide the evidence of his breaches of divine law can take different forms. The fact that women seeking to interrupt their pregnancies in the capital were familiar with a version of this apocryphal tale is unsurprising. The narration of the story *at an abortion clinic*, however, is striking. Relating this tale to the other women who had arrived to interrupt their pregnancies offered a way to exonerate them: priests too are complicit in violating the religious rules they espouse. People often used the term *doble moral* (double morality) to refer to the church's tendency to publicly champion a set of moral positions and norms while breaching them in private.[19] Nowhere was cynicism about moral lapses in the church more palpable than in discussions about the clerical sexual abuse scandals that have made global headlines in recent years. When I asked María Puerto, the assistant director of the ILE program, what she thought about the Catholic Church's position on abortion, she invoked the scandals directly. "Look," María told me, "it's contradictory, because priests are not saints. How many pederast priests are there who rape little boys?"

Her objections echoed national discussions about the *doble morality* of Catholic leaders that were unfolding at the time. One media story ran on April 28, 2014, just a few months into my fieldwork, in *La Jornada*: "The Dark History of John Paul II, Accessory to Pedophiles, Canonized along with John XXIII." The day before, crowds numbering in the hundreds of thousands had packed into St. Peter's Square in Rome to observe as late Pope John Paul II was made into a saint along with late Pope John XXIII. Pope John Paul had been widely embraced in Mexico, which he had visited several times during his tenure from 1978 to 2005. As the 2014 headlines from *La Jornada* relate, the later years of his papacy were mired in scandal. His canonization was deeply contentious. Many people were angry about his inaction in the face of allegations of sexual abuse that surfaced at end of his papacy.

Prominent among the accused was Mexican priest Marcial Maciel Degollado, known for establishing the Legionaries of Christ, a Roman Catholic order that thrived in and outside Mexico in the latter half of the twentieth century. Degollado too had been a revered figure in Mexico, particularly among the wealthy classes, many of whose children were educated in the elite private schools run by the Legion. Degollado's success in recruiting new students and securing abundant donations made him a favorite of Pope John Paul II. Reverend Degollado's reputation was spoiled when the public learned, just a few years before his death in 2008, that he had sexually abused dozens of young seminarians, sustained marital relationships with multiple women in different countries simultaneously, and engaged in illegal drug use. Pope John Paul II patched over the scandal to exonerate his friend and preserve the reputation of the church. Anger about the cover-up boiled over in the weeks leading up to John Paul II's canonization, and political cartoons circulated widely in the media.

In one cartoon a choirboy muses to himself about the pope: "Of course he's a saint who performs miracles! For example, when he saved Maciel from the trash bin after the pederasty accusations." In a different cartoon, Maciel grabs the wrist of a young boy. As the boy resists the priest's advances, Maciel threatens: "Come on, or God will punish you," while flashing a photo of his friend and protector Pope John Paul II. The cartoons were successful as political satire because news of the Maciel scandal was all too predictable—one more in a series of incidents of clerical sexual abuse unearthed throughout the 1990s and early aughts. Like the tale related in Santa Marta's waiting room about the deceitful priest who coerced his illicit lover into an abortion and like the story of Padre Amaro, the cartoons embody popular disillusionment with the church that has grown more acute in recent years. Negative attitudes about the

FIGURE 2. Political cartoon critiquing the canonization of Pope John Paul II. Published on April 28, 2014, in *El Economista*. Image by Chavo del Torro.

FIGURE 3. Political cartoon critiquing Pope John Paul II for covering up the sexual abuse scandal of Mexican Legion of Christ leader Marcial Maciel Degollado. Published on December 29, 2014, in *El Economista*. Image by El Perujo.

church permeated my conversations with abortion patients. For many of these women, clerical corruption served to extenuate their own sacrilegious decisions.

When I asked ILE patients about religious injunctions on abortion they were quick to emphasize contradictions in Catholic dogma and the behavior of church officials and lay Catholics. Their responses became predictable. One young woman told me, "I've seen so many things among Catholic people, and people who represent the Catholic Church, like priests. [We assume that] the pope, or someone studying to become a priest, must be such a good person. It's not true at all. That's why I don't think God is going to punish me [for having an abortion]. I've seen that Catholicism, my family's religion, is so hypocriti-cal. Maybe the Catholic Church is not okay with [abortion], but [look at] all of the children that have been raped by priests."

I remember sitting in the clinical sonogram room with Sandra, a twenty-six-year-old architecture student, who outlined these contradictions with a story. As part of her university training she had learned about the graves of babies discovered beneath convents in different parts of the country. The re-mains, she told me wide-eyed, were the babies of nuns who had aborted their pregnancies! "So, it's silly to me that the church is against abortion, when it appears [that its representatives] have raped nuns. I mean they rape children [too], it's bad." Sandra's rendition of this familiar story—yet another version of the Padre Amaro tale—included a curious twist. As we have seen, the story is generally narrated as a stealth romance between priests and nuns who conspire to bury the evidence of their illicit affair. In Sandra's version nuns were the vic-tims of priestly rape. Her retelling wove long-standing anticlerical sentiment together with more recent sex abuse scandals that have eroded the church's reputation. For Sandra, the church's double morality around abortion (and rape), manifest in the architecture of its institutions, offered a degree of moral absolution for those defying Catholic teachings.

Along with critiquing the way church officials flouted religious doctrine to defend the morality of abortion, women lamented the punitive character of the church. "Instead of approaching you and helping you out of the hole," one ILE patient articulated, "[the church] drowns you, they push you down until you can't get up again, and afterwards they turn around and leave you there." Abortion patients were quick to critique the church for hypocrisy in other ways as well. Amalia, a Tacalco resident whom I met at Santa Marta, called the Catholic Church "un negocio" (a business). She said, "There is this thing [that people do]. One swears that they won't drink alcohol for a year [for example], you go to church and declare the oath, they give you a little paper and say, 'Okay, you cannot drink alcohol for a year, or for a month.' But say, during that time, you have to attend a wedding. You can go and *pay* the priest for permission to break the oath that day, it's silly." Although Amalia was estranged from the church, her father remained a loyal parishioner. At his church the pastor drove a flashy new car and lived in an ostentatious house. "All of the money [that the pastor] pulls together," she said, "he brings home. So where is the [practice of] 'Though shalt not rob?' I think he's robbing. Where is the [practice of] 'Though shalt not kill?' How I see it, [depriving children of food] amounts to killing."

Other women underscored the church's attempts to counter widespread poverty as duplicitous. "I do not like that they [priests] always profess things that they themselves contradict," one patient told me. "They simply pray for people who have nothing to eat, yet they have all the money. I've even seen priests who take money from the alms to pay for their cell phones. Even the pope and his colleagues are not without sin, and therefore they should not be judging others." Perceived economic corruption on the part of religious leaders was an especially grave offense for the women in my study, many of whose abortion decisions were carried out precisely because of economic constraints that prevented them from taking a pregnancy to term.

Even if women rejected religious edicts or did not identify as Catholic, they all had to contend with religious condemnation at the site of the ILE clinic.[20] In my research at Santa Marta, many women confused the crisis pregnancy center (CPC) that had been erected next door with the ILE clinic. When Adela arrived at Santa Marta with her boyfriend and their three-year-old daughter in August 2014 they mistakenly entered the CPC first. Inside, a male staff member discouraged the young couple from pursuing an abortion, promising assistance after their child was born. Adela was certain about her decision to interrupt her pregnancy and made her intentions clear to the staff person before leaving to find the ILE clinic. But it was too late. All ten ILE slots had been claimed by the time she appeared at the entrance to Santa Marta.

Back at home Adela's boyfriend ruminated on the messages dispensed at the CPC and began to have second thoughts about the abortion. "I was clear him with him," Adela told me. "'That man doesn't know how we live, he's fooling you, you think he is going help you? No.' I told him, 'We have to be responsible, we have to think economically about how we live, because bringing a baby into the world to suffer, to watch us fight [isn't right].'" After a few days of discussion, he acceded, and together the couple battled the city traffic once more to return to Santa Marta. On the second visit, when the CPC worker approached them again, Adela was more forceful. She said to him, "The truth is, there are a lot of things that you are not going to be able to fix in my life. You are not going to solve my problems. I'm not going to show up here and cry to you [when something happens in my life]." Reflecting on the experience with me later, Adela observed that the prolife activists "give you a nice brainwashing, and the one who ends up losing is you. They tell you, 'A baby is beautiful; God sends a baby.' I already have one in the flesh, and I know very well what it entails to care for a baby."

While religious institutions are central to processes of reproductive governance, religion can be an important moral resource in reproductive decision-making.[21] For anthropologists religiosity is fluid, malleable, and open to creative adaptation, rather than a "pill that people can decide to swallow or not."[22] In the context of rural Mexico, anthropologist Jennifer Hirsch has drawn attention to the way that "people manipulate ideology, strategically reinterpreting religious teachings" that ban contraception in order to control their fertility without jeopardizing their status as good Catholics.[23] Eugenia Georges has examined the tendency among Greek Orthodox women to emphasize economic circumstances that would prevent them from fulfilling their social responsibility to care for their unborn child in order to exonerate themselves from the sin of abortion.[24] Working in another context, Joanna Mishtal and Rachel Dannefer found that for many Catholic women in Poland the church's condemnation of birth control had only limited influence over reproductive decision-making in the face of post-Soviet economic scarcity.[25] Research from around the world, in sum, shows that people adapt, repurpose, or selectively overlook religious teachings in the context of their everyday lives to meet their own reproductive aspirations without jeopardizing their faith or identity as adherents of a particular religious tradition.

Such was the case in urban Mexico, where women articulated the absolute necessity of abortion despite religious classification of the practice as sinful. Unlike the "grassroots theologians" that Jennifer Hirsch encountered in her research among Catholic women in rural Mexico, the urbanites I came to know did not generally feel the need to justify their behavior using religious logics, although they did often note that bringing a child into poverty represented a graver sin than interrupting a pregnancy.[26] More often women took the Catholic Church to task, critiquing its directives and looking to God for forgiveness. Far from passively accepting religious directives, many of the women in my research maneuvered to obtain, and later justify, abortion. To absolve themselves they pointed to entrenched patterns of clerical corruption and invoked adverse public knowledge about the church that has surfaced in recent years. For many women, the Catholic Church had lost its moral authority. While the church still claimed to set the moral standards by which people should live their lives, it had fallen from grace. Many people scoffed at the church for failing to abide by its own moral code. In the capital's impoverished neighborhoods, as we will see, abortion was an unavoidable aspect of women's reproductive lives.

POVERTY, POPULATION, AND THE PRECLUSION OF LIFE

It was an ordinary autumn morning in 2014 when Dr. Alexa entered the Santa Marta counseling office with uncharacteristic urgency. Had we seen the morning news? A sixteen-year-old had abandoned her newborn in the toilet at Metro Xini! The final stop on Tacalco's main line, the Metro Xini station was the second-to-last leg of my regular commute to Santa Marta. I knew the place well. A continuous mass of commuters moved through its wide hallways during peak hours (*horas picos*). Others made a living panhandling, riding the lines back and forth all day. On that morning when a janitor discovered a tiny body in the public toilet, the masses swarmed in. The infant was still covered in white vernix, umbilical cord intact, according to reports later released. The police dispersed the crowds. Onlookers stepped aside as paramedics rushed the baby out of the building to a nearby emergency room. The young mother had experienced contractions in the metro and given birth in the bathroom. Minutes later, she fled, likely in shock. Though she later returned to retrieve her infant, the janitor had already contacted the authorities. While the adolescent mother was taken into police custody and would later have to appear in court, media headlines hailed the janitor as a hero. A mother and grandmother herself, the public worker had felt compelled to act when she heard the baby's cries, she later told reporters. Unable to part with the neonate, she rode in the ambulance all the way to the hospital.

"Que poca madre" (How awful), Dr. Alexa whispered under her breath after relating the story to all of us in the counseling office. Roberta and Carolina shook their heads in disbelief. How, they wondered aloud, could a mother leave her baby to die in a public toilet? *Poca madre* is a Mexican idiom sometimes used to express indignation or offense. The literal translation is "unmotherly." When Dr. Alexa used the phrase to describe the young woman featured in the news that morning, both meanings applied. The indignation of the ILE personnel initially confounded me, particularly in light of their exposure to comparable situations that compelled nearly two dozen women from the area to seek abortion services at their clinic each day. But I came to see that the personnel were angry, if not entirely at women themselves, then at the social circumstances that forced them into situations of utter desperation. Dr. Rios later told me that she had stopped reading the media stories about abandoned infants because they were too upsetting. It was the only way she kept from misdirecting her anger about the unlivable social conditions toward her patients.

While the Metro Xini incident was the first time I heard about abandoned infants during my research, it was not the last. Once I started paying attention news of abandoned infants was all around me. During some months multiple infants appeared—in the trash, in cardboard boxes on street corners, and in plain sight in busy shopping malls. The problem was concentrated in poorer sections of the city and poor *pueblos* outside the capital. When a birth mother was identified, she was often young and desperate. ILE patients invoked the figure of the abandoned baby as a trope—the tragic alternative to abortion in an overpopulated context with limited resources to go around. When I asked one patient about her stance on abortion, she turned the question back on me. "What's worse," she prompted me to consider, "that someone aborts, or that so many infants end up in the trash?" In some cases, women insisted, the foreclosure of a new life made good moral sense.

Poverty was not the only reason that women in my sample sought abortion. Some spoke of "life projects" centered on education and career advancement, plans for the future that a new baby would encumber. Others cited instability with a romantic partner or medical reasons. And many more mentioned some combination of these factors. Regardless of their own situations, many women emphasized that national conditions of stark inequality, environmental degradation, overpopulation, and violence could make abortion a profoundly moral act. One ILE patient summed up women's concerns when she told me, "It is important to protect the [fetus] from such adverse conditions, so much social injustice, inequity. Having a child in this country is like depriving it of life. There's so much violence, pollution, injustice." The fact that women shouldered the burden of adverse social conditions was not lost on them. As another patient told me,

> It falls on us, it falls on women. Those of us who are [of the working class], we struggle so that our children can have a good education, we try to give them everything. But in many cases, we can't afford it. To fix this problem, the politicians and presidents and the rest [of the figures in power] would have to give up their salaries and invest that money in education, but that's inconvenient for them. I have seen how in other countries, in the US and elsewhere, children learn to read and write, to play sports. Here there is nothing, they defraud us. It is horrible in Mexico.

Concerns about the size of the national population also formed an important backdrop for individual and collective deliberations about abortion. When ILE patients referenced the population, it was only sometimes to evince anxiety about political stability or national progress—concerns that had preoccupied state leaders late in the twentieth century when "overpopulation" was first defined as a national problem. More often, "overpopulation" was a way for women to talk about the dismal economic circumstances in which they lived, conditions that shaped their considerations around family formation. Ines, a Tacalco resident with three kids, was thirty-two when she sought an abortion through the ILE program. She had initially tried her luck at a health center near her house, but a receptionist informed her that abortion services were not available there because the hospital director objected to the procedure.

"What do you mean you object to abortion?" Ines asked aloud in our conversation, as if in response to the medical administrator himself. "Then why don't you go outside and create a shelter for all of the homeless kids who roam the streets asking for money? When there are so many children living in the street, so many mothers who push their daughters into prostitution to get by, people drugging themselves, drinking? Things are bad here in Mexico, really bad. These people should defend those of us who are already here rather than making the population bigger, because there is not enough to go around as it is." For people in working-class boroughs, social and demographic conditions bore down on moral deliberations around childbearing, forming an inescapable aspect of reproductive decision-making. As Ines's comments laid bare, many of these women did not have the luxury of conscientiously objecting to abortion as the hospital administrator had done, even if some of them did harbor moral reservations about the procedure.

The tendency of the women I met to cite "overpopulation" when justifying the need for abortion reflects a curious adaptation of the logic that motivated late twentieth-century population control campaigns in Mexico and elsewhere in Latin America, which in many cases worked to constrain reproductive options through heavy-handed state directives.[27] Other studies show that wealthier women can more easily sidestep the challenges and paradoxes of reproduction in this densely populated context. In her ethnography of fertility clinics in Mexico City, for instance, Lara Braff found that women struggling to become pregnant justified their pursuit of (expensive) fertility treatments by distinguishing themselves from the poor, rural, and dark-skinned women whose "hyperfertility" they imagined to be out of control.[28] The generally poor and working-class women in my study—the imagined "reproductive Others" whose fertility state officials and wealthy lay people define as problematic—invoked national conditions of overpopulation to defend the moral integrity of abortion.

Exemplary is the experience of twenty-year-old Viane, who traveled five hours to the capital from her avowedly Catholic home state of Guanajuato with her one-year-old son in tow. I met Viane in the waiting room of Santa Marta Clinic. Her ultrasound revealed that she was 10.6 weeks pregnant, which meant that she needed an EVA procedure that was not being offered at Santa Marta at the time. Viane asked me to accompany her across the city to Reina María

Clinic, where she would seek the procedure the following day. We met in the chilly predawn hours, accompanied by prolife activists who had assumed their regular position outside and fifteen or so other women who had already lined up to secure an ILE appointment. I stayed with Viane throughout the morning and during the abortion.

Viane worked in a clothing store earning 700 pesos a week ($38 USD). Her boyfriend was nine years her senior and married with three small children of his own. While he promised to support her, she sensed his growing distance upon learning of her pregnancy, and she did not trust his word. Although he had discouraged her from ending the pregnancy, Viane saw no other option. Deep down, she knew he would never leave his wife. As if in response to her boyfriend, during our conversation in the clinic she asked aloud,

> What can one do with 700 pesos a week? With rent and food, diapers for two, milk for two, clothing for two, and there'd be three of us including myself. It would be really hard. I've gone to church, and maybe I'm doing something wrong in their [Catholic priests'] view, but the way I see it—it's not that I'm excusing it, but—I'm going to bring a baby into the world for what? So it is undernourished, sick? So I wouldn't have clothing to dress him, or diapers, or milk, so I wouldn't be able to take care of either of them?

Viane had doubted her first pregnancy as well. Her ex-boyfriend, the father of her one-year-old son, had discouraged her from having the baby, and she had gone to seek the advice of a priest. "The priest told me that aborting my pregnancy was a serious sin, that if I, as its mother, wouldn't defend it, who would?" Viane took the priest's message to heart and resolved to keep her first child. This time, though, things were different. Her cousin in the capital had told her that the procedure was now legal and accessible there. Viane knew that her parents would stop providing financial assistance if she had a second child, especially if they learned that the man involved was married. She reflected aloud, "It's a hard decision, I know I'm coming here to kill a living being, but at the same time, how I see it, it's not the same as killing my one-year-old son. I would have to sacrifice one to take care of the other."

For Viane, bringing another baby into the world to suffer would amount to neglect both of her would-be child and of her toddler. "Catholic leaders have always had their beliefs," she said, "that abortion is wrong, it's a sin, God will punish you. They never put themselves in your place, they always judge. Let them say what they will, these people are not going to support me, they are not going to put food on my table." Pregnant but unable to support a second child, Viane was compelled to act in ways that were inconsistent with her religious beliefs. As she reconciled the divergence, "Maybe [abortion] is a sin, but [under certain circumstances] one has to do it, one needs to do it. And one keeps believing in what they believe, that doesn't change." Abortion was a means for Viane to make good on her responsibilities to her son and to shield her would-be child from a destitute fate, moral commitments that aligned with her personal sense of right and wrong independent of religious mandates.

Other women also expressed disdain for the rigidity of Catholic doctrine. "The church makes us feel guilty for taking away someone's life," thirty-four-year-old Elsa told me. She worked in a sewing shop a few blocks from Santa Marta. "And yeah, I feel bad, but the church is not going to provide for me so I can feed my children; nor is God going to come down and pay for my children's school fees. I mean sometimes one has to work [to make money], and you can't take care of your children if you are also working." Elsa was tearful and guilty when I interviewed her in the operating theater of Santa Marta. We talked through her circumstances for a good while. She had dropped out of school after the seventh grade. Though she had wanted to keep the pregnancy, she already had three children and worked ten-hour days for a meager monthly wage of 3,000 pesos ($163 USD). With this schedule and income she could barely make ends meet as it was.

Prior to seeking an abortion Elsa had gone to discuss her decision with a priest. She asked him why God would send her another baby if he knew that she could not take care of it. The priest reasoned that God knew that even with all of the problems that life presents, she was capable of taking care of five or ten babies if that was what God wanted for her. He reiterated that abortion was a grave sin. Still wanting for the solace she had sought from the priest, Elsa prayed that everything would go smoothly before coming to the clinic, asking God to watch over the process. Despite her feelings of guilt, she concluded, "For the church, she who aborts is a sinner and is going to hell, because life is sacred for God, and God decides who comes [to be born] and who doesn't. We [humans] can't decide. But we are women, and women who now have to work a double shift, so we have to decide." Elsa's observation that the lack of social supports to assist women with child care made "the double shift" of maternal and wage labor burdensome highlighted what she and others perceived as the antiquated character of Catholic doctrine on abortion. Limited options for wage labor left Elsa in poverty, preventing her from accepting "all of the babies that God sent," and she reconciled her decision with this in mind. For Elsa and others, selectively accepting "God's children" was not a rejection of motherhood. It was a means to mother well.

Twenty-three-year-old Margarita had a two-year-old daughter and had recently broken up with her boyfriend when she learned she was pregnant. Margarita described herself as *creyente*, hesitating to call herself a Catholic because she did not regularly attend mass. When she got pregnant again, Margarita felt bad. "I didn't want to do this. For me this is ugly, to take someone's life away. But here in Mexico, economically, you can't make ends meet with two kids." Despite the misgivings she felt about her decision, Margarita supported the legalization of abortion. "There are a lot of women who have children, and they neglect them. I don't know if you've seen in the news that women are throwing babies in the trash. It's good that they legalized abortion, this way we don't run the risk of so much hunger in Mexico, so many abandoned children without parents." For Margarita, the virtue of abortion stemmed from her profound concern about the social and moral abandonment of children.

Other women expressed that they had the means to care for a new child but wanted to carve out a life that was not defined entirely by motherhood. Women in this situation often wrestled with how to incorporate maternity into other life plans centered on educational achievement and career development. Young motherhood, in their view, could foreclose possibilities that had historically been out of reach for women. Many Mexican women today have greater access to higher education, formal employment, and lifestyles that do not involve marriage and children.[29] Yet opportunities are not evenly distributed. Residents of major urban centers like Mexico City have better access to social mobility and are more able to craft feminine identities that deviate from patriarchal norms. For low-income families, people living outside urban settings, and older generations, these opportunities are more limited.

ILE patients who associated their abortion decisions with personal and career development generally came from middle-class families or had widened their horizons by excelling in school. At the age of twenty-two, Gaby traveled to the capital from her home in Mexico State to access ILE services in 2014. She had grown up in one of Mexico City's well-to-do boroughs but had since moved outside city bounds. Gaby had been raised in a Protestant household, but she had stopped believing in God. She was studying psychology at the Universidad Nacional Autónoma de México (UNAM), the competitive national university that is almost entirely free to students who are accepted. While the national university and other public universities can offer a pathway to social mobility, they most often benefit people like Gaby who already come from privileged backgrounds.

Born in 1992, Gaby had come of age in an era when fertility control was already a national priority. The lasting imprint of the Mexican family planning campaigns was evident in her explicit association between unplanned pregnancy and national cultural decline. "I see that many Mexican families have the problems that they do precisely because a baby appears and it wasn't planned," she told me in the context of explaining her decision to abort. "I don't want to have those kinds of problems. As primitive as the capital is, it's not as primitive as many other states. Where I live [in Mexico State], and in many other states outside of the capital, there are a lot of people who don't know anything [about family planning] and unfortunately now *somos muchos* [we are so many], and that's why we are poor. The families are so big, and the jobs, the salaries, are very small. They are not enough to support a family of two that lives modestly, let alone to allow for luxuries."

Gaby worked part-time as a receptionist at a health center when she wasn't commuting into the capital for school. She found it difficult to juggle her various commitments. When her pregnancy test turned up positive, she and her partner decided together on an abortion.

> The rhythm of life that I lead makes me realize that right now a baby would only be an obstacle. I don't want to pause what I've completed so far in my studies in order to take care of a baby. I have a lot of life left to live, and I

think I'm going to be a really successful person, so I want an abortion. I realize
that I have the ability to keep it. I have a stable life, a house, a car, a job . . .
[but] I don't want to limit myself right now. I have a lot of growing to do, and
if I've achieved this much at my young age, I think I'll have more. . . . I'd like
to have a baby, but at the right moment, when I decide.

The promise of a "successful" future defined by material acquisition and career
advancement fit within the conceptual and economic horizons of Gaby's life.
Abortion, as she saw it, was a pathway to that future.

This did not mean that Gaby had no qualms. She had been indecisive at
first. "I think abortion is a right, but it's justifiable only in grave circumstances,
for women who get pregnant really young, or don't have support from a partner, or have no money or no job. Fortunately, I have all of that, but I don't
want to sell myself short." She felt confident that abortion was the best option
for her but was stuck on what she saw as the "selfishness" of her decision. In
the end, with the support of her partner, she opted to undergo the procedure.
"But that doesn't mean I think women should take it lightly," she added before
we finished our conversation. "Abortion is not a game."

Other ILE patients with access to more economic and educational resources
voiced similar reasons. Lucinda was twenty-six and had been dating her boyfriend Ivan for almost three years when she sought ILE services at Santa Marta
in 2014. By the time we met, she had finished her college degree and had recently begun working as a quality control specialist in a snack food company in
the capital. Ivan, one year younger, was still working toward his college degree
in biochemical engineering. Lucinda had been raised in a Catholic family, she
said, but went to mass only out of respect for her grandparents. She believed
in God, but not in the way that the church painted him.

Lucinda and Ivan wanted a baby, but not yet. "We were protecting our-
selves [using contraception] and we had talked about the possibility of having
a child, but our idea was—not like my cousins or my siblings who say, 'Well,
the baby arrived, so what else are we going to do?' Our idea was, let's get to
work. We wanted to finish our educations, start our careers, and then make
the decision." Lucinda had avoided pregnancy for two years with an IUD, but
she assumed it had fallen out. Even though Lucinda and Ivan agreed that it
was the wrong time for a baby, it wasn't an easy decision. "It was hard for us

because we've thought about the possibility of having a child, it's a desire that we share, but it wasn't the right moment. So we analyzed all of the pros and cons, like—okay if we have it, Ivan has to interrupt his education and find work right away, and without a college degree in Mexico that means working wherever, earning whatever."

Much like Gaby, Lucinda was struggling to juggle her own (and her partner's) career ambitions with her desire for motherhood and the familial and societal pressures that mandated maternity. She explained,

> The problem is, how should I put this? Mexico is odd in the cultural aspect, it has very traditional ideas . . . and there are even more traditional people in *los pueblos* [outside the capital]. There are Mexican people who think that women exist to have children, that having children is what makes you a woman. She can have a successful career, a car, this and that, a huge house, but if she doesn't have children, she isn't a woman. I can have a degree or win a competition in Japan or Canada, and it's like, oh, that's nice, and when are you going to have kids?

Women like Gaby, Lucinda, and others had observed the ways in which young motherhood had curtailed opportunities for other women in their lives who were saddled with domestic obligations. While they were open to having a baby down the line, at the time they became pregnant their energies were focused elsewhere. When a pregnancy did not square with their personal goals, they pursued an abortion to bring their life plans to fruition and forge feminine identities that were not confined to motherhood. While abortion could be a tricky decision, they emphasized that it was a bridge to a better future for themselves and for the country, a place where so many women struggled to get by because they were encumbered by mothering obligations and expenses. In retrospect, both Gaby and Lucinda expressed that ending their pregnancies had been the right decision.

Regardless of their own economic circumstances, most ILE patients pointed to the dearth of collective national resources that would be necessary to sustain all pregnancies from conception to birth. When deciding on the outcome of a pregnancy the women I met accounted for the conditions of daily existence, pointing to economic hardship, mothering work, and violence, as well as their own ambitions and desires for a better life. Many women held that the elimination of future suffering overruled a categorical imperative to protect life in all circumstances. Unlike the moral absolutism of the church, women's moral approach to abortion was moored in the context of everyday life in the city's working-class boroughs. These factors made "selective mothering" a morally defensible, if existentially challenging, practice, and women defended it as such. While some ILE patients were pregnant for the first time, many made wrenching decisions to terminate their pregnancies as mothers seeking to care for their children in the context of profound economic insecurity. Decisions to reject individual pregnancies cannot be divorced from the mothering work in which many women were already engaged. Women's moral justifications for abortion consistently emphasized the importance of caring for the living as well as the unborn.

Even when women did not already have children, their accounts of seeking abortion emphasized the kind of mothers they aspired to be and the quality of life that a baby deserved. Given the circumstances that made supporting multiple children a difficult prospect, women defended the morality of abortion despite church (and state) prohibitions and occasional feelings of guilt. For many living in the city's poor boroughs, pregnancy termination, like the specter of abandoned babies, was a hard fact of life. The Catholic Church and the state (except in Mexico City, and now Oaxaca, Hidalgo, and Veracruz) promoted the sanctity of life as a moral imperative while neglecting millions of indigent citizens. It was this contradiction that women across the ILE clinics identified and articulated.

DIVINE AND MORTAL LAW

Many women related that they would not have considered abortion if it had remained illegal. In that case, they often said, they would have had to *aguantar* (endure) the pregnancy. Although they were well aware of instances of illegal abortion, this was not an option that most seemed to consider for themselves, or at least not when I asked about it hypothetically. Many of the ILE patients knew of others who had procured an abortion before the procedure was legal yet few admitted that they had done so. Legalization thus seemed to open new practical possibilities for managing one's reproductive life. Although many had, at one point or another, contemplated their moral position on abortion in abstract terms, the presentation of an inopportune pregnancy demanded a more intimate reckoning with these questions.

Along with explaining that legalization was the starting point for their moral deliberations about abortion, women referenced the health risks of clandestine illegal abortion as well as the gendered burdens of unwanted pregnancy. As one woman put it, "In all honesty the person who bears all of the responsibility [of parenting] is the woman. If you get pregnant and have an unwanted child, how is that child going to end up? Many people think abortion is wrong, but now that it is legal, many people are going to be able to have a better quality of life." Women's vocal support of legalization suggests that it provided a source of moral legitimation for controversial reproductive decisions. While some women harbored reservations or grappled with guilt, many others expressed confidence and peace of mind about interrupting their pregnancies.

At the same time, support of legal abortion did not mean that women necessarily conceived of abortion as a "woman's right" or thought of themselves as subjects of abortion rights. On occasion patients invoked feminist frameworks of "women's choice" and "reproductive rights" when describing their positions yet generally it was only after I asked them directly. More often, support of the procedure among the ILE patients was context specific. There were certain circumstances that justified an abortion in their view but for most it was not a transcendent right. In interviews and casual conversations throughout the clinic women voiced adamant rejection of *repeat* abortion, frequently admonishing the irresponsibility of those who "used it like a form of birth control." They worried deeply that women would take advantage of the progressive law and the ILE program and approach abortion as an "easy out," abdicating what they saw as a moral responsibility to take seriously their reproductive potential. Gaby, the psychology student at the UNAM, put it like this: "I think it is a right, but there also has to be a limit, because abortion is not a contraceptive method. It's not as if 'instead of using a condom I'll go get an abortion.' Mexicans have demonstrated that *mientras más apertura, más la gente se aprovecha negativamente de los servicios* [the more openings there are, the more people take advantage of social services]. So, if several clinics like this one existed, I think women would abuse the service, and our own bodies."

Most women, moreover, agreed with the twelve-week gestational limit, after which they generally thought abortion should be regulated. Beyond the first trimester the fetus was considered "más formadito" (more developed) and to interrupt it at that stage could threaten a woman's health or cause pain to the fetus. For most of the ILE patients I met, abortion rights were to be used with caution, profound moral responsibility, and careful consideration of the contextual factors that rendered the procedure necessary under certain circumstances. Abortion, they repeated time and again, was a serious decision.

On occasion, state sanction and extreme circumstances offered little in the way of moral consolation. For women in this group, pregnancy placed them at a moral impasse. Every direction they turned presented new moral conundrums. Even though carrying the pregnancy to term could pose unbearable economic and other burdens, abortion felt gravely wrong. Sari and Luz, whose stories I relate below, described themselves as Catholic and were overcome with guilt when they returned to Santa Marta for a sonogram scan two weeks after they had interrupted their pregnancies. Their inability to reconcile their decisions was rare according to my findings. It is plausible, nonetheless, that other women may have felt similarly and avoided abortion when confronted with an inopportune pregnancy.

Phantoms of Abortion

Sari arrived at Santa Marta Clinic for a second abortion in May 2014. Though she had studied cosmetology, she was unemployed at the time and spent her days caring for her three kids, the youngest of whom was seven months old. Fearful of how the providers might react to her return, she had tried to interrupt her fifth pregnancy on her own. The abortifacient tea that her husband procured from a local *yerbera* [herbalist]—a mixture of chamomile, rue, cinnamon, chocolate, and other herbs—had failed to produce contractions. She also tried taking misoprostol that she had purchased at a local pharmacy, but without luck. The failed abortions were a sign, Sari's sister-in-law had told her, that the baby wanted to stay with its mother. Sari's husband was optimistic. "We can rise to the challenge," he said. "*Donde comen tres, comen cuatro* [If there is enough food for three, there is enough food for four]. But the decision is yours." Sari's husband was more than twenty years older than her and had been struggling to hold down a job. "I started thinking," she said to me at the clinic, "what will happen when he gets older and can no longer work?" Overwhelmed by care obligations at both ends of the life cycle, Sari managed to swallow her fear and return to the clinic.

"I felt tremendous guilt," she recalled. "I went to a Mother's Day celebration at my children's school after and started to bleed so much that I had to go home and change. My son told me to lie down and rest. I felt terrible, a terrible weight because it was Mother's Day and everything." After the bleeding began it took a long time for Sari to pass the embryonic tissue, making the process physically painful. She saw this as God's way of punishing her. "In the end you are killing a life, and I feel that God sends us a life and we are no one to take it away. If one day I am judged, I'll know why. Before the law of God and the law of man, I am a murderer, and I am aware of that." Sari had concealed the pregnancy and the abortion from her kids. "I don't like to lie to my children," she said, "but I can't teach my daughter that babies are meant to be thrown away."

The decision continued to grate at her in the night. The following morning she awoke in her bed surrounded by her three children. "Suddenly—it wasn't just me who heard it, that's how I know it wasn't just a phantom of my conscience. My daughter heard it too. We heard 'Mama,' a little voice, and then everything was silent." Sari would have had a fourth baby, she told me, if her circumstances had allowed it. "If I had more economic solvency, it would have been possible. I would have been able to offer it something." She had asked God not to send her "another little angel" because she knew she would have to send it back. Now she worried that God would turn his back on her. "I'm really scared that in some moment he will punish me or take one of my children away. When the cramps began, after I took the pills, I said 'God, no, don't punish me. I want to be there for my children. I know I've made mistakes, but I am asking for forgiveness.'"

God's Law and the Authority over Life

After Luz agreed to an interview, I led her through the Santa Marta waiting room and into a small office where we could speak privately. She settled into a chair and I sat on rolling stool across from her. "*Hice mal* [I did wrong]," she blurted before I could turn on my digital recorder. "God knows that my apologies are sincere. I won't do it again. This wouldn't have happened if it weren't for my *tonterías* [foolish behavior]." Luz was a single mother of three children from a past relationship: an eighteen-year-old, a fourteen-year-old, and a three-year-old. Desperate for money, she had abandoned her studies after the eighth grade and found work in a computer assembly factory in Tacalco. Life was uneventful in the borough. The days flowed into each other, blurring across cycles of child care and factory work. But things had changed about a year and a half earlier when a neighborhood youth stole her son's motorcycle. Recovering the bike led Luz to the errant teenager's father, Eduardo. They had been dating ever since. While the romance had captivated her at first, Luz's voice cracked with frustration as she explained that Eduardo had been planning, and failing, to leave his wife for months. Luz hadn't told Eduardo about the pregnancy or the abortion. It was easier this way, she decided. "He would want me to keep the baby." They had used the withdrawal method for the duration of their relationship, but this time Eduardo had failed to pull out. She was furious at him for putting her in this situation and tired of waiting for him to make good on his promises. Under other circumstances, she said, she might have wanted a fourth child. But not like this. I believed her when she swore loudly that she would never see Eduardo again.

Despite her resolve, coming to terms with ending her pregnancy was not easy. "It was hard to accept," she said. "At first I said, okay I'm going to have it, I'm going to do this, and then I said no, but if I have it, I'll be alone, who will take care of my kids? I need to work. No, it's better not to. I didn't see it so clearly. It's really difficult to accept between yes and no, yes and no." Luz's doubts were rooted in part in her Catholic upbringing. "*Solo Dios nos puede quitar la vida* [Only God can decide when life ends]," she told me. "From childhood I was always one of the ones who said no, this is wrong, to have gotten into this situation now as an adult, *me remuerde, se siente feo* [it stings, it feels bad]." Although she had asked for God's forgiveness and repented, the situation weighed on her. "In reality, how can I ask God to protect my children if I am killing one of them just like that?" she ruminated. "For God, this is not valid. It's he who can take life away and no one else, not you because you want to or me because [I choose to]. It's God who decides."

As a single mother of three, Luz saw no alternative but to take God's work into her own hands. She swallowed a dose of mifepristone at Santa Marta. Exactly twenty-four hours later, in the bathroom of the factory where she worked, she placed the misoprostol pills under her tongue as instructed. Luz checked her watch several times over the next few hours, slipping away to the bathroom when she could to check for signs that the medicine was taking effect. Finally, she was overcome by powerful cramps. "The saddest part—I was filled with remorse because *el globito* [the little sphere] fell into the toilet," Luz related. She scanned the toilet for signs of life or death, unsure of what she was looking for or why she wanted to see. When she made out what looked like "a peeled grape," she reached in to retrieve it. There were no visible body parts, no arms or legs, she said, fixated on what had emerged from her body.

"How did you feel when you saw it?" I asked, unsure of how to respond.

"I felt bad," Luz told me. "He knew. He knew [he was supposed to pull out]. This wouldn't have happened if it weren't for my foolish behavior." As her story evolved the blame shifted between herself and her boyfriend and back. And all of my attempts to soften her guilt fell flat. "[Abortion] is a foolish thing on women's part," Luz asserted. "Maybe sometimes it's necessary but no, no it is not a right." If the procedure had still been illegal, Luz acknowledged, she would have had the baby. In addition to opening practical options, then, the legal status of abortion seemed, from the outside, to offer a degree of moral absolution for her decision, if not entirely mitigating her guilt. But she did not describe it this way. "I have to work, to take care of my children," she told me, resigning herself to the misgivings that plagued her decision. "*Tengo que sacarles adelante* [I have to help them get ahead.]" It was this commitment that Luz had clung to that day in the factory bathroom. She asked God for forgiveness once more, she said, before flushing the toilet and returning to work.

REPRODUCTIVE MORALITY EMPLACED

The moral absolutes reflected in religious edicts and liberal frameworks of reproductive rights ignored the context of women's lives, which in many cases were marked by poverty and limited opportunities for formal employment. Abortion decisions entailed moral calculations about the quality of life that prospective parents might offer to a child born into a society plagued by scarcity, violence, and lopsided opportunities. Most of the women in my study did not assess the morality of abortion in abstract terms. They evaluated the viability of bringing about new life in the context of pressing financial constraints as well as interpersonal entanglements that precluded multiple children even when pregnancies were desired.

Many women saw the termination of a pregnancy as a means to be better mothers for their existing children or to shield their would-be children from destitution. Others saw it as a way to expand their prospects beyond mothering and domestic obligations, roles that had defined opportunities for older generations of women. Rights-based approaches to abortion, much like religious decrees, glossed over the local conditions that determined whether it was viable for a pregnancy in urban Mexico to come to term.

In working-class zones of the capital like Tacalco, precarious economic conditions, perhaps more than any other force, governed women's reproductive options. Current neoliberal labor market structures defined by low wages and decreasing public supports such as child care, quality public education, and welfare, made abortion a basic aspect of women's reproductive repertoires and something that many felt justified in seeking. The attenuation of state services has had severe consequences for women. My findings revealed a context in which the state has failed to provide the structural supports that would facilitate reproduction and parenting for women with desired pregnancies. Women's narratives point to the limitations of a feminist vision focused narrowly on securing legal options for limiting fertility. At their core, these stories confirm the value of frameworks of reproductive justice that pair the struggle for abortion rights with wider concerns around wage equity, environmental safety, and social supports for women and families to reproduce and parent in dignified conditions.[30]

Church condemnation was of small consequence to many of the women I came to know through the ILE program, regardless of their declared religious allegiances. Women like Viane, Elsa, Margarita, and others were keenly aware that the church opposed their nonprocreative reproductive decisions, but that did not stop them. Many of them pointed to the hypocrisy of male authority figures in the church (and the state) who claimed to occupy the moral high ground despite being publicly outed for moral transgressions, corruption, and abuse. It was women who bore the psychic and moral culpability imposed by male leaders who reneged on their responsibilities and accountability. It became clearer and clearer that the women I met, and the broader public, were coming to terms with the consequences of listening to these bankrupt voices of moral authority. While some accepted the guilt that officials in the church and the state laid at their feet, many more had stopped listening.

CHAPTER THREE

BEING (A) PATIENT
The Making of Public Abortion

EVERY WEEKDAY MORNING, two long lines formed outside the Santa Marta Community Health Center. In one line stood families waiting for prenatal care, child checkups, and other services offered through the local clinic. In the other line, just a few paces away, stood women waiting to enter the ILE wing. Although it took me some time to read this scene, everyone in the neighborhood could see who had arrived for an abortion and who had not. Indeed, the 2007 reform made abortion *public* in multiple ways. The transformation of abortion into a legal right of women in the capital brought the procedure out of the secret realm of private clinics and into public view. And the creation of the ILE program provided the institutional infrastructure through which broad sectors of the population might realize their abortion rights through the public health sector. Yet abortion services have been largely severed from other aspects of health care in Mexico City—a model of abortion care that will feel familiar to US readers—so that abortion, and abortion patients, have assumed a new kind of visibility or "publicness" at the site of the clinic, where they must wait, sometimes for hours on end, in plain sight. My account of women's experiences obtaining ILE services in this chapter reveals what happened after abortion became a new element of public health care in the capital and how the women availing themselves of this state service make sense of the care they receive.

To understand women's experiences, we must appreciate the institutional and affective arrangements of care that define the ILE program, which exists at the lowest rung of the public health system designed early in the twentieth century to serve the poor and unemployed who could not access employer-based health care. While health in Mexico is ostensibly a public good, the national health system has suffered severe funding cuts and resultant erosion in recent decades amid wider neoliberal reforms and structural adjustment. The MOH has been especially hard hit. Health services there are free (aside from copays assessed on a sliding scale), but the system is marked by tremendous resource scarcity and overwhelming demand, and its personnel are notorious for their gruff dispositions. Women who obtain ILE services are thus cared for in the lowest tier of a crumbling state health system by overwhelmed personnel with limited resources at their disposal. Their experiences reflect the moral uncertainties that trouble abortion in this context, as well as the equivocal tenor of the public care afforded to the country's poorest citizens. Before we move into the ILE clinics, a brief tour of the Mexican health system elucidates how the MOH figures in the broader health care landscape, as well as the meanings it conjures for ordinary people.

THE PROMISE OF HEALTH AND THE
"SLOW DEATH" OF PUBLIC CARE

The right to universal health care formed a key promise of the Mexican Revolution and is protected in the 1917 Constitution. Health, at least theoretically, is a right of citizenship to which all are entitled by virtue of belonging to the nation-state. In reality, access to health care is deeply unequal in Mexico, mirroring the stark social inequalities that have long plagued the country. It took several decades for postrevolutionary leaders to establish social security institutions that would meet the health care needs of working people.[1] And even these institutions only partially fulfilled the revolutionary promise of health, as they left millions of already economically vulnerable Mexicans unprotected, ramifying preexisting inequalities. Until a popular health insurance program known as the Seguro Popular was established in 2004 to cover the roughly fifty-four million previously uninsured citizens, health care in Mexico had been attached to formal employment. The public hospitals erected throughout the country in the middle of the twentieth century were designed to broadcast the national commitment to the health of the citizenry. Yet when muralists like David Alfaro Siqueiros were hired to paint their walls with nationalist imagery, the artists used the institutional canvases to convey their own subversive message: "Hospital walls became contested spaces where art depicted Mexico's embrace of modern technology and medical practices while also showcasing, in vivid color, citizens challenging the government's broken revolutionary promises, especially the right of all to health and social security," writes historian Gabriela Soto Laveaga.[2]

Under Mexico's current president the national health system is undergoing dramatic changes, but at the time of my research the population was carved into three main categories with regard to health care coverage that were tiered in quality and public esteem.[3] A privileged sector of the population with the resources to purchase private health insurance and/or pay out of pocket for expensive treatments in private hospitals and clinics enjoyed the highest standard of care. It was mostly wealthy Mexicans and foreigners living in the country who made up this category, yet people who counted on employer-based health care sometimes opted to purchase care through private clinics when they could afford to because it was known to be superior to any type of public care.[4]

People who depended on employer-based health care gained access to a very different set of public institutions. Those who made up this second category—formal-sector workers and their families—enjoyed a medium standard of care through the Mexican social security institutions that were established in the first half of the twentieth century. Most noteworthy is the Mexican Social Security Institute (IMSS), which serves workers employed in the private sector. Established in 1943, IMSS is the largest arm of the social security system, covering roughly half of the population, or 62 million Mexicans. It embodies a curious mixture of state-of-the-art medical equipment and a dearth of basic supplies. The Institute for Social Service and Security of State Workers (ISSSTE), established in 1959, has a smaller reach, covering around 12.9 million people working in the public sector as well as their dependents.[5] Despite resource shortages and high demand, social security institutions like IMSS and ISSSTE were generally well regarded by those in my research.

The most vulnerable segment of the population working in the informal economy, as well as the self-employed, the unemployed, and their families, were subject to the poorest standard of health care through the MOH. This system was designed in 1938 to "catch" the un- and underemployed without coverage and today houses the ILE program. With the inauguration of Seguro Popular in the early aughts, unemployed individuals continued to obtain care through the MOH, but their copays were covered. If the entire public health sector has suffered funding cuts in recent decades, the MOH, more than any other sector, embodies the broken revolutionary promise of health. Resource and personnel shortages, together with enormous patient demand, hamper the kinds of care that even the most qualified and well-intentioned clinicians are able to supply.

Spending time in MOH clinics meant witnessing firsthand that materials such as toilet paper often run out. Patients were housed together in shared rooms with little privacy because of space shortages and high demand. In many instances, patients had to bring their own bandages, saline solution, and other medical provisions to appointments. It was to the MOH, instructively, that incarcerated individuals in need of medical care were generally transported when health services were unavailable within the prison system. When I visited the MOH General Hospital of Tacalco, about twenty minutes from Santa Marta Clinic, several patients were shackled to benches in an overflow room. One adolescent boy had an IV in one wrist and a handcuff on the other—a striking embodiment of the carceral and caring capacities of the state. For a time, incarcerated women visited Santa Marta Clinic to procure abortions. Some were serving sixty-year sentences on charges of kidnapping and organized crime; they would not get out in time to care for a child. Eventually, Dr. Rios decided it was too complicated to accommodate their security teams alongside the general population of patients, and the MOH channeled them to a different facility.

ILE services are not offered through the social security institutions, such as IMSS and ISSSTE. This means that unless a woman can afford to purchase costly services through a private abortion clinic, the ILE program is the primary option for abortion care. Because the social security institutions are federally run, they were not required to implement ILE services when the procedure became legal in the capital. No one I asked could say why they chose not to, though most clinicians cited political controversy around abortion. Even Maria Puerto, an ILE program administrator, could not say definitively why the social security institutions failed to incorporate ILE after the 2007 reform. "Maybe because the MOH hasn't had the power to interfere or govern [the public health norms] on this topic within these organizations, that might be a reason," she hedged. Whatever the reasons, all ILE personnel and program administrators seemed to agree that the result was an enormous burden of abortion patients on the MOH, already the most overstretched tier of the public health system.[6]

For philosopher Milton Fisk, the "slow death" of public health care formed part of a broader neoliberal turn that unfolded in the 1980s in the context of a national debt crisis that shattered the Mexican economy.[7] The government cut public health funding, devastating the social security institutions and the MOH. Between the years of 1982 and 1987, health care spending per individual plummeted 50 percent among those with social security and 60 percent among the uninsured.[8] As local industry shuttered, many people found themselves out of work and unable to access the employer-based health care they had relied on through IMSS and ISSSTE. The ranks of the unemployed, underemployed, and informally employed swelled. With nowhere else to turn, more and more people sought health care services through the MOH. Facing unprecedented demand and fewer resources than ever, the MOH could no longer serve everyone who entered its doors.

Funding cuts weakened every dimension of these public health institutions. Personnel wages decreased, working conditions worsened, and physical infrastructures deteriorated.[9] The corrosion, writes former Mexico City health minister Asa Laurell, "laid the groundwork for an ideological attack that presented public institutions and social programs as intrinsically inefficient, bureaucratic, inhumane, and so forth."[10] The history of the neoliberal attrition forms the backdrop for the delivery of public abortion services through the MOH. This is a system that many people critique even as they depend on it for basic health care needs.[11] A spray-painted mural a few blocks from Santa Marta Clinic signaled the perspectives of people in this Tacalco community: "We demand more medicines and surgical equipment in the clinic." Resource shortages were not the only concern of those who made use of public health services in the capital. Many people harbored suspicions about the public health institutions themselves and the state workers who staffed them—patterns reflecting a broader sense of popular mistrust in state authorities that has grown more pronounced in recent years.

LEGACIES OF VIOLENCE IN A SLIPPERY STATE

I didn't expect to hear reflections on the status of Mexican democracy when I interviewed Ines, a single mother in her early thirties who sold clothing for a living in Tacalco's informal economy. We were sitting together in an empty room at Santa Marta in the summer of 2014 when I asked her if she remembered the passage of the 2007 reform. "I remember," she said, recalling the religious and political leaders who had denounced the law. "The Mexican government is a joke," she went on. "We citizens don't have a voice or a vote." Ines had supported the reform and she found the organized backlash on behalf of the church and its PAN allies disturbing. "I think resistance to abortion legalization is political, economic," she mused. "In Mexico, there is a huge organ-trafficking market, so if there are no children around, there won't be a source of organs." I didn't know what to make of Ines's comment at the time. I wouldn't learn until after our conversation that her suspicion, however far-fetched it had seemed, was rooted in a media story that had broken earlier that year.[12] At the time, police had recently arrested a member of the Michoacán cartel Los Caballeros Templarios (the Knights Templar). The Templario leader stood accused of participating in an underground network that abducted children from differ-

FIGURE 4. Graffiti near Santa Marta Clinic. "We demand more medicines and surgical equipment for the clinic." Photograph by author, 2014.

ent parts of the country and transported them to sites equipped with medical technologies to harvest their organs. Offering up evidence of the culpability of the detained cartel leader, a member of a local Michoacán vigilante group that had organized to combat the brutal drug-related violence asserted to the media that he and his team had once stopped a suspicious vehicle on the road. Inside, he told reporters, they found several Mexico City schoolchildren swaddled in blankets in a refrigerated box. The uses of the child organs in the underground network were not entirely clear. While some media stories cited economic motivations and trafficking, others posited that the organs were used in initiation rites for the cartel, which required new recruits to eat them as a test of loyalty.[13]

Later that summer, shortly after I interviewed Ines, a video circulated across the media outlets, adding another layer of confusion to the story. The footage captured a conversation on political strategy between the son of Michoacán's former PRI governor, Fausto Vallejo, and "La Tuta," a notorious leader in the Templarios cartel. The video established the governor's collusion with the organization, deepening popular suspicion about the blurry boundaries between state officials and organized crime. But questions still lingered. Was the man featured in the footage really La Tuta? To what degree was Governor Vallejo conspiring with the cartel, and on what issues? Was his son, as he claimed after the video became public, a victim of cartel exploitation, or was he an accomplice? Who took the footage, and who released it? Was the video itself a political strategy, and if so, whose? As anthropologist Claudio Lomnitz observed in an opinion piece that he published shortly thereafter in *La Jornada*, "With each media operation, society as a whole loses more and more of a sense of the 'floor' with respect to what the true reality is."[14] There were no easy answers that summer, but for Lomnitz some things were clear.[15] "Today we know that the Vallejo government had a bridge of communication and negotiation with the Templarios," he wrote. "And we know, as well, that it is expedient for someone powerful that this information is known."

Ines was the only ILE patient I met to voice the theory that political opposition to legal abortion stemmed from economic interests in maintaining a steady supply of children whose organs could be harvested and trafficked on the illegal market. Her concern, however, condensed a more pervasive angst that had metastasized within the general public about who, and what, could be trusted. It was just two months after our conversation at the clinic that forty-three teachers in training were disappeared in the southern city of Iguala, in the state of Guerrero, in September 2014. The group of student teachers had traveled by bus from their college in the nearby town of Ayotzinapa to protest educational reforms that disadvantaged rural students. Their journey was interrupted when local police and federal military troops fired upon the buses, killing six students and terrorizing those who escaped the bullets. After the events, forty-three of the student teachers were missing. The massacre called to collective memory the governmental slaughter of hundreds of student protesters under PRI rule on the eve of the Olympic Games in 1968, becoming emblematic of how little had changed with the "democratic transition."[16] The Enrique Peña Nieto presidential administration, in power at the time, is now known to have obstructed the investigation of the crimes, and some suspect collusion.

Conditions of profound political insecurity and brutal violence have penetrated everyday life in Mexico in recent decades, creating "a floating border between the state of law and the state of exception."[17] Organized criminals have infiltrated state organisms and institutions, generating a crisis in the legitimacy of the state.[18] Popular anger is directed as much at cartel bosses as political leaders, whom many people fault for failing to address the drug-related violence and corruption, or worse, for conspiring to produce it. Kari, an ILE patient whom I spoke with casually at Santa Marta, evoked the general mistrust in the Mexican government during a conversation about the rash of school shootings that have terrorized US cities in recent decades. We had been sitting in the waiting room when she asked for me for an explanation of what she saw as a peculiarly US phenomenon. "In the United States citizens kill each other," Kari said. "Here in Mexico, the government kills us." I understood what Kari meant. News of the Guerrero massacre was fresh, and protesters were still flooding the city streets all around us. But her comment struck me because she made it from within a government clinic where she would obtain a state-sponsored abortion at no cost, something, of course, entirely unavailable in the US.

The paradox at the center of Kari's observation is captured in anthropologist Megan Crowley-Matoka's theorization of Mexico as a "slippery state," whose citizens see governmental insitutions and functionaries as a source of indispensable assistance and benefits, yet also as fundamentally unpredictable,

unreliable, and potentially threatening.[19] Slippery states furnish their populations with life-sustaining services such as health care, but those services may
vary in quality and dependability, may fail to materialize altogether, or may
take harmful forms. This "slippery" characteristic, observes Emily Wentzell,
has been a defining aspect of the postrevolutionary Mexican state, capturing "a
destabilizing inconsistency in the availability of promised care and resources,
based on what might feel to citizens like chance (for instance, whether you get
an honest or competent doctor in a state system)."[20] During the PRI regime
that defined much of the twentieth century state services and benefits were
attached to loyalty to the ruling party or were acquired through personal relations. Political clientelism has long shaped the delivery of public health services
in Mexico, where patients in public institutions are often treated as privileged
recipients of government benevolence rather than as citizens endowed with
rights.[21] Legacies of clientelism bear on how citizens imagine their entitlement
to state services as well. "The construction of a subject of rights has not been a
substantial part [of] socialization in Mexico, let alone [of] experiences of relationship to the state," observe Ana Amuchástegui and Edith Flores.[22] It is thus
in the context of a "slippery state" marked by decades of neoliberal attenuation,
endemic corruption, and pernicious gendered violence that ILE services have
been made publicly available through the MOH. What kind of care emerges in
such a context? And how do recipients of ILE services, a population made up
primarily of poor and working women, experience the care afforded through
the public clinics?

PUBLIC WAITING

Most of the patients that I interviewed in the ILE clinics related that tedious
waiting suffused every step of the process of obtaining an abortion through the
public sector. It was often the first thing they mentioned when I asked about
their abortion experiences. At the same time, many of these lifelong recipients of
public health services saw extensive waiting as an unremarkable, if cumbersome,
aspect of going to the doctor. Waits that feel interminable, women often told
me, define care in the ILE program and in the public health sector generally.

To wait is to surrender to the power of another over one's time. Pierre

Bourdieu describes the medical universe as "one of the sites par excellence of anxious, powerless waiting."[23] And waiting, for Bourdieu, "implies submission." Social scientists have begun to attend to the micropolitics of waiting for health care and its undue burdens on the lifeworlds of the poor.[24] Anthropologist Javier Auyero sees waiting as "a process in and through which political subordination is reproduced."[25] Waiting has subjective effects, shaping how people come to conceive of their social value and their position in the political order. The poor and marginalized, so much of whose time is eaten up waiting on state services like public transit and public health care, experience their subordination in a visceral and embodied way. In the process of waiting in state institutions for public services that may or may not materialize, the poor learn that their time is subject to the whims of more powerful actors for whom it holds little value.

By and large, it was poor and working women who had to endure the lethargic pace of the MOH to claim their right to an abortion, as wealthy women could rely on private clinics, where demand was lower and waiting was limited. In the course of waiting hours and sometimes days on end to receive a state-sponsored abortion, patients confronted their subjection to state and biomedical control over their time. Long periods of apprehensive waiting rendered women seeking ILE services "patient" in two senses: as recipients of a biomedicalized reproductive health service and as tolerant withstanders of the sluggish rhythms of the overburdened MOH.[26] In the ILE clinics women came to understand that to access their right to an abortion they had to be patient, keep quiet, and suffer the wait.

The waiting began long before women entered the clinic. Daily openings were limited, and most women could not make appointments ahead of time. Women and their accompaniers subjected themselves to uncomfortable circumstances to secure a *ficha* (appointment) in the clinic. The gestational limit on ILE care meant that bureaucratic and other delays posed serious ramifications, as women's pregnancies continued to progress despite postponements they encountered. The length of the delay could mean the difference between securing an abortion or not. At the time of my study, women whose pregnancies had advanced just one day beyond twelve weeks could be turned away from the program and denied care.

FIGURE 5. Waiting at Santa Marta Clinic. Photograph by author, 2014.

Depending on where she lived, a woman might board three forms of pub-lic transit before sunrise to arrive at an ILE clinic in the hopes of obtaining a *ficha*. In the congested capital, this was no small task. The city and surround-ing metropolitan area are home to roughly twenty million people. During peak commuting hours (*horas picos*) it can easily take over two hours to travel a few miles by car. The metro is faster, since it operates underground, unless it's rain-ing, in which case people rush in for shelter and the lines move more slowly. Despite its discomforts, the metro is fairly accessible. A single ride costs five *pesos* (twenty-five cents USD), and the system operates from 5:00 a.m. to midnight Monday through Saturday, with more limited hours on Sundays. Most Mexico City residents who do not own private cars have a strategy for navigating the city that involves a combination of public transit (either the metro, an aboveg-round system called the *metrobús*, or a *pesero* bus), taxis, and increasingly a ride-share option like Uber. Since many women had to leave home even earlier than 5:00 a.m. to arrive at an ILE clinic, they could not always rely on the metro.

Taxis were a common form of transit among the ILE clientele, but this op-tion was not without risks. Rates of taxi-related robbery and kidnapping are lower than they once were, but anyone will advise caution. Unless someone purchases a ride from a more expensive regulated taxi (*taxi sitio*), hailing a cab indiscriminately off the street can be dangerous, particularly for women. People use the term *secuestro exprés* to describe the phenomenon whereby a taxi driver holds passengers hostage and forces them to drain their accounts at a bank win-dow. Whichever kind of transportation one uses, navigating the city requires energy, caution, and above all, a tremendous amount of time.

I made a point to use public transit as much as I could throughout my fieldwork. My commute to Santa Marta Clinic from the apartment I rented in an adjacent borough was over an hour each way and, depending on the traffic, sometimes closer to two. I often raced myself to see if I could get there faster than I had the day before. On most mornings I arrived exhausted after pushing through walls of people to board a metro car, where I was regularly so wedged between people that only their bodies were sustaining my weight, and then walking a few miles between the metro lines. I almost always hailed a taxi on the last leg of the trip because I was too tired to wait for the bus, a luxury that some ILE patients did not have. For many of the women I met at the clinic the trip was even longer and more arduous. Given the time-sensitive nature of abortion, their journeys were borne of absolute necessity.

It was hard for Abril and her partner Damian to ignore the burden of time as they made preparations to obtain an abortion at Santa Marta Clinic. Nei-ther of them had stable jobs or the economic means to support a new baby, they told me when we met in the clinical waiting room, and they wanted to finish their college degrees before having a family. Both of Abril's sisters had been adolescent mothers, so she was familiar with the enormous sacrifices that parenthood entails. When Abril's friend told her about the ILE program, she and Damian made plans to get there as soon as possible. Even though the couple lived within city bounds, Damian traveled to Santa Marta twice before the day of the procedure—first to solicit information about how the abortion process worked and later to test out the most convenient public transit route from their apartment to the clinic to ensure that they arrived early enough to secure an appointment. Time bore down on the couple as they arranged their visit to the clinic. "We planned the visit against the clock," Abril said. "I couldn't let the pregnancy get any bigger. By my calculations, I was three weeks along. But when the ultrasound came [obtained outside of the ILE program], it said seven weeks. So I said no, I can't let that much time pass. A private clinic charges 6,000 pesos [$300 USD]. We didn't have the money, so I wouldn't have been able to have the abortion [if I didn't get to the ILE clinic in time for the twelve-week cutoff]."

Two full weeks passed from the time Abril learned she was pregnant to the day she was able to obtain an abortion at Santa Marta. "More than anything it was the lack of resources," Abril said, accounting for the time lapse. "Because from where we live the clinic is far. We had to get there really early, at 3:00 a.m., and figure out when the buses leave and what time we had to arrive, because they only give out ten appointments a day. I didn't want to wait another week. It was already a difficult week with Damian. I was totally desperate, and he also felt the pressure—I have to admit that I pressured him because of how bad I was feeling. I told him to find the money [for the abortion-related travel]. I wanted to get it over with. So, basically, it took time to figure out who could lend us a little money. Even though the ILE service is free, we had to pay for a taxi, bus tickets, and a hotel near the clinic so we could get there faster the morning of the procedure to secure a spot in line. Damian was at the clinic practically from 2:00 a.m. onwards in order to get me an appointment because the staff scare you and tell you that there are only ten available slots. There are people who come, they practically spend the night outside the clinic. So he said, 'Whatever I have to do.'"

I was incredulous when I first learned that women and their accompaniers arrived so early at the clinics. But Damian and Abril were not the only ones to endure uncomfortable circumstances to secure an appointment. "I came to get information yesterday," Amalia, a Tacalco resident and mother of two studying to become an engineer, recounted about her own journey to Santa Marta. "A policeman outside the clinic entrance told me to arrive before 6:00 a.m., but I asked him honestly what time people started coming, because I know how things work at this type of clinic [referencing public clinics], that people start lining up much earlier. He said the first people start arriving at 4:00 a.m. The girl who was waiting here with me yesterday arrived at 6:00 a.m. and she didn't get an appointment. So today she came at 3:30 am, before me. When I got here, she was already waiting. By 5:00 a.m. there were like six people, all sitting in the dark."

When the abortifacient pills dispensed in the clinic failed to produce an abortion (known as a *resistencia*), women had to make the trip all over again. Graciela, a thirty-nine-year-old mother of two studying to become a hairdresser, returned to Santa Marta for this reason. On the day we met she would undergo an EVA abortion to empty her uterus. Graciela had initially wanted to keep the pregnancy, her third, but her doctor issued several warnings. Her age plus her diabetes meant that the pregnancy posed risks to her health. On their second visit to Santa Marta, Graciela and her husband heeded the receptionist's admonition to arrive early. They made it to the clinic by 2 a.m. "They only let ten to twenty people in a day," Graciela said. "You *have* to get here early. Thank God we were the second ones to arrive. The first in line said they got here at 2:00 a.m."

Almost every woman I met through the ILE program described the long wait times as onerous, but waiting produced added emotional strain for women who did not have the emotional support of a friend or partner. Ximena, an office worker in her midtwenties with two kids, was in the middle of a messy divorce from an abusive partner when she became pregnant for the third time. She cried throughout our conversation in one of Santa Marta's offices, explaining that she had been dating someone else since things had collapsed with her husband. Because of the change in partners, she was unsure by whom she was pregnant. Nervous to confide in anyone about the situation, she had asked a taxi driver to accompany her to the clinic. "I was going to come here with a complete stranger who would drop me off," she related. "I was scared to stay at the clinic because it's pretty far from my house and it's really hidden. The fact that I didn't know what awaited me, and that I had to arrive at the crack of dawn and go to an unknown place, was terrifying." For Ximena, waiting with a stranger at the clinic in the early morning hours added another layer of distress to an already daunting process.

Other patients made light of the long wait times, using humor as an emotional release. Lucinda described the long stretch of time she and her boyfriend Ivan had spent at the clinic on their first visit. She had gotten time off from the snack food company where she worked, and he had been able to fit the visit into his schedule as a university student. "He didn't come with me this time [the second time], because it took forever, *fue tardadísimo* [it took so long]," she said.

> At least we [the patients] were inside the clinic. But the accompaniers were outside from like—we got here at like 7:30 a.m. and we didn't leave until 12:30 p.m., more or less. So he would sit—I watched as he sat on the stoop, then he would walk up the clinic stairs. The sun came out and he would move to the other side. He got cold and tired and almost fell asleep. He didn't know what to do with himself! I even joked around with my boyfriend. I told him they make us wait *so long* so we don't come back. If you think for one second that you might need another abortion one day, you know you'll have to wait like five hours.

Even though Lucinda and her partner brought levity to the situation, women's experiences obtaining ILE care were generally marked by discomfort, uncertainty, and anxiety.

It took me several months of talking to patients to learn that there were ways to maneuver to secure a *ficha* but that doing so required a measure of savvy and know-how not afforded to the majority of ILE patients. This was a population, by and large, that was accustomed to waiting for public health services. Pulling strings to circumvent the wait was a realistic option only for the well connected. At age thirty-two, Mariana had recently completed her college degree in actuarial science when I met her. She had called a local nonprofit organization that serves women to inquire about ILE services prior to seeking abortion care. The organization sent her to Santa Marta, the clinic closest to her house, and alerted the staff to her pending arrival. I asked Mariana if she thought she was able to secure a spot the first time she came because the organization had given the clinic her name. "Yes, yes, because I was like the twelfth or thirteenth person in line, and when they opened the clinic doors, the policeman came out and called my name and that was that. I entered first. Ten of us entered, but there were two who didn't get in." And what of the others waiting in line, I asked Mariana, did they get mad? "No. If I were one of the ones who couldn't enter that day, I would have raised Cain. But we're in a country where the majority of people don't demand what is rightfully theirs, they stay quiet."

Staying quiet when denied a public service after a long and uncomfortable wait is a powerful example of acquiescence to state and biomedical power over one's time. With few other viable options for interrupting their pregnancies, most women had no choice. The ease with which Mariana passed to the front of the line reflected her own fortunate position as a college-educated person with promising career prospects, advantages that allowed her to feel comfortable and confident "demanding what was rightfully hers" even as the women around her kept quiet. The facility with which she navigated the public health bureaucracy marked her out as possessing what Megan Crowley-Matoka has called "agility" (*agilizar* is the verb form more commonly used in Spanish). For Crowley-Matoka, the term conveys "a certain cultural style to how things get done in daily life in Mexico, for the way in which institutions of all kinds are assumed to be labyrinthine, obstructive, and often corrupt bureaucracies, best navigated by circumventing the official processes and rules through a combination of favors, personal connections, winsome appeals, and the politically astute application of pressure."[27] Instead of testing her luck by arriving at Santa Marta Clinic like rest of the women who had lined up outside before dawn, Mariana knew to contact a nonprofit organization that might facilitate the process, shepherding her through and securing her an appointment on the first try and with relative ease. By skipping to the front of the line and past at least two women who would be denied abortion services that day, even though they had gone out of their way to arrive at the clinic before her, Mariana publicly performed the importance of "agility" in getting one's needs met in the public health sector. Not everyone was so savvy.

While most women had little choice but to resign themselves to the long stretches of time that made visits to the clinic burdensome and boring, occasionally time emerged as a point of tension in the clinic. Almost every patient I met through the ILE program described to me in detail how she had waited patiently for hours on end, sometimes more than once, to secure an appointment. I was surprised, then, when Roberta, a Santa Marta social worker, bemoaned the reluctance of ILE patients to endure long wait times. "They want to go and be attended in that moment. They want everything fast! They come to the ILE clinic and sometimes demand that you attend to them quickly, when in reality here we give them everything in one single day, in a few hours. We don't take that long!" The discord between Roberta's assessment and the reflections of patients like Amalia, Ximena, Lucinda, and others is striking. Long wait times, though inconvenient, were hardly enough to dissuade women from seeking abortion care.

On occasion, patients resisted temporal regimes in the clinic to demand that their needs be met. I remember a fall morning at Reina María when patients crowded every corner of the small clinic, some fading in and out of sleep or else delirious with boredom. Many had been there for several hours patiently waiting. A nurse named Julia sat hunched over her record book, lifting her gaze now and again to survey the waiting room and instruct the patients to stay quiet. The other personnel shifted about, finalizing paperwork before the abortifacient pills could be dispensed. But for everyone else, time seemed to stand still. When she could no longer tolerate the wait, a patient named Berta asked Julia how much longer it would be. The nurse snapped at Berta, letting her know that the personnel were moving as fast as they could.

"Well, you should really respect our time," Berta stated on behalf of the other patients.

"There are protocols in this clinic, *señorita*, we can't move any faster."

"Well, the protocols should really respect our time," Berta continued. "We've been here all day without eating. And don't think you're doing us a favor," she added. "We pay your salary with our taxes." Unnerved by the conflict, I looked away from the scene, but Julia sought an outlet.

"It's not my fault she didn't take care of herself," she whispered to me.

Although women sometimes asked questions of the personnel, I had never observed an ILE patient confront a medical worker so directly. Berta contested the notion that the program was supplying her with a gift, rather than a health service that was rightfully hers. As a tax-paying citizen, she emphasized, she was entitled to public health services, including abortion. And it was her prerogative, she implied, to express grievances when that care did not emerge in a timely fashion. Julia seemed taken aback by the exchange. She shifted her (and my) attention away from deficiencies in the program and back onto her patient. I didn't get a chance to interview Berta, but when I prompted Julia to reflect on the encounter later on, she had this to say: "The wealthy patients are more work, they are disobedient. They feel powerful."

Most women had few alternatives but to surrender to the slow tick of bureaucratic time in order to access their right to an abortion. They simply could not afford an abortion through the private sector, where plentiful resources and reduced demand would have allowed for a faster and more comfortable experience and more privacy from the visibility of the public clinics. Yet submission to clinical temporalities did not mean that women were entirely passive. When awaiting ILE care, many found or forged cracks in the clinical protocol to ensure that their needs were met more efficiently, or at least to communicate grievances. Some, like Mariana and Berta, flatly refused to yield to the clinic's temporal order, working around or pushing against bureaucratic rhythms and procedures. While there was some room for reshuffling clinical timescales, the vast majority of patients had to endure uncomfortable and often very public waits, which they tolerated without confrontation or complaint.

BUREAUCRATIC DELAYS AND THE OPACITY OF PUBLIC CARE

Abortion services are ostensibly available to all women who arrive at an ILE clinic within the first trimester of pregnancy. However, to obtain the procedure, women must arrive with certain documents. Documentation requirements vary slightly between ILE clinics and hospitals, but most require (1) an official form of identification; (2) proof of residence, such as a bill; (3) a birth certificate; and (4) an official form of identification for the person accompanying the woman seeking abortion. Minors and women arriving from outside the capital have additional documentation requirements.[28]

In her early thirties, Lety was working full-time, finishing a college degree, and raising a daughter together with her partner when we met at her postabortion follow-up visit to Santa Marta Clinic. Her decision to interrupt the pregnancy was straightforward, but the process of accessing an abortion through the ILE program had proved far more complicated. After Lety learned she was pregnant, it took her and her partner two weeks to arrive at Santa Marta Clinic. "It was the bureaucracy of the documents," she said.

The only thing I had was a bank statement [as proof of residence]. I brought it, and when we were lining up [the clinic staff] said, "No, you have to go back, we can't accept this." They told me to go back to my house for the document and then return. I asked them to treat me that day because it was the only day that I had permission to miss work. At first they said no, and then later they agreed to attend to me if I promised to bring the proof of residence later on. But really, this type of bureaucracy—they sent another woman home! The truth is, the clinic is *really* far from my house, like an hour away. This type of thing has a really big impact because, as I told them, I only had permission to miss work for *this* day. I can't change my day off now that I'm here.

Lety was able to secure an appointment by pressing the personnel to appreciate her situation. She resorted to pleading with the clinicians to consider her circumstances. In the process, she emerged not as a subject who had been afforded a set of social and political rights but as someone who needed to beg for state protection.

As a symbolic tie to the state, documents both establish and legitimate sociopolitical belonging. They can trigger the distribution of needed resources or disqualify someone from accessing state benefits.[29] As scholars of undocumented migration have long observed, documents, and the kinds of sociopolitical inclusion they signal, also get under the skin to alter subjectivities. They legitimate existence in legal and moral terms, transforming individuals from "non-subject[s] incapable of taking stands or making demands" into subjects whose demands warrant recognition and response.[30] In the ILE program documents served to distinguish those who could access a public abortion from those who would be denied state care. These bureaucratic demands could make the process of accessing ILE remarkably difficult, sometimes forcing women to return to the clinic multiple times before they had gathered the proper documentation. They also had lasting symbolic effects, shaping women's experiences of their relationship to the state and its public health institutions and functionaries. Most women found the documentation requirements exasperating. Not only did they make the process of obtaining an abortion convoluted, they also produced a great deal of anxiety and uncertainty. Women arriving at a clinic were rarely confident that they would be able to obtain the care they sought, despite jumping through a series of hoops to get there and scrambling, often from one end of the city to the other, to gather the requisite paperwork.

Araceli returned to Santa Marta for an EVA procedure after experiencing a *resistencia* (resistance, or failed abortion). On her second visit, a conflict erupted outside the clinic at 4:30 a.m. when a sixteen-year-old patient named Edith arrived with her mother. The trio sat uncomfortably in the dark, confiding in each other about the circumstances that had drawn them from different corners of the sprawling capital to this out-of-the-way clinic before sunrise. Araceli was forthright about the challenging pregnancy she had endured with her daughter, now a healthy five-year-old. A second pregnancy felt risky given her reproductive history, so she had decided on the abortion. Edith had been diagnosed with cancer. She too needed an abortion for medical reasons. Even if she had wanted to keep the pregnancy, the cancer therapies she would undergo, in all likelihood, would have provoked a miscarriage.

After a few hours, the clinic security guard interrupted their conversation to solicit identification documents from all of the patients lined up outside. When Edith's mother realized that she had forgotten her daughter's birth certificate, the guard was unyielding. Desperate, Edith's mother asked if she could retrieve the document from home. She would be no more than thirty minutes, she entreated. "I was the third [in line]," Araceli recalled about the events that morning.

> [Edith, the sixteen-year-old] was the second. So I told her [mother] to go quickly. It was only like seven in the morning, they weren't going to let us into [the clinic] yet. But when she came back, they didn't want to attend to her, even though they had not yet given out all of the appointments. They hadn't even gotten to number ten. So, it was a mess, it was a giant mess outside because everyone [asked why they couldn't just attend to her]. Edith's mother left to get the birth certificate, but Edith was *here* [at Santa Marta] the whole time, so technically she didn't lose her place in line. I don't know what the protocol is, but it seemed logical to give her a spot.

In the end, the clinic staff gave Edith the last appointment of the day. "But she should not have had to go through all of that," Araceli emphasized, still troubled by the incident. Although Edith was able to interrupt her pregnancy, all of the patients at the clinic that day could see the power of documentation to confer (or not) time-sensitive treatment. They could also see the arbitrariness of documentation requirements, without which care could be withheld even from patients who needed it the most.

Blanca, a single mother of two in her early thirties, had crossed into the capital from her home in Mexico State to arrive at Santa Marta by 5:30 a.m. in the hopes of obtaining an abortion. We met at her follow-up appointment two weeks later. "Ever since I learned I was pregnant I've felt anxious," she told me. Even though Blanca had been using birth control pills, when she missed a period she knew something was wrong. Blanca had interrupted her education during middle school and was working as a waitress. Her kids demanded most of her time and energy. When Blanca told the man she had been seeing about the pregnancy, he stopped returning her calls. Though a friend had agreed to accompany her to the clinic for the abortion, being there made her feel even more alone. "In the clinic I saw people who had come with their children and mothers, women with their husbands, and then me, alone. I felt bad. I thought, how can this be happening?" Lonely and despairing, Blanca had been eager to get the abortion over with, but she encountered several difficulties.

Originally from the southern state of Oaxaca, Blanca had moved to central Mexico years earlier in search of a better life. She left behind many of her belongings, including a variety of documents. When she arrived at Santa Marta, the personnel initially turned her away because she lacked the proper paperwork. I could hardly follow the story she narrated about arriving at clinic because her experience was so convoluted. "Two weeks ago, I lost my ID," she said,

> and I couldn't find my birth certificate. As I understood it, I had to go get a new birth certificate, it was going to be impossible. I said to myself, if I already made the decision to interrupt my pregnancy why do I have to go all the way to the IFE [National Electoral Institute] so they can give me a birth certificate, and from there jump through more hoops to get an ID? On the Internet my friend and I found the phone number for IFE and I called. They said they could help me, but in the IFE there was no way they could attend to me, so it was all taking forever. I thought, what am I going to do? But then I remembered that I had left my birth certificate with a neighbor. I contacted her, but she had moved. Two days went by and I told her I was coming for the

certificate. The night I was headed there it started to pour, so I turned around. I said I would go tomorrow and get it and then go directly to the ILE clinic. It took forever. I had to wait fifteen days because I had lost my ID. So, from the moment I learned I was pregnant—first I lost the ID and then, because I was trying to remember where I left it, the process was worrisome, maddening!

As she moved through a maze of state institutions, Blanca was thwarted at every turn.

She was eventually able to retrieve her birth certificate and arrive at the ILE clinic with the accompaniment of her friend. Inside, the personnel asked for a document for proof of residence. She had brought an electricity bill, but it was a year old.

So, when I arrived at the ILE clinic the receptionist noticed and said no, that I needed to bring a different proof of residence. I said, "Even though I'm already here?" I told her that my friend [the accompanier] knows where I live, and I can tell him to go there and get a different bill. They said that they stopped providing attention in the clinic at 1:00 p.m., so there wasn't much time. Then they said that they would attend to me but that it would cost money. I had to pay 100 pesos [about $5.00 USD required because she was not a Mexico City resident].

In the end, Blanca was able to interrupt her pregnancy. But she had the hardest time accessing ILE care of all of the patients I met. Every time she seemed to advance in her search for documents another hurdle appeared in her path. Fortunately, the sonogram scan in the clinic measured her pregnancy at 5.3 weeks. Had her pregnancy been farther along, the bureaucratic delays might have precluded her from accessing a legal abortion. Even though Blanca was ultimately able to obtain the procedure, the bureaucracy of the public health system left her defeated.

Naomi was in her midtwenties and had recently finished her college degree in psychology when we met at Santa Marta. The pregnancy came as a surprise. She suffered from several health conditions that affected her fertility, and pregnancy had always seemed out of the question. Naomi and her boyfriend had broken up when news of the pregnancy came, and she knew that if she carried it to term she would have to raise the child alone.

At first, I said yeah, I can do this, and then I got really scared because I thought, okay, I finished college. Normally, the culturally established thing, at least where I live in Tacalco, is "Okay, you finished your college degree and you're an adult now, you aren't that young, it would be bad if you were eighteen, but you're twenty-four so you should have the baby." But I thought, I don't want just this. I want so much more. Really what pushes me to have the abortion is the question of wanting to achieve more and not staying in the same position as my parents. I saw how my mom worked day and night to raise my sister and me.

Like so many other women, Naomi's route to obtaining an abortion was meandering and complex, requiring her to navigate a dizzying maze of clinics and health centers across the city for two weeks. Even though she lived near Santa Marta Clinic, her friend had encouraged her to seek care in a different ILE clinic, which she described as having more resources and more compassionate personnel. When Naomi arrived at the clinic that her friend had suggested, the clinicians asked for a *gratuidad* form (a kind of public health care), which she didn't have. When she went to a local health center to obtain the form, a social worker scolded her: "Abortion isn't any old thing, *señorita*, you don't even have a health emergency." Naomi visited several other hospitals in search of the form without success. Eventually, she returned to Tacalco to try her luck at the general hospital. From there, the clinicians sent her to Santa Marta, where she was eventually able to obtain a medical abortion.

A number of scholars have explored how intractable bureaucracy is a core feature of citizens' experiences of the state in contexts across Latin America.[31] In addition to interrupting the exercise of social rights, scholars note, inefficient bureaucracy can dampen citizen trust in public institutions. In the Mexican capital, bureaucratic hurdles and delays could make the process of exercising one's right to public abortion care remarkably unpredictable. Many women, like Lety, Edith, Blanca, and Naomi, made halting journeys through the ILE program. Piloting a course through the labyrinthine public health sector occasioned confusion and distress for women even before they arrived at the clinic. Some found ways to demand that they be attended even when they lacked the required paperwork, entreating clinic personnel with impassioned appeals.

Occasionally clinicians were moved to bend the rules, succumbing to pathos. But for many patients the effects of the process were powerful and lasting. Many women were subject to requirements that felt illogical and at times inhumane. While some ILE patients were accustomed to seeking care through the MOH, others came to experience a relationship with the state that is generally reserved for the poorest citizens.

OBSTETRIC VIOLENCE?

If getting to an ILE clinic and securing an appointment there upon arrival were fraught with uncertainty and stress, inside the clinic the care provided was marked by moral ambiguities. I spent countless mornings with the social workers in the Santa Marta counseling office as patients filed in and out. As I replay those scenes in my memory now, some of the details have faded with time. I had never seen her before, but Roberta and Carolina both recognized the young woman who folded herself into the plastic chair on the short edge of the counseling table one autumn morning. I don't recall her name, but I remember thinking that she couldn't have been older than I was at the time, not yet thirty. When Roberta asked her why she had returned to the clinic for a second abortion, why she had found herself in this situation again, the patient resigned herself to the tenor of the conversation. Had the first abortion been pleasant? Roberta pushed, confronting her patient with an insoluble question. That was why she had returned, wasn't it, Roberta tested, because the first abortion hadn't hurt enough? I can't remember if or how the young woman responded that morning, just that she thanked us, and before long another patient emerged from the waiting room and appeared in the doorway.

I often struggled throughout this research to reconcile the brusque demeanor and hassled tone of the providers with my own expectations for how abortion care should unfold. Early on, I searched for evidence that patients agreed with me that the clinicians were inappropriate, reading exchanges like this one as instances of "obstetric violence" (OV)—hostile doctor-patient interactions that collude with wider social inequities to threaten women's reproductive rights and assault their personhood. Yet while patients occasionally complained about the ILE providers, most approved of the care they received.

Ultimately, my material from the ILE clinics has prompted me to consider what the OV framework misses.

A legal and advocacy framework originally developed in Venezuela in 2006, OV has gained currency among reproductive health advocates, midwives, and academics concerned with abuse or disrespect of women seeking of obstetric care.[32] The framework has since overwhelmed reproductive health advocacy discourse across Latin America, becoming what Paula Sesia has called "a new epistemic category."[33] While OV can take different forms, individual medical personnel as well as entire health systems are implicated in victimizing birthing women through degrading comments, physical injury, excessive medical interventions, and generally undignified treatment.[34] The concept has proved an expedient means to frame discrete instances of obstetric harm as expressions of wider inequities in women's health as well as broader societal patterns of violence against women. Midwives and reproductive health advocates across Mexico have adopted the framework as a rallying cry to denounce mistreatment on maternity wards as an epiphenomenon of the gendered violence that women face in their everyday lives.[35] Research conducted in Mexican public and private health institutions has documented sexist and humiliating comments as well as more egregious bodily violations such as unconsented insertion of IUDs and coerced sterilization, all of which are directed disproportionately at poor, indigenous, and dark-skinned mestiza women.[36] One meta-analysis of national obstetric data from 2016 concluded that as many as 32 percent of women who had given birth in the previous five years were subject to OV.[37] By 2017, twenty federal entities had updated their laws to define OV as a form of gendered violence.[38] And yet, with a few exceptions, little is known about the degree to which this framework is applicable to the delivery of controversial aspects of reproductive health care such as abortion in or outside Mexico.[39]

In the ILE clinics I never witnessed instances of involuntary sterilization, unconsented insertion of IUDs, slapping, or other kinds of overt physical harm documented in health care settings elsewhere in the country. Nevertheless, at times I had trouble resolving my own discomfort with certain aspects of ILE care, such as scolding and cajoling, with the accounts of providers and patients, for whom such care practices often held different meanings. However, as my research progressed and my relationships with providers deepened, I found it harder and harder to square their manifest concern for their patients with an analytic of "violence." These were not the terms through which most patients or clinicians understood the delivery of public abortion services. Many women accepted clinical scolding as a recognizable expression of medical paternalism that linked them to clinicians. Providers, for their part, saw scolding as a means to foster responsibility in their patients, a way to call them into a relationship of care. I found more nuance, more equivocation, and more gratitude in patient-provider relationships—spaces of epistemic uncertainty that are eclipsed by the absolutist frame of "violence."

I have come to see the kinds of clinical scolding and coaxing that are central to the provision of ILE services as intimate expressions of paternalistic care in a context where abortion, unlike childbirth, proved morally disquieting for many patients and providers alike. Care is an elusive concept. I use it to describe intimate gestures of moral engagement between clinicians and their patients, as well as the wider political and biomedical infrastructures that organize such minute relational exchanges. Care, in other words, unfolds in intersubjective and institutional modes. To be clear, framing medical paternalism as care does not excuse instances of verbal or physical harm. My point, rather, is that care is never as straightforward or as innocent as it may appear.[40] Anthropologists have argued that care is everywhere "embroiled in complex politics," as it unfolds in arrangements of stark hierarchy and at times can produce new power imbalances.[41] Ethnographic research shows that care can motivate practices of overt bodily harm and, paradoxically, form a central aspect of the work performed in punitive institutions like jails.[42] Care and harm can fold in on one another, becoming difficult to parse.[43] For all its ambiguity, what is clear is that care "can blur the lines between ethical and unethical, coercion and aid, responsibility and negligence, help and harm."[44] In the ILE clinic, how clinicians approach their patients—along a continuum from genuine concern to contempt—comes to shape patients' assessments of public abortion services. At the same time, a broader landscape of political and economic configurations influences the kind of care, both technical and affective, that even the best ILE clinicians are able to furnish.

During interviews I always asked patients for their reflections on the services they received through the ILE clinics. I made a point to remind them that I was a researcher in the clinic and that any complaints they expressed would remain anonymous and have no bearing on the care they received. Despite the long waits and bureaucratic hurdles that most women described, overwhelmingly, patients evinced support and gratitude for the ILE program.

Karen was finishing her high school degree when she became pregnant for the fourth time. When I met her she had been a patient at Santa Marta Clinic before. "I live nearby here," she told me. "I notice how many women come to the clinic. There are lines every day, there are so many women that come. It makes you think about how many children do not end up neglected. I think about how much it helps a woman to change her life. Women don't just come from Mexico City but from far away. They wake up super early, they sleep outside the clinic. If you ask each of these women, I think more than half would tell you, and I am included, that they are thankful that clinics like this exist."

Along with feeling grateful for the existence of the program, most patients described *un buen servicio* (a good service). In their endorsements of ILE services patients emphasized technical aspects of the care provided, such as the cleanliness of facilities, the safe conditions under which abortions were performed, and the comprehensive information offered, as well as affective dimensions of care, including gentle and respectful treatment by the personnel. When I asked a patient named Lety, who was finishing her college degree, about how the providers treated her, she said, "Very good, all of the nurses, the truth is that they treat you very well. The doctor was very professional, she answered all of our questions. In reality they are very professional. They are very human, they get up close to the patients, that is important." For Lety, the clinicians struck a balance between upholding standards of professionalism and also allowing patients feel close to them, physically and emotionally. "It was very good," a college student named Monserrat said about her experience seeking her first abortion at Santa Marta. "The receptionist is really nice, and the nurses the same, even the doctor. I felt like it was a really good service honestly, because they work to ensure that everything is safe in terms of your health in order to perform the procedure."

At times women contrasted the care offered through the ILE clinic to negative experiences they had endured in other public clinics. Yolanda, an uninsured office worker, said, "Everything was great, honestly very good, they attend to you well, and the hospital is clean. They are good people, all of the nurses, they don't have that face like 'Ugh, don't bother me.' In some hospitals, you go, and they are tyrannical, they tell you, 'I don't know, go ask someone else.'"

Accustomed as they were to seeking care in public hospitals, women sometimes anticipated hostility from the ILE personnel. Paula, a single mother with a high school education and no health insurance, expected the clinicians to be antagonistic. When I asked her why, she said, "In government hospitals, when you give birth for instance, they treat you horribly, they tell you 'Push, faster, *mamacita*, you have to open your legs,' they treat you ugly. So, imagine going to a place where obviously you are going to interrupt a pregnancy. So, yeah, I had that image of what it would be like, aggressive." In the end Paula was pleased to learn that the personnel were warm. "They never acted rudely, far from it. In fact, this is the first time in a public hospital that they treat you well. They speak to you with affection, they make you aware of what this means, but not with violence, nor trying to attack you or anything. In other places health workers use violent language, but not in this case, at no time did I feel that way."

When complaints about the care offered through the ILE program did surface, they tended to center on the affective states of the personnel. Even as many women praised the tenderness and respectful treatment of providers, others described them variously as despotic, rude, or pushy. "The attitude of the personnel is not very nice," said Dani, a college graduate who had obtained an abortion at Reina María Clinic. "[But] you go to any public health center and they are going to treat you the same. It's not just this clinic, it's in general. The attitude is very rude, even arrogant, I do not like it." In private clinics, she continued, the treatment is decidedly different. "Staff there are like 'Hi, good morning, how have you been, can I offer you some water or tea or coffee?' I don't understand why these people are the way they are in *this* department [ILE], because abortion is delicate. I mean, a woman doesn't wake up and say, 'Today I'm going to get an abortion, even though I've already had three or four.' No, everything has its consequence. You can see their faces, they come fearful, nervous, sad, crying. And to encounter someone who is mean makes it even harder."

My conversations with patients revealed that women who had returned to the clinic for repeat abortion care were generally subjected to harsher treatment, a pattern that might explain the divergent accounts of ILE care that patients articulated. "*Me regañaron* [they scolded me]," said Clara, a college student seeking her second abortion. "They asked me if I wasn't afraid of dying." Karen was twenty-three and seeking her fourth abortion when I met her at Santa Marta. She had been trying to complete her high school degree while working in a clothing store. Karen told me that she had induced one abortion at home using misoprostol years earlier, and later had obtained two abortions through the ILE program. When we met at Santa Marta, she was overcome with remorse and cried throughout our conversation. Her last experience in the clinic had been traumatic. "When I came last year, it was really ugly how the doctor treated me. I'm not complaining or anything, but I—" Karen cut herself off. When she collected herself enough to continue, she revealed that she had been lying on the operating table before an EVA procedure when she burst into tears. "*Ponte flojita* [relax your body]," the doctor reproached, before wedging her knees apart. "The doctor said, 'Stop crying, because if you don't, we could perforate your uterus or worse, you could be transferred to the hospital, do you want to die?' The personnel told me, 'This is not the first time you are coming, and you are acting as if it's the first time, as if you were recently raped.' It was ugly." As we continued to talk, she divulged that she had sought her second abortion three years earlier when she learned she was pregnant after being raped, an aspect of her personal history that made the doctor's nasty comment even more painful. "The first time you come is hard enough," she said solemnly. "And the second time, [the attitude of the personnel is like] 'If you've already been through this, we are not going to be all sweet with you.'"

Karen was not the only patient I met to note that the personnel treated repeat abortion patients with more contempt. Sari had been ashamed to return to Santa Marta for a second abortion. "One, it's not cool to be coming here to abort babies," she told me, "and two, human beings are always preoccupied with what others will think, so to come here again with my face of 'Oops, I'm back again' [made me nervous]." Sari and her partner simply could not afford a fourth child. At the clinic, she had been completing a reproductive history form in the waiting room when the receptionist addressed her in front of all of the patients: "You're back again?" For Sari the comment was humiliating, but she didn't fault the receptionist.

> I think one benefits from them saying this stuff. If we don't want them to say anything, then we should prevent this from happening. In a sense the receptionist was right. If the personnel were to applaud us, how many people would be coming through the doors? If they were to applaud us, every day this clinic would be extremely full. We don't like that they say these things to us, but they have to say them. They make you see things how they are. They let you know that abortion is not okay, that you're putting your life at risk, and that you have to take care of yourself. So they scolded me. But it doesn't matter. Or, well, it matters, but they weren't rude. They are right to scold me. At the end of the day, I am back here to take out a baby, right? And it doesn't feel good, coming to kill a baby.

Like Sari, many patients did not feel good about arriving for an abortion, even if they felt confident that it was the best option for them. In instances when women were overcome with guilt, or when they understood abortion to be the moral equivalent of murder, as in Sari's case, it is possible that they may have been more inclined to acquiesce to clinical scoldings. At the same time, for Sari and others who agreed with the providers that abortion was not to be taken lightly, clinical scoldings, though unpleasant, hurtful, and at times embarrassing, were appropriate expressions of clinicians' care.

VALUATIONS OF CARE AND VIOLENCE

The contours of ILE care raise a number of questions for the anthropology of reproduction: How are we to account for troubling acts of harm in reproductive health settings while also attending to the moral and affective registers of care that bind clinicians together with their patients? Who defines what constitutes violence in reproductive health care? If a patient or provider sees "care" but an anthropologist or a woman's health advocate sees "violence," which account are we to accept? Is there a way to make sense of patients' approval of what may look, from the outside, like "bad care" without resorting to explanations of false consciousness? And which approach, ultimately, might improve women's experiences and their health?

In Mexico, legacies of state violence including outright neglect and public health care crises conditioned many women to expect negative experiences in the ILE clinic. Ultimately, however, despite advocacy discourse and my own early interpretation of events, most did not frame their experiences of accessing public abortion care in terms of "violence." Excepting a handful of complaints, primarily among those who had returned to the clinic for repeat abortion services, most women approved of both the technical and affective aspects of the care offered through the ILE program, pinning their satisfaction on the availability of the service, the safety of procedures, and the considerate treatment by personnel. Even when women described harsh treatment, it was rare for them to interpret this practice as a damaging or "violent" assault on their personhood. More often patients distinguished ILE care from the poor treatment they had experienced in *other* public hospitals. Clinical scoldings, in this context, emerged as an expected and appropriate reminder about the limits of abortion rights and a recognizable expression of compassionate concern on the part of medical personnel. Submission to clinical admonishments reflected a shared understanding between providers and patients that abortion, as women often told me, is "serious and delicate, not just any old thing."

If we take patients' perspectives seriously, clinical transactions in the ILE program cannot be defined neatly as instances of care *or* violence. ILE care, like abortion itself, is ambiguous and indeterminate. Women who needed a way to interrupt pregnancies they could not continue generally felt cared for in the public clinics, where clinicians demonstrated technical skill, offered helpful information, and in most cases, provided a concrete means for them to terminate their pregnancies safely. While many felt ashamed to return for repeat abortion care, they were grateful, ultimately, that there was a place to turn. Although the process of obtaining a public abortion could be burdensome, this did not seem to diminish women's assessments of ILE as "good care." Practices of scolding and shaming on the part of providers, likewise, did not seem to detract from patients' positive valuations, even though some found these practices to be insensitive or embarrassing.

When we are talking about a kind of care as fraught as abortion, it is important to consider whether a woman considers herself deserving of the care she receives—what some scholars call "reproductive citizenship." The concept encompasses juridical protections afforded by the state as well as the subjective processes whereby individuals come to embrace reproductive rights and their prerogative to act on them.[45] Most ILE patients conveyed that abortion should be an option for women, yet they did not generally see it as a categorical right. "I think that one should be able to choose [abortion], but there have to be parameters," one patient told me in a representative comment. "It is not okay to be coming here all the time, that's not the objective of these clinics." As another patient commented, "Women have the right to decide whether or not to continue on with a pregnancy. But they also have the obligation, after one abortion, to protect themselves and take care of themselves [with contraception]. There was one woman who came to the clinic for the second time. What's up with that? You are using your right to abortion, but you are not making good on your obligation to protect yourself."

Women's understandings of their own contingent entitlement to abortion may have shaped their appraisals of ILE care, leading them to excuse certain aspects of treatment. If they did not see abortion as their right, in other words, perhaps they did not feel they deserved "good" abortion care. In a context of what we might call "precarious reproductive citizenship," it is plausible that some may have been inclined to resign themselves to insensitive treatment. The desperation that many women faced when confronted with an ill-timed pregnancy may also have shaped their assessments, leading them to surrender to daunting waits and hurtful comments because they had limited viable options to resolve their pregnancies. While these are plausible explanations for patients' general approval of ILE care, their narratives allowed for critique of the program.

Studies of OV have focused overwhelmingly on what separates obstetric patients from their health care providers. While this research has made an important conceptual intervention into understandings of how class, gender, and racialized bias can lead some clinicians to mistreat their patients, I found that women seeking ILE generally agreed with their medical providers that abortion was unlike other medical procedures. A sense of recognition and mutual agreement cut across the patient-provider divide. Moral ambivalences can form a central aspect of the delivery of controversial reproductive health care such as abortion. Attention to these dimensions can guide future inquiries into the care practices that emerge around contentious aspects of health, affording new insights into doctor-patient relationships and the ethics of biomedical practice. A full account of care practices in the ILE program demands closer attention to the perspectives of the personnel, including their understandings of abortion risk and responsibility. It is to these dynamics that I turn in the next chapter.

CHAPTER FOUR

ABORTION AS SOCIAL LABOR

Protection and Responsibility in
Public Abortion Care

BY THE TIME WE FIRST MET at Santa Marta Clinic Dr. Rios had been on the front lines of the ILE program for five years, all the while battling severe resource shortages, overwhelming demand, and occupational stigma. Her clinic brimmed with patients. Most were Tacalco residents, but over the years Dr. Rios and her staff had facilitated thousands of abortions for women who arrived from across the country. The job had marked her in ways she could not have anticipated when she accepted the position. "I've seen extremely difficult cases," she told me from behind an oversized metal desk in one of the clinical consultation rooms in the winter of 2014, "an eleven-year-old girl who was raped by her father, a pediatrician; women who were sexually abused by their partners; incarcerated women who became pregnant. I feel very fortunate as a woman, as a person, with what I have. And it was exactly for that reason that I said to myself, with all of my privileges, why don't I help those who are unprotected?" Dr. Rios beamed proudly that day about her role as the medical director of an ILE clinic. "ILE," she said, "is a very important social labor." For her, I came to see, this work was not about emboldening women to exercise agency and individual choice; it was about *protecting* her patients and the broader social whole.

Dr. Rios seemed to understand intuitively the perspective within medical anthropology that hospitals offer far more than technical solutions to bodily ailments.[1] The care dispensed there ascribes symbolic value to its recipients, marking them as worthy beneficiaries of investment and concern.[2] In contexts where health is defined as a social right—such as Mexico and other Latin American countries—medical professionals come to embody the state, reflecting, for some patients, governmental investment in their welfare and biopolitical inclusion.[3] Clinical encounters are charged transactions, what anthropologist Amy Cooper has called "sites of political negotiation and contestation . . . effect[ing] changes that reverberate beyond the resolution of bodily afflictions to transform subjectivities and social relations."[4] These are loaded micro interactions through which processes of subject formation are made manifest.

If the role of medical caregivers everywhere holds a political charge, the stakes of working as an ILE clinician are particularly pronounced. In Mexico City, public health care workers like Dr. Rios have been tasked with translating abortion rights from abstract political constructs into technical and affective forms of care. Through medical skill and subtle moral gestures, they give concrete shape and consequence to the political directives handed down from the Mexico City Legislative Assembly. These health professionals are more than mere gatekeepers for abortion services. In their encounters with patients, I want to suggest, ILE providers instantiate abortion rights, defining their terms and conditions. Although we typically think of reproductive laws as emanating entirely "from above," anthropologist Mara Buchbinder has shown how abortion providers in the US context help to create and enact abortion laws "from the middle out."[5] Because of their unique role in translating legal directives into medical care, abortion providers play a central role in materializing abortion rights.

Unlike the private abortion providers who animate accounts of freestanding clinics in the United States, the ILE personnel did not generally approach their patients as empowered subjects exercising their right to choose.[6] They assumed protective postures toward their patients, urging women to exercise caution in their reproductive lives and minimize recourse to abortion as a means to take responsibility for the vitality of Mexican society.[7] Even as they realized abortion rights on a daily basis—doling out abortifacient pills and performing aspirations—a key aspect of their work entailed discouraging women from returning to the clinic. A central tension thus defined their role: they sought to limit the very procedure they provided. While their approach may be uncomfortable to some audiences, the ILE personnel cared deeply for their patients and for the welfare of the Mexican public. To appreciate their perspectives, it is helpful to consider how these public health workers landed in the ILE program as well as the kinds of social and professional ostracism they faced upon entering a disparaged line of work.

SCARE STORKS IN HEALTH

The rapid introduction of ILE services into MOH hospitals after the 2007 reform meant that medical personnel had to assess their beliefs about abortion and openly stake themselves on either side of an impassioned national debate. Many grappled with conflicting pressures and allegiances. While the medical establishment called on public clinicians to participate in the provision of abortion care, the Catholic hierarchy in conjunction with prolife political leaders urged them to object and defect. Many medical professionals put their religious and moral commitments above their medical call of duty. At the inception of the ILE program, the vast majority of MOH workers invoked their right to conscientious objection.[8] This makes it all the more interesting to consider why some clinicians decided to participate.

In many cases, particularly for midlevel providers such as social workers and nurses, it was occupational opportunity, rather than a long-standing political commitment to reproductive rights, that drove them to join the ranks of the ILE program. Many personnel had worked in other sectors of the MOH before they applied or were recruited to join the ILE program. And many had little, if any, prior professional experience with abortion before undergoing the MOH training required of all ILE workers. This kind of "opportunistic" entry into abortion care is markedly different from the politicized trajectories of abortion providers in contexts where the procedure has been severed from the broader medical system. In the United States, for instance, where abortion care exists almost entirely in freestanding clinics, reproductive rights activism and professional careers have, until recently, been coterminous.[9] The occupational paths of ILE personnel are significant in shaping their moral reservations about abortion and its free provision through the public health sector. Even though most

ILE employees did not set out to work in abortion care when they began their medical careers, they all came to inhabit a stigmatized occupational world.

Dr. Rios, who trained as a general practitioner, had worked in a different ward of the Santa Marta Community Health Center prior to transitioning into the ILE wing. When the director of reproductive health at the MOH invited her to direct the Santa Marta ILE clinic, she did not have a firm position on abortion either way. Even though Dr. Rios was not a longtime advocate of reproductive rights, the clinical directorship offered a promising job opportunity and she accepted enthusiastically. Sturdy in frame and standing at about five foot nine, Dr. Rios had a reputation among the ILE personnel for her brusque demeanor. She commanded the attention of everyone in the room. Her lips were always painted with maroon lipstick, and she was elegant even in the unbecoming navy uniform required of MOH workers. When she wasn't attending to a patient, Dr. Rios told me, she made a point to sit at the nursing station in the center of the clinic. From that vantage she could keep an eye on her staff as well as each patient who filed in and out of the crowded waiting room Monday through Friday. Even as I grew closer to social workers Carolina and Roberta across countless shared afternoons in the counseling office, I danced around Dr. Rios for months before mustering the courage to ask her for an interview.

"I love helping women," she told me, once we got a chance to talk. "More than anything, those who are disadvantaged." Dr. Rios was passionate about her work, but the job was not without its costs. As a longtime resident of Tacalco, she was known in the community around the clinic. As she moved about the neighborhood she sometimes recognized women whom she had assisted in interrupting their pregnancies. Yet to the degree she could, Dr. Rios strove to keep her work a secret. "Where we live, in a *barrio* right near Tacalco, people are really parochial," she said. "They grew up in this *pueblo* and they have really traditional customs. They're *really* Catholic, *de hueso colorado* [to the bone], so I prefer not to say a word about where I work."

Dr. Rios had expected people in her Catholic neighborhood to condemn her work, but she was surprised to encounter criticism from medical colleagues in other departments of the Santa Marta Community Health Center. "I have been working at Santa Marta for ten years and all of the doctors and medical personnel next door know me," she said. "Ever since the ILE wing opened many people have stopped talking to me. They call us *espanta cigüeñas* [scare storks]. They are always whispering." Other ILE personnel repeated similar versions of this curious phrase, and it took me some time to piece together the meaning. "Scare stork," I eventually realized, represented a clever play on the imagined purpose of a scarecrow. Some health care workers accused the ILE personnel of "scaring" or in other cases "murdering" storks—that quintessential symbol of procreation. "People judge us as evil, killers, assassins, that's what they call us," Roberta told me in a separate conversation. "They've always excluded us ILE workers. They don't spend time with with us because they say we kill babies here. They use very grotesque expressions like 'You kill children over there, you are stork murderers,' just imagine."

Roberta and Carolina were both hired as social workers at Santa Marta when the ILE clinic opened, and they had worked under Dr. Rios for nearly five years when we met. The trio had come to know each other well. Like Dr. Rios, Roberta and Carolina had never imagined themselves working in abortion care; they had simply ended up there. "It wasn't exactly that I was interested in abortion," said Roberta, the forty-something mother of an adolescent son. "But when I went to the MOH general offices in search of work, this was the only position open, in the ILE clinic." Roberta's radiant smile and porcelain skin drew eyes. Her blonde hair blew in the wind every time she came and left the clinic on her boyfriend's motorbike. She spent her days working closely with Carolina in the counseling office, so I often thought of them as a pair. But they were different in appearance and disposition. If Roberta was serious and poised, Carolina was her playful foil. By the time we met, Carolina had divorced the father of her adolescent son and daughter and taken a boyfriend. I remember how the MOH uniform hung loose on her petite frame, particularly when she was in the midst of one of her frequent weight loss regimens. Much like her colleagues, Carolina's path into abortion care was unanticipated. After finishing her social work degree years earlier she had been assigned to a hospital very far from her house. "I had to travel two and a half hours there and back, five hours a day lost." When I asked her why she had opted to join the ILE program, her answer was simple: "I asked for a change of post and they sent me here."

Others working across the ILE program were assigned or invited to an ILE clinic from another post within the MOH. Dr. Iberro, a general practitioner, had been working for one year at the Reina María Health Center when the ILE wing opened there. When an MOH administrator invited her to transfer to the ILE clinic, she agreed. "The truth is, I never imagined myself working in an abortion clinic," Dr. Iberro told me, peering over a pair of glasses that slid down the bridge of her nose. "It wasn't my thing. Gynecology wasn't really my interest." With time Dr. Iberro had come to value her job as an ILE provider, which she supplemented with a higher-paying position in a private diabetes clinic.

Even though most of the clinicians I came to know had stumbled into abortion care, for some the decision to participate reflected political commitments that predated their affiliation with the ILE program. A gynecologist at Reina María named Dr. Jimenez was, as he told me, "convinced about the ILE program from the beginning." He had logged six years by the time we met and stood out for regularly harnessing feminist discourse to describe his work. "Mexican women have not been given the right to reproductive health or reproductive freedom unconditioned by the husband, the mother," he told me the first time we spoke. "So, this situation is what makes us think that we [doctors] can be useful in that aspect, by giving women their rights to reproductive health, giving them their rights as human beings, as legal persons, as social beings, and not merely as producers of children." Over the years Dr. Jimenez had become frustrated with some of his ILE colleagues, whom he described as lacking a political commitment to reproductive rights. While his support of abortion was categorical, many of the ILE providers I encountered grappled with moral reservations about the procedure and ethical questions about the extent to which Mexican women were entitled to public abortion care.

WHO DESERVES PUBLIC ABORTION CARE?

For anthropologist Sarah Willen, "deservingness" is the inverse of rights. If rights are categorical, "deservingness" is subjective, variable, and negotiated contextually.[10] My research with the ILE personnel revealed that even when health-related rights are in place (albeit relatively new), the question of who *deserves* public care is not necessarily a settled matter. For many providers, much like the women under their care, abortion rights were meaningful and legitimate only in conjunction with ongoing collective responsibilities and interpersonal obligations. When I asked providers about their position on abortion, their statements were tempered by correspondent expectations and conditions on the part of women seeking the procedure. "With all rights come obligations," Dr. Iberro put it succinctly. "ILE patients are obligated to prevent this from happening again." In the ILE clinic abortion rights were a slippery slope that portended abuse and exploitation. Circumstantial factors were thus important in mediating clinician support for abortion. How, then, did providers assess which patients were worthy (or not) of their emotional, moral, and material investment? And how did these moral assessments bear on the kinds of care they offered?

In the ILE clinic abortion deservingness hinged on three central axes: (1) *who* was seeking the abortion (e.g., How old was the woman? What was her class background? (2) *why* a woman was seeking it (e.g., What were the circumstances of the pregnancy? How badly did she need it?) and (3) *how* she was seeking it (e.g., How had she conducted her reproductive life before now? Had she had a prior abortion? Was she using birth control when she became pregnant?). Tony, the nursing intern at Reina María Clinic, was explicit about the boundaries of abortion-related deservingness. "I consider abortion a right, but I'll say it again. It is not a game. There are situations in which one really needs an abortion, but that is not the same thing as 'Oh, I'm pregnant again, I'm going to get an abortion.' That's when I think there should not be a right, like for women who have had *so many* abortions."

For Tony and other ILE personnel, women who approached abortion as "a game" forfeited their right to the procedure. Abortion rights in this line of moral reasoning more closely resembled privileges; they could be retracted when used for the wrong reasons, too many times, or without careful reflection. ILE personnel articulated a hierarchy of acceptable reasons for undergoing an abortion, with pregnancy resulting from rape at the top and individual "carelessness" at the bottom. "If a woman was raped, in that case you say, well, it wasn't an absence of responsibility on her part but rather she was attacked," Roberta told me. "Other patients were taking care of themselves [using contraception], but for health reasons a doctor suggested the abortion. So there are some responsible individuals, but there are also the irresponsible ones." In Roberta's scheme of deservingness, rape addressed the "how" and "why" questions simultaneously, precluding further moral probing. In the case of rape, moreover, the *why* of abortion seemed always to outweigh and nullify the *how*. The question of whether a woman was using birth control, in other words, was secondary to the pressing reason that she needed an abortion: to redress the violent circumstances under which the pregnancy came about. Women who sought abortion at the direction of a doctor likewise largely escaped blame. In these cases, the reason for the abortion exceeded a woman's desire because it was determined to be medically necessary to preserve her health. In other cases, when the personnel found the motivations for pursuing an abortion less compelling, a woman's reproductive conduct was central to their assessments of deservingness. This was what Roberta meant when she told me, "There are also the irresponsible ones." Clinicians generally saw women who had not taken appropriate steps to prevent an unintended pregnancy and who lacked what they deemed a compelling reason to obtain the procedure to be the least deserving of ILE care.

Assessments of deservingness mediated the possibility of moral redemption after an abortion. "I'm in favor of abortion among women who were raped or who got pregnant because their birth control failed them," Tony told me. "We can *concientizar* [awaken] that type of woman, and she can begin to take care of herself after the abortion." In context, his statement captures the idea shared by other personnel that women who used abortion "recklessly" were exploiting their right to the procedure and were beyond "awakening." Providers framed abortion as a juncture from which to begin a personal project of moral change and enhancement in their reproductive lives, emphasizing that patients must *tomar conciencia* (become aware) after the procedure to avoid "recidivism," or repeat abortion. With each abortion, the window for "moral awakening" diminished and the chances of moral redemption waned.

The language of the ILE personnel bears a striking similarity to the Mexican clinicians that anthropologist Vania Smith-Oka describes in her ethnography of Oportunidades—a conditional cash transfer program implemented in the early aughts to mitigate the effects of poverty by inducing poor (and largely indigenous) women into "modern" motherhood through economic incentives.[11]

When women adopted regimens of family planning according to program goals, clinicians described them as *concientizadas*—awake, aware, "modern" in disposition, and dutifully compliant with medical mandates. Such was the kind of moral transformation that ILE personnel like Tony hoped to inspire among the largely poor and working-class ILE clientele. The language of "awakening," observes Vania Smith-Oka, "assumes that prior to being *concientizada*, [a woman is] either willfully ignorant or irretrievably stupid."[12]

At the same time that ILE personnel outlined a variety of contingencies that hampered abortion rights in their understanding, they also voiced compassion for women whom they considered more deserving of abortion care. The figure of the pregnant rape victim—generally a young girl who had fallen prey to sexual abuse by an older male—emerged as a trope in clinical appraisals of deservingness. ILE personnel recounted the lasting emotional impact of such cases, which were one of the hardest aspects of their work. A Santa Marta nurse called Vanessa recalled her profound emotional disturbance with regard to one case. "There was a young girl, thirteen years old, who was sexually abused by her biological father. Her mom didn't support her in the situation, so she came for the abortion with her grandmother. And it was only then that the grandmother realized that her son [the patient's father] was the abuser. Cases like this don't leave you, more than anything when you have daughters. You think about your own children a lot."

The thirteen-year-old whom clinicians spoke of is a quintessential example of a deserving abortion patient in the ILE clinic. Her situation left no lingering questions for the personnel about the reasons for pursuing an abortion or the direness of her circumstances. Rape was an exceptional situation that seemed to annul clinicians' moral reservations about abortion and its free provision through the public health sector. Rape exceptionalism, it bears reiterating, is codified in Mexican abortion law, representing the only condition under which the procedure is permitted in every state. It is important here to recall the experience of Paulina, the thirteen-year-old who was ultimately denied her right to an abortion after being raped by a burglar at her home in Baja California in 1999. Her experience marked a turning point in the national abortion debate, as the public could see the devastating toll of the country's harsh abortion laws.[13] Feminist scholars have roundly critiqued rape exceptions for abortion, pointing to the moral freight of legislation that conditions access to abortion on women's consent (or lack thereof) to sex. As legal scholar Lisa Kelley observes, "The logic of rape exceptions disciplines women and girls to consent to heterosexual intercourse only when they can bear its potential reproductive consequences,"[14] consequences that men can more readily elude. For the ILE providers, considerations of reproductive conduct, such as whether the sexual act resulting in pregnancy was consensual and whether birth control was used, were significant in moral appraisals about who deserved a state-funded abortion. Even though abortion rights in the capital are protected by law, the public health care workers responsible for delivering abortion care evaluated questions of deservingness on a case-by-case basis.

I never witnessed a provider deny a woman an abortion so long as she arrived at the clinic in time to secure a *ficha*, met the gestational limits of the program, and brought with her the appropriate documents. Nevertheless, ambivalence formed a key aspect of the delivery of ILE care. While meting out limited public health resources, providers grappled with ethical questions about who merited these services and who might be exploiting the program. It may be tempting to reduce ambivalence on the part the providers to prejudice against abortion or against the largely poor and working-class ILE clientele. But this is only part of the story. Equally important was an understanding among ILE providers that abortion was a tremendously risky procedure that should be avoided at all costs. Although numerous studies disprove this assertion, showing that first-trimester abortion is in fact remarkably safe, the providers associated abortion with manifold risks, threats that in their conception reached far beyond physical danger.

ABORTION AS SOCIAL SPECTER

"Patients might have the perspective that 'abortion is my right, and I can exercise it as many times as I want,' but I always say, 'Why expose yourself to risk again and again?'" Dr. Iberro stated from within the small ultrasound room of Reina María Clinic. We sometimes talked there on weekday afternoons once all the patients had passed through. I looked on as she sorted patient files and tinkered with the sonogram machine, her golden hair hanging low on her shoulders. It was common for the providers to emphasize the risks of abortion.[15]

Their fixation on risk might be chalked up to "abortion stigma" or evidence of outdated medical knowledge on abortion safety. Early on in my research I sometimes arrived at these kinds of conclusions. With time, however, I came to see that the ILE personnel were working with a more capacious concept of "abortion risk" that encompassed threats to the bodies of individual women and the Mexican social body.

During daily informational sessions in the clinic waiting room, social workers emphasized to patients and their accompaniers that abortion was a procedure that threatened to place them and their loved ones in imminent danger. They made impassioned appeals: "Abortion is not ordinary. What are the risks, *chicas*? Hemorrhage, hysterectomy, death, that is why you're never going to come back, right?" Rhetorical questions like these formed a standard aspect of informational *pláticas* (talks) at the ILE clinic. I often found these scare tactics troubling, particularly against the background of an organized national prolife movement that might exploit such information for its own ends. My early fieldnotes are littered with my own reactions of disbelief at the outsized notions of abortion risk communicated in the clinic. But ILE providers defended their approach. Abortion, they insisted, was different from other medical procedures.

"In informational sessions we tell the patients we are not joking when we say you could become infertile, your uterus could be perforated, you could need a hysterectomy, you could even *die* from ILE," Dr. Iberro said. "Fortunately, not everyone has complications from multiple abortions, but imagine a patient who wants to have a child in the future and now she can't. We want patients to understand that once they come here, the risks are high. It's like Russian Roulette. If a patient returns for a repeat abortion, there is a greater likelihood that something will happen to her." Dr. Iberro's comments are striking in their contrast to the findings of medical research. Studies show that when performed in adequate conditions, first-trimester abortion is remarkably safe, far safer, in fact, than childbirth.[16] So why were ILE providers like Dr. Iberro preoccupied with the "risks" of abortion? And why were they so forceful in conveying a hyperbolic understanding of abortion risk to their patients?

Anthropologists emphasize that valuations of "reproductive risk" are not free-floating assessments. They emerge, rather, in specific cultural, biomedical, and political contexts.[17] As anthropologist Laury Oaks puts it, "understandings of risk are not simply based on scientific evidence but also on the social and political evaluation of what is deemed dangerous."[18] Scholars have thoroughly considered how pregnant women are disciplined in and beyond the biomedical setting to avert risks to the health of the fetuses they gestate. In biomedical discourse and practice, woman and fetus exist in an adversarial, rather than a symbiotic, relationship, in which the well-being of the fetus often takes precedence over that of the woman. When pregnancy or childbirth go awry, women thus absorb much of the blame for "failing" to effectively keep risk at bay. Less research considers how concepts of risk bear on abortion practices in biomedical settings, though Joanna Mishtal and Elise Andaya have observed that in the US context intense cultural "concern about the physical danger posed by abortions—especially relative to statistically more risky yet less regulated procedures—[can be] viewed as a moral response to the danger caused by a transgression of expected gender categories."[19] The risk of childbirth—roughly fourteen times higher than that of a legal first-trimester abortion—hardly provokes such impassioned concern.[20]

ILE providers' notions of abortion risk are rooted in a national context of abortion criminalization and resulting rates of extremely high abortion-related morbidity and mortality. This is a setting quite apart from the United States, where abortion has been legal and available in clinical contexts for nearly half a century. The threat of abortion-related injury and death in Mexico, by contrast, is impossible to ignore. As recently as 2001, just six years before the inauguration of the ILE program, illegal abortion caused the deaths of 1,500 women a year.[21] Stories about death and injury from unsafe abortion circulated too frequently here to feel like improbable outcomes. Many patients and clinicians knew someone, or knew of someone, who had procured an illegal abortion and suffered complications as a result. Considered in this light, ILE providers had good reason to be concerned about the physical risks of abortion, even if they found themselves working in a clinical environment in which the procedure, barring rare complications, was generally safe.

But there was something else, an aspect of Santa Marta's clinical history that I learned about only in pieces over the course of several months, shreds of conversation and clues that I was left to reconstruct on my own. There had been an accident at the clinic. It had happened shortly after my research began and

I had not been at the clinic that day. It had been an ordinary morning when a woman returned to Santa Marta after a *resistencia*, a failed medical abortion. The personnel prepared the operating room for a routine EVA to empty her uterus. They donned smocks. All was normal. During the procedure, however, things went awry. As the doctor on call that day aspirated, the cannula pierced the woman's uterus. When the patient began to hemorrhage, the clinicians transported her to a nearby hospital, where she was placed under close medical watch. The doctor who had performed the abortion was wracked with guilt and worry, as were the other ILE staff. They visited the woman at the hospital in shifts over the course of the week, relaying the information they could gather back to the other Santa Marta personnel. In the end, the doctors were unable to repair the uterine perforation and they performed a hysterectomy.[22] The woman made a full recovery and was released from the hospital after one week, now without her uterus.

The accident shocked the ILE personnel, and especially Dr. Rios, who, in her capacity as the medical director of the clinic, decided to stop offering aspiration abortions there as a precaution, choosing instead to channel patients in need to a different ILE clinic across the city. I had noticed when, shortly thereafter, a physician working for a reproductive rights NGO showed up to assist with aspiration techniques. At the time, no one explained his presence at the clinic, and I got the sense that they did not want to talk about it. Some of the providers answered my questions in vague terms, gesturing to the accident and even mentioning a uterine perforation, but without revealing specific details. It wasn't until years after my formal research ended that one of the Santa Marta clinicians reconstructed the story in detail for me over the phone, rehearsing the anxiety that had overcome them all on that day years earlier.

Even when performed in adequate circumstances like those provided at Santa Marta, abortion, like any medical procedure, carries a small amount of risk. Recounting an accident within the ILE program—one of the few public abortion programs in the world that is subject to tremendous political opposition—also carries some danger. I am not interested in or qualified to question the technical competence of the ILE personnel. "There can only be a handful of gynecologists who have not perforated a uterus during [an aspiration abortion] procedure," write clinicians Fevzi Shakir and Yasser Diab.[23] That this was the only serious complication I learned of during my time in the ILE program should be instructive on the infrequency of this extreme outcome. My intention in recounting this accident, rather, is to offer context for concepts of abortion risk that featured centrally at Santa Marta. The incident was deeply troubling for the providers, threatening their conscience, their status as competent professionals, and their job security, as well as the reputation of the clinic and the entire ILE program. There was a good deal on the line for these medical workers, particularly in a context in which their work already attracted public backlash. The accident was a sobering reminder of the stakes of their maligned labor, and it made the statistically rare risks of induced first-trimester abortion feel too close to ignore, haunting the providers in subsequent months and years.

While political opposition to abortion certainly troubled the personnel, I am convinced that something else was going on for these public providers, something beyond inward or outward "abortion stigma." These health care workers toiled each day in the pressured environment of the ILE clinic for modest compensation when many other medical personnel in the public system were unwilling to do so. This was a taxing job, and they performed it despite contempt from medical colleagues and the broader public. With time I realized that understandings of risk among ILE personnel extended far beyond medical threats to the physical bodies of their patients. Theirs was a more capacious definition of risk, encompassing concerns about the social and moral well-being of the body politic. Abortion, as they saw it, had the potential to unravel families. If a woman died during a procedure her children would be left without a mother. Although the ILE personnel were quicker to emphasize the medical risks of abortion, our private discussions revealed that they harbored a deeper angst grounded in their understanding of the more menacing psychological, familial, and societal risks. This comprehensive understanding of abortion risk was rooted in providers' deep valuation of women's social roles as caretakers and mothers.

Julia, a Reina María nurse, expounded on the social ramifications of women's ill health, which she construed as one potential result of abortion. "Women are very important for the family nucleus," she told me. "If there is no money, they find it, because their kids are not going to starve. It's rare that a man really supports his kids. If the woman dies, the children are the ones that are going to suffer." Julia's comments were curious because she emphasized the unequal gendered burdens that so often befall women in order to articulate the dangers of abortion—a procedure, of course, that Mexican activists have long placed at the center of struggles for women's equality. Her fears about the health risks of abortion make sense in a context where botched abortions (almost always in contexts of legal restriction) have claimed the lives of many women. The central idea captured in her comment, that women must take their children into account when assessing abortion risk, is one that ILE providers regularly communicated to their patients. Personnel called on patients to be responsible not only for themselves but also to their families and to the social body. For ILE personnel, abortion, and particularly repeat abortion, posed risks that reverberated beyond individual women. By enjoining women to take their health seriously, clinicians sought to protect the Mexican family, and by extension society at large. If abortion was for these providers a looming social threat, it was their role to avert it. Theirs was what Dr. Rios had aptly called "a social labor."

Some ILE providers worried that abortion could produce psychological damage, emphasizing the relationship between a woman and her fetus that for them rendered abortion necessarily troubling. "You see [the patients' attitude is one of] 'I don't care,'" Roberta lamented, conveying what she observed as a pattern of flippancy among ILE patients. "But really, deep down inside, in their conscience, in their subconscious, they feel what they are doing. You can ask any one of them, and none are going to tell you, 'For me abortion is excellent.' They will never say that because they are women who have already conceived. And conception is one of the most wonderful things in our life, because it's a miracle, the fact that one can give life to another being. Patients are always aware of this."

Dr. Iberro expressed a similar sentiment when I asked her whether she thought that most of her patients approached abortion as a political right. "I don't think so," she said. "They still come as social martyrs with the idea that 'I'm going to do it, but I don't want anyone to find out.' I don't think they see it as a right, they see it as a way out. They all come suffering in one way or another. They have their procedure, and they suffer. They leave, and they keep suffering." When I pushed her to elaborate, Dr. Iberro continued, "The patients start crying and say, 'I don't want to lose [the pregnancy] but my partner won't support me,' or 'My mom doesn't know because if she finds out she will kick me out of the house.' They'll tell us, 'I don't want anyone to find out at home because my family is very Catholic.' That's how we come to see that they don't exercise it as a right but as a way out of a problematic situation."

In the Santa Marta counseling office Carolina and Dr. Alexa sometimes discussed the *carga emocional* (emotional load) that burdens ILE patients. "You can tell from the moment they walk in. They enter the ultrasound room, and they want to see the photo [of the fetus]. If they're coming to abort, then why do they want to see that?" Dr. Alexa asked. "Or why do they ask you if it will hurt [the fetus]?" Carolina added. "Like, what does it matter? You're here, you're going to [abort]. If I tell you it hurts [the fetus], you're not going to do it?" For personnel, women's curiosity about the sonogram and concerns about fetal pain were evidence of an affective attachment to the fetus that precluded interruption of the pregnancy. Though many patients (like the providers) grappled with ambivalence around abortion, there was little room in the clinic to express or resolve moral misgivings.

Some patients, the providers told me one afternoon, developed "postabortion syndrome" (PAS). I was unsettled to hear mention of PAS in a legal abortion clinic. PAS is a pseudomedical affliction introduced by the US antiabortion lobby a decade after *Roe v. Wade*.[24] At the time, prolife activists were adapting their strategies and shifting focus.[25] In the context of growing public and professional concern over the psychological trauma afflicting Vietnam veterans, prolife activists repositioned abortion as an event that could traumatize women.[26] Undergoing an abortion, like being sent to battle, produced lasting psychological sequelae, or so they claimed. For decades mental health professionals in the US have discredited PAS. The research is decisive: there is no causal link between induced abortion and psychological trauma; nor is there a patterned clustering of symptoms following from an abortion that can constitute a discrete, diagnosable syndrome.[27] Emotional and psychological responses to abortion are circumstantial, reflecting "culturally and historically specific ideologies about gender, motherhood, femininity, kinship, and personhood."[28] Although some women may experience negative reactions to an abortion, research suggests that women who are denied the procedure fare worse psychologically.[29]

What *does* shape negative emotional responses to induced abortion is the presence of "abortion stigma"—defined as "a negative attribute ascribed to women who seek to terminate a pregnancy that marks them, internally or externally, as inferior to ideals of womanhood."[30] Abortion stigma is not a universal phenomenon. When present, it derives from the moral breach that pregnancy termination poses to hegemonic gender roles that conflate femininity with motherhood, posit a maternal instinct, and restrict feminine sexuality to procreation.[31] Women who have internalized abortion stigma, or who live in contexts where it is pervasive, may experience more upset after an abortion due to a social context in which it is condemned. In Mexico abortion stigma is ubiquitous. Even as popular attitudes on the procedure shift toward support, particularly in major urban centers like Mexico City, abortion is widely understood as evidence of sexual promiscuity, irresponsibility, and selfish egoism.[32] One recent study found that ILE patients in the capital generally felt confident in their abortion decisions and evinced low rates of "internalized abortion stigma"; what troubled women was not whether they had made an irrevocable mistake but how *others* might respond to their decisions.[33]

Nevertheless, that afternoon in the Santa Marta counseling office Dr. Alexa spoke with conviction about the psychological threat that abortion presents for Mexican women, "a lot of whom," she related, "don't have the culture to cope with the procedure." I asked her what she meant, and she told me, "They get an abortion because someone forced them, or they didn't have support. I am positive that the majority of women, 50 percent, 60 percent, are negatively affected by having an abortion. At the end of the day, it's a child. It's a dead child, a child that you interrupted, but it existed. That's why in the clinical history we ask how many pregnancies a woman has had, and we count *all* of them [including those that ended in abortion], because at the end of the day, it existed. ILE sticks with them." Carolina nodded in agreement as her colleague spoke, and then added, "I can assure you that all of them, without exception even if they look tough, they all bear this weight for the rest of their days."

"For the rest of their lives," Dr. Alexa affirmed.

"For the rest of their lives, *amiga*," repeated Carolina.

The sincere invocation of PAS by ILE workers raises a number of questions:

What criteria are used to evaluate "willing" clinicians hired to the ILE program? How do questions around abortion stigma (or even PAS) figure into regular ILE staff trainings? Have psychologists and mental health professionals in Mexico explored (or debunked) "postabortion syndrome"? That afternoon at the clinic, Carolina and Dr. Alexa articulated an uncomfortable position: "Mexican women don't have the culture [to undergo an abortion without emotional or psychological turmoil]." While abortion rights proponents have worked in the past four decades to normalize the idea that "motherhood is voluntary" and to emphasize the centrality of reproductive rights to women's citizenship, women in the capital inhabit a cultural and moral milieu in which maternity is valued and abortion is penalized. ILE providers, like the women they serve, are exposed to antiabortion discourse emanating from the Catholic Church and evangelical churches, some of which, like PAS, originated from the US prolife movement. Public clinicians like Carolina and Dr. Alexa endeavor to protect their patients while navigating a cultural climate that is extremely adversarial to abortion.

ILE providers, in short, did not generally see abortion as an ordinary aspect of reproductive health care or as a political right to which women were categorically entitled. Abortion was for them a profoundly risky practice that had the potential to damage women's bodies and psyches, tip the balance of the family unit, and threaten the welfare of Mexican society. When ILE personnel underlined for their patients the statistically unlikely risks of induced abortion, their objective was not to amplify stigma or generate shame. Nor were they intent on disciplining women into ideal subjects of biomedical and state control, though at times their cajoling had this effect. In their professional capacity as health care professionals, these workers strove to protect women and the broader society from harms related to abortion that felt real and menacing, harms for which there was evidence all around them.

PROFESSIONALISM AS PERFORMANCE

"I don't know if I'm Catholic. I don't profess any religion ardently. But if I were pregnant, my absolute decision, my position on abortion, is no. I would not abort," Dr. Rios told me one afternoon after the patients had left the clinic for the day. Comments like this one sometimes led me to question the staff's position on abortion. When I asked Dr. Rios directly, she was unwavering in her support of patients' decisions. "I know what my values are. Helping women in their decision to abort doesn't cause me any conflict," she told me unequivocally, extinguishing my doubts with the same confidence with which she regularly addressed her patients and staff. "I have always said that the decision is theirs." Yet Dr. Rios's support of abortion was strictly professional, a position that guided her work but did not obtain in her personal life. "The patients are the ones terminating the pregnancy," she clarified, "not me." Delivering public abortion care entailed ongoing moral questions. As unforeseen situations arose, ILE personnel sometimes found themselves on shaky ground, obliged to weigh their beliefs against their professional responsibilities. These public clinicians are among those whom anthropologist Rayna Rapp has famously called "moral pioneers," individuals who are made to navigate uncharted bioethical terrain afforded by new medical possibilities.[34]

Most ILE personnel balked when I asked if they would ever consider having an abortion themselves, and I often wondered how providers facilitated a procedure about which they held such profound misgivings. Roberta's comments were clarifying: "Well, you have to learn to separate that part, you are just orienting the patients who will have abortions. I consider it a job. Patients have abortions, not me." Even Maria Puerto, an ILE program administrator, had learned to separate her private views from her work. "I keep my beliefs to one side. I have them, but I don't involve them. I respect the women, their decision, the reasons they seek an abortion. Even though I don't like [the decision], I respect them. I do my job as I should, with sensitivity, quality, responding to their doubts, and informing them that they have the right to a sexual life."

All medical personnel in the MOH have a right to conscientiously object to participating in the ILE program. When I began this research, I had imagined that the fact of opting in, therefore, indicated prochoice values among "willing" clinicians. This turned out to be to a mistaken assumption. Personal, professional, and political commitments did not always harmonize in the ILE program. Many personnel supported abortion *enough* to work in ILE, particularly when other occupational opportunities were scarce. They all felt that abortion should be an option for women, but this did not mean they considered it a viable option for themselves. All explained that abortion should be legal but rare, a last resort.

To navigate the ethical doubts that surfaced in their day-to-day work, the personnel made an effort to evince "professionalism," divorcing their own moral positions from their occupational responsibilities. In the ILE clinic, professionalism was an affective and performative mode that mediated the contradictions between privately held beliefs and public duties. Cultivating a professional ethos could be challenging for ILE providers, especially at first. "Look, at the beginning it was extremely taxing," Carolina recalled about her entry into the ILE program. "This program is one of the toughest because you deal directly with the emotional life of people, and obviously because it's ILE, the patients have a lot of emotional burdens. As a new worker it takes a lot out of you, but once you gain experience. . . . Obviously, everything is professional here. You can't involve your emotions. You have to be professional in order to help the patient." When grappling with their own moral or religious uncertainties about abortion, in other words, ILE providers did not act merely as individuals but as what Mara Buchbinder calls "representatives of a larger community of practice."[35] In this context, professionalism entailed evincing a neutral, emotionally detached stance with regard to a patient's decision to abort a pregnancy, even when that decision presented personal moral qualms for the provider.

When Dr. Rios was hired, she had recently become pregnant. As her abdomen swelled, she worried that her presence in the ILE clinic might pose a conflict of interest—an insensitive embodied reminder of fertility to patients seeking to terminate their pregnancies. After the director of reproductive health at the MOH allayed her concerns, Dr. Rios continued to show up for work as usual. Everyday life in the clinic was ordinary, except for the new burdens of morning sickness. Toward the end of her first trimester, however, something unexpected happened. Dr. Rios had been conducting a routine ultrasound on a patient with the exact same gestational age as her—eleven weeks—when she began to cry suddenly and darted out of the room. "My emotions overwhelmed me," she said. It had been difficult to imagine the fate of the fetus inside her patient against the background of her own pregnancy, which she planned to carry to term. "That night I talked about it with my husband, and he said, 'Look, not everyone is fortunate enough to have the kind of life that you have. You don't know if the baby that she interrupted is the result of an unwanted pregnancy, an unplanned pregnancy.' My husband, he made me see things clearly." From that moment on Dr. Rios vowed privately not to judge the abortion decisions of her patients, whose situations, in many cases, differed considerably from her own. Compartmentalizing the emotionally disquieting aspects of abortion from her daily work allowed her to be an upstanding professional.

While the beginning of one's career in the ILE program was the hardest, the challenges did not necessarily abate over time. When I asked Carolina whether her perspective on abortion had changed after years of working in ILE, she said, "I have the same position on abortion that I always have. I respect the decision of each person. For me, personally, I consider it a life. But I have to be professional." Carolina had told me more than once that she would never consider abortion as an option for herself. I found her answer hard to believe at first, so I asked her several times. Her voice rose dramatically in pitch every time she answered the question. When I prompted her to reflect on the process of reconciling her beliefs with her work in the clinic, she conceded, "Of course there is a contradiction, a [guilty] conscience that weighs on me because I am an accomplice in a sense. But it is my job, and I focus on the fact that I am a professional and I cannot involve my emotions or what I believe in what I am doing at work."

Learning to draw emotional boundaries was a crucial aspect of navigating the morally fraught work of public abortion care. Striving to separate personal views from one's professional duties offered the ILE providers a way to care optimally for their patients, fulfilling professional obligations even when their work collided with their beliefs or confronted them with uncertainty. Despite their efforts at emotional detachment and neutrality, however, I found that providers' moral doubts impinged on their work at the clinic. Such cracks in the veneer of "professionalism," as we will see, shaped clinical encounters in consequential ways.

CONTINGENT RIGHTS AND ATTENDANT RESPONSIBILITIES

"What happened? Why are you back here for a second time?" Roberta asked a patient named Aremis as she took a seat in the Santa Marta counseling office.

"How were you taking care of yourself when you became pregnant?" Roberta proceeded with a standard battery of questions.

"The condom."

"You're here for your second abortion," Roberta noted, scanning Aremis's medical file. "You have three kids. You're a single mother. Who is going to take care of your kids if something happens to you? Abortion is no joke. It's your health you're putting at risk. *You have to be more responsible.* Which contraceptive method are you going to choose so that we don't see you back here again?" Aremis asked for the implant before slinking back into the waiting room.

As this scene from my fieldwork conveys, messages about responsibility were inseparable from state and clinical discourse on ILE services. Vanessa, a Santa Marta nurse, once told me: "The MOH has two objectives, that ILE procedures are successful and that the patient leaves well oriented about family planning methods. Once a patient *se responsibiliza* [responsibilizes] by correctly using a family planning method, there will be fewer abortions." Providers saw patients like Aremis as in need of intimate reminders about their social and moral responsibilities to protect their health, their families, and the strength of the Mexican social whole. Almost every day in the ILE program clinicians pushed their patients to "be more responsible" in their reproductive lives.

The emphasis on responsibility in the ILE clinics is not new. Mexican reproductive governance has long cohered around the figure of the "responsible subject." Despite fluctuating demographic targets and evolving population rationalities that have guided national reproductive policy in the last century, women, and to a lesser extent, men, have consistently been seen as "responsible for reproducing [a] rational social and national bod[y]."[36] While today women in the capital have been granted the right to interrupt their pregnancies, they have also been charged with exercising that liberty with tremendous responsibility. This idea is built into the abortion law passed in the capital on April 24, 2007:[37] "The government will permanently and intensively foster comprehensive policies that promote sexual health, reproductive rights, and responsible parenthood. Its family planning and contraceptive services have the principal objective of reducing the incidence of abortion through the prevention of unplanned and undesired pregnancies, the diminishment of reproductive risk, and the prevention of sexually transmitted diseases to contribute to the full exercise of [reproductive rights]."[38]

For sociologist Nikolas Rose, "responsibilization" is a style of governance deployed increasingly in late liberal societies, whereby "the problems of problematic persons are reformulated as moral [problems in the way] such persons . . . conduct themselves and their existence."[39] The state and an array of institutions such as hospitals, churches, and schools act from afar, steering human behavior to cultivate self-managing subjects who come to internalize and embody responsible dispositions. The process he traces is not simply a form of neoliberal governmentality whereby the state privatizes responsibility, offloading its biopolitical obligations onto individual citizens. For Rose, a defining feature of this process is that governance is attached to "technologies of freedom."[40] Rather than curtailing freedom, governance in this mode can filter through expanded choices. This is a generative form of power that fosters moral reconstruction. "Autonomy is now represented in terms of personal power and the capacity to accept responsibility . . . [to] plan one's life as an orderly enterprise and take responsibility for its course and outcome," writes Rose.[41] Inclusion in the moral community hinges on the capacity of individuals to assume responsibility and self-governance. "Responsibilization" offers a productive analytic for thinking through the regulation of reproduction in Mexico, where state, medical, and educational leaders have long enjoined women to exercise responsibility in their reproductive lives, even as that injunction has assumed new meanings over time.

Women in the Mexican capital today have been redefined as legal subjects of abortion rights, a shift that would seem to suggest a transformation in their citizenship. Feminist advocates and scholars have described the abortion reform in this way, celebrating the symbolic power of the reform in reconfiguring women's relationship to the state. While the reform is presented in feminist organizational messaging and recent scholarship as ushering in a transformative moment for women's citizenship, I found that it also reinstates familiar styles of governance that have long defined reproductive policy in Mexico. ILE clinicians approached the act of abortion as an instance of failed responsibility, but also a redemptive moment for moral awakening. Women making use of ILE services were called to assume responsibility by adopting contraception to avoid recourse to abortion.

At the same time, processes of subject formation in the ILE clinic were not exclusively about fostering *individual* responsibility. As state workers, ILE personnel sought to instill in their patients a sense of personal as well as *collective* responsibility.[42] In a context of limited public health monies, they entreated their patients to become guardians of their reproductive health to benefit the welfare of the Mexican collective. Even as the ILE program preserved established agendas of Mexican reproductive governance that have long prioritized women's sexual responsibility, this was not a context in which the state had offloaded all liability for health onto individuals. The public health system has eroded in the context of neoliberal reforms, yet health, at least theoretically, is a social right. And the ILE program is publicly funded. When ILE providers like Roberta prompted patients to consider who would take care of their children if they succumbed to an abortion, they were asking them to contemplate the interpersonal obligations that tied them into a social and moral community with others.[43]

From the perspective of personnel, patients who accepted ILE services incurred a biopolitical responsibility to adopt a contraceptive method and prevent future recourse to more costly forms of state care, such as abortion. There is nothing in the 2007 abortion law or ILE program guidelines to prohibit a woman from obtaining multiple abortions. Providers were adamant, however, that abortion was a one-time solution, and they communicated this perspective to all of their patients. "We raise awareness in women about sexual and reproductive health," Roberta said about her role as a social worker. "We orient them. We don't want to promote abortion no holds barred; rather, we promote sexual responsibility." In the clinics, "sexual responsibility" was synonymous with the reliable use of birth control. Roberta went on to explain, "Even though you talk to patients again and again about birth control—here it's not only the social workers, but the nurses, the doctors, we all repeat the information—they still come back [for an abortion]. And then you think, there's no responsibility on the part of the patient. Sometimes we even ask them, 'Do you not love yourself or what? Why don't you take care of yourself? Maybe they don't have money to buy contraception, but the public health centers offer it for free.'"

Although providers pushed patients to adopt a contraceptive method on the day of the abortion, they were not always successful. "We can't obligate them [to take a method]," Carolina told me. "Many get annoyed, they don't do it. Many become very aggressive, and what can we do? They don't want the method, they say no, and you feel stunned, you think, What is going on here? There is a lot of indifference among patients; they don't want to take care of themselves." Guided by ILE program objectives and their own conviction that abortion should not be repeated, providers regularly pressed women to "llevar un método" (take a contraceptive method) on the day of the abortion. During the daily *pláticas*, social workers emphasized the benefits of long-acting methods in particular, pushing intrauterine devices (IUDs), hormonal injections, and implants above user-dependent methods such as the pill, the condom, and the patch. ILE personnel preferred long-acting methods because their success did not rely on women, whom in most cases they imagined as undependable stewards of their reproductive health. To make their pitch more effective, providers drew attention to the high cost of the long-acting methods with statements like "These methods are very expensive, up to 5,000 pesos [roughly $260 USD], but today you can get them for free." Staff emphasized that once placed in a woman's body, long-acting birth control methods were not to be removed because of the high cost incurred by the MOH. Patients owed it to the MOH, in other words, to leave the method in their bodies even when doubts surfaced.

In addition to emphasizing the cost of long-acting methods, personnel also downplayed their side effects. On more than one occasion I watched second-time abortion patients justify their repeat pregnancies to staff by explaining that they had removed the implant after experiencing unexpected dizziness or weight gain, side effects they had not been aware of when they elected the method at the ILE clinic. "The methods don't make us fat," staff would reply, "eating fattening foods makes us fat." In cases when patients became pregnant despite properly using a method, provider would say: "No son los métodos que fallan, son ustedes!" (It's not the birth control that fails, it's you all). Rejoinders like these reaffirmed the notion perpetuated in the ILE program that women needed to be more responsible stewards of their health, even as they adopted birth control methods as instructed.

Birth control has been legal and available through the Mexican public health sector since 1974, although circumstances still limit access and use. By official accounts, national efforts to make contraception widely available have been remarkably effective. At the time of my research in 2014, 75 percent of women of reproductive age across the country used a contraceptive method, and in the capital rates were as high as 79 percent.[44] Almost all of the sixty ILE patients I formally interviewed for this study reported having used some type of birth control in their lifetime, and many conveyed that they were using birth control at the time they became pregnant. Because of their role in the abortion clinic, ILE providers were regularly exposed to portions of the population that were not using birth control or whose birth control method had failed. For this reason, perhaps, they had exaggerated frustrations about the putative "failure" of Mexican women to prevent unwanted pregnancies.

At Santa Marta Clinic one afternoon, Roberta and I were receiving patients in the counseling office when a young woman named Milagros appeared at the doorway. She sank into the plastic chair at the short edge of the glass-top table, her shoulders curled inwards. Roberta and I sat across from one another on the long edges of the table, and Dr. Alexa peered out from behind a desktop computer in one corner of the room. The hurried pace of ILE counseling typically did not allow for social workers to spend more than a few minutes with each patient. Everyone agreed, however, that Milagros needed more time. Roberta's eyes widened as she paged through Milagros's medical file: "two live children; five abortions."

"You've had five abortions! How is that possible? *Que bárbara* [a local expression of disbelief]. It doesn't scare you?" Roberta asked, incredulous.

Milagros nodded. She was very scared. Her husband, she told us, had purchased the misoprostol pills at a pharmacy so she could induce the abortions at home.

"But the important thing is that you take care of yourself," Roberta interjected. "Abortion has a lot of risks. Who will take care of your kids if something happens to you? *Aguas con el aborto* [you have to be careful with abortion]. What we just finished explaining in the *plática* is true! We've seen patients who had to go to the hospital after an abortion because of a hemorrhage. What if you have an overdose and die?"

Wiping away tears, Milagros called her husband "machista." She had considered the implant, she insisted, but he would not allow her to use any kind of birth control. "I feel like he wants to fill me up with kids to feel more secure about the relationship because he's older than me, but I can't do this anymore.

This is not living." Her comment confused me, since she had aborted her pregnancies with her husband's permission. But the providers did not probe. Milagros told us that she wanted a divorce. She had been trying to leave her husband for some time. But without work of her own, she depended on him to get by. As the conversation proceeded, Milagros's emotional state unraveled. "I have to endure the pain of the abortions, not him," she sobbed. Dr. Alexa peered out from behind the computer screen, moved by Milagros's account.

"You've been lucky," she added from across the room.

"That's exactly what I told her," Roberta said. "There are patients who after two abortions . . ."

"They die." Dr. Alexa finished her coworker's sentence.

Roberta continued to talk at length with Milagros, encouraging her to leave her husband and escape the abuse. Milagros was receptive to her appeals, but there was nowhere for her and her two children to go, and no money to take them there. She seemed utterly stuck. After about thirty minutes, Roberta followed Milagros into the waiting room. Before then I had never seen a social worker address a woman's partner in the space of a counseling session. Male partners tended to hang in the background of daily activities at clinic, serving primarily to transport their wives and girlfriends there and back home. Although they were present for educational *pláticas* on birth control methods, they were more able to escape the scoldings of the personnel, whose energies were trained primarily on women. But when an opportunity arose that day at Santa Marta to address a male partner, Roberta felt compelled to intervene.

"Follow me," she said to Milagros' husband, walking him back to the counseling office as Milagros stayed behind in the waiting room. After listening to Milagros describe the power he wielded over her at home, I hadn't expected him to submit so readily to Roberta's admonishments. But sitting there, in the same plastic chair usually occupied by women patients, he was quiet and withdrawn. He kept his gaze fixed on the floor.

"Do you love your wife?" Roberta asked. When he nodded in humiliation, she urged him to prove his love by using a condom or pursuing a vasectomy. Abortion, she cautioned, is not a family planning method. By using contraception, Roberta entreated, he could take better care of his wife, he could prove his love for her. He conceded, eventually joining his wife back in the waiting room. None of us in the counseling office that day knew what happened after the couple left the clinic a few hours later.

As rational-actor approaches have come to predominate in global family planning projects, medical anthropologists have thoroughly questioned the assumptions built into this model.[45] Family planning paradigms generally approach the use of birth control as a matter of knowledge and choice. Such models hold that if someone has accurate information about how to use birth control as well as access to a method, then she will use it to prevent an undesired pregnancy. Information plus access equals "rational choice." Pushing back against these models, anthropologists have drawn attention to the circumstances that circumscribe "choice." They have also called into question the liberal assumptions that underlie such frameworks, which posit that reproduction is everywhere understood as subject to human design. Lauren Fordyce observes that Haitian immigrant women's understanding that "God sends babies" explodes secular liberal paradigms.[46] In Cuba, moreover, where abortion has been legal since 1965 and available through the public health system since 1979, Elise Andaya found that women characterize their frequent repeat abortions as a sign of modernity and responsibility, even as state officials lament their failure to avoid unwanted pregnancy (and abortion) by using birth control.[47] Working in Greece, Heather Paxson has examined how state projects to "rationalize sex" fail to account for gendered power dynamics that make multiple abortions more feasible for many Athenian women than insisting one's partner wear a condom.[48] In a context where condoms conjure associations of extramarital affairs or sex work, campaigns to promote their use are unlikely to gain traction. Such ethnographic research shows that people do not passively accept state regulations; they adapt and rework state imperatives in pursuit of their own reproductive goals.[49]

Milagros's situation points to some of the relational circumstances that may inhibit Mexican urbanites from using birth control even when they desire it. For Milagros's husband, fertility and reproduction were embodied evidence of the stability of their romantic union and his masculine competency. For Milagros and the providers, the repeat pregnancies and abortions were evidence of *machismo* and gendered abuse. Women like Milagros negotiate birth control as relational beings embedded in romantic and other interpersonal configurations, and in the context of wider economic and political circumstances over which they may wield limited control.

Nevertheless, for ILE providers, the interpersonal circumstances that shape fertility management sometimes slipped to the background. "This is our struggle," Tony said about the ILE program and the MOH more broadly, detailing the institutional efforts to promote sexual health and responsibility through massive campaigns and publicity. Evincing a comparable sense of cynicism about women's ability to use birth control effectively, Carolina once told me, "There is a very small percentage of women whose birth control fails them. Others simply don't want to use it because they don't have a partner or for a million different reasons. When we have staff trainings," she continued, "we talk about this stuff. We can't force them to take a method or to keep using it. Before, we thought that maybe we were providing bad counseling because patients kept coming back for abortions. We would ask them what happened. They'd say, 'I didn't use it, I didn't want it, I broke up with my boyfriend and had it removed.'"

Occasionally staff considered other factors that prevented women from obtaining birth control. Roberta acknowledged the long wait times at public clinics, for instance, and the physical burdens of surgical sterilization. "Sometimes we recommend that patients undergo vasectomy or tubal ligation, surgeries so that they don't have any more kids," she said. "But they don't go to the institutions that offer these services because the idea of going and standing in line, it is burdensome, because obviously a surgery entails multiple steps." ILE personnel also described conditions of poverty, lack of time to visit public clinics, interminable traffic and resulting long commutes, a cultural aversion to open discussions of sex, and the persistence of "machismo" (contributing, in their view, to men's unwillingness to use condoms). "A lot of times women are afraid because of all of the myths that exist about contraceptive methods," Dr. Iberro once speculated about additional factors preventing the adoption of birth control. "They think that something bad might happen when the method is poorly placed. Patients tend to think, if this happened to her then it will happen to me too, they inherit these fears. Sometimes a woman's family won't permit her to use birth control, so the patient leaves the ILE clinic with the pill but doesn't use it, or doesn't refill it because patients are lazy, because someone caught them, because they don't have money. Or sometimes they leave very convinced about a [family planning regimen], but then they have trouble acquiring a refill and end up returning [for an abortion]." At times ILE personnel tempered their complaints, emphasizing that they could not generalize about all patients. Nevertheless, frustrations about reproductive irresponsibility permeated provider conversations at the clinic.

Tony cast irresponsibility as a cultural trait to account for the failure of the Mexican populace to use birth control effectively. In one of our many conversations, he described the prevalence of *desidia* (laziness). "It's like tomorrow I'll go, today I can't, I can't go this day either because I had something to do, we call this *desidia*. Here, people leave their health for tomorrow." For personnel like Tony, patients' refusal to adopt modern birth control methods represented an exasperating disavowal of enduring public health efforts to combat unintended pregnancy as well as a disregard for their own painstaking labor within the ILE program. Their frustration must be understood against the backdrop of several decades of governmental expenditure on birth control, first implemented in the national family planning campaigns of the 1970s. For ILE personnel, abortion, which they usually read as a personal failure to prevent unwanted pregnancy with birth control, diverted limited public health resources and represented a burden on the already-strapped MOH. If the ILE personnel saw the pursuit of abortion in general as frustrating evidence of sexual irresponsibility, far and above the most vexing aspect of working in the ILE program was the return of patients for repeat abortions.

IS ABORTION CHRONIC? RECIDIVISM AND THE LIMITS OF DESERVINGNESS

"Very good, Lore," Dr. Rosaldo addressed a young woman who lay on the operating table recovering from an EVA procedure. I had positioned myself by Lore's head to hold her hand at her request. I watched from the same vantage point as she did throughout the procedure and afterwards, as Dr. Rosaldo kneaded her uterus with his fist to stimulate contractions and slow the bleeding. Lore's eyes glassed over, and her breathing deepened with each contraction. "*Ya casi, ya casi* [almost there]," Dr. Rosaldo exclaimed from the other end of the operating table before clapping his hands together to mark the end of the procedure. "We don't want to see you back here now," he addressed Lore, "only if you're coming to say hi."

With his joke, Dr. Rosaldo communicated a loaded message about the limits of abortion rights and the assumptions that many providers brought to clinical encounters across the ILE program, even during painful and vulnerable moments such as this one. In the ILE clinic abortion was expected to be a singular event. Whereas clinicians were generally supportive of one-time abortion, repetitive abortion caused horror and dismay. The repeat abortion patient, real or imagined, crystallized the tension at the heart of working in ILE: these public workers were responsible for providing a public health service while also working to limit it. "Abortion recidivism," as they sometimes referred to repeat abortion, thus legitimated their role in the clinic while also challenging it. Implicit in the notion of recidivism—a concept associated with a second offense or return to criminal behavior—is the moral transgression that (repeat) abortion represented for clinicians.

Dr. Rosaldo was not alone in his frustration over second-time patients. Repeat abortion exasperated clinicians working in different roles throughout the program. The topic figured prominently in casual conversations across the clinic, as ILE personnel vented about patients who approached abortion "like a form of birth control." "What's frustrating is that you counsel them," Roberta said. "You tell them the risks that they are running when they come for an abortion, and they come back! They come back knowing it is dangerous for their health. They abuse the program. With all of the counseling we provide, the whole range of information provided here, they come back, not once, twice, they come back up to five times! To have so many women who keep messing up means that they are using it like a family planning method." ILE providers constantly puzzled over what might compel a woman to return to the ILE clinic for multiple abortions, especially in a context where contraceptive methods were widely available. Dr. Iberro shared her bewilderment with me. "I've never been one to criticize people who undergo abortions, everyone has their circumstances," she said. "But one has to learn her lesson. The fact that women treat it like a contraceptive method bothers me. If the patient comes back ten times, I will attend to her each of those ten times. But I would tell her, 'You know what? You shouldn't [do this] because there is a whole gamut of methods, why don't you choose one?'"

For many personnel, repeat abortion was frustrating because it signaled that women were not taking care of themselves. Carolina elaborated: "A one-time [abortion], okay, but then one should learn from that, I mean, it's your life, it's not like we're talking about any old thing, it's your life! I'm saying that really these women are very troubled emotionally, the ones who come back several times." Dr. Rios agreed with her colleagues. "Sometimes," she vented, "I feel angry, for example with women who come back more than two, three times. I tell you that it makes me angry and confused, I say why again? Why this attitude of 'I don't give a shit'? 'It's my decision' [as if impersonating a patient]. Yes, it's your right, but sometimes I ask myself what is going on with these women?"

According to ILE program protocols, women are allowed to access abortion services as many times as needed. While data on repeat abortion in the ILE program are no longer available, in 2017, ten years after the program's inauguration, only 5.5 percent of women had accessed ILE services more than once.[50] This figure does not include abortions procured outside the ILE program (e.g., in a private clinic, or induced at home with misoprostol purchased over the counter, as in Milagros's case). Perhaps for this reason, when I showed the figure to Dr. Alexa, she was incredulous, expecting the rate to be higher. It is possible that ILE personnel, who were familiar with the reproductive histories of each woman, knew more about general rates of repeat abortion than the MOH data reflected. Yet the "problem" of repeat abortion, at least within the ILE program, seemed to exist largely in the minds and fears of clinical personnel, who worked hard to prevent this outcome. The "repeat aborter" captured a host of anxieties among clinicians about the potential exploitation of abortion rights and the possibility that women had come to devalue their reproductive capabilities.

Throughout this research, I occasionally encountered women who had undergone multiple abortions, both within and outside the ILE program, and most often when their birth control failed. The vast majority of women I met, however, were obtaining an abortion for the first time. I sometimes pushed the ILE personnel, therefore, to be more specific: Who were these women that "used abortion as a contraceptive method"? Tony leaned in close, placing his right elbow on the table between us and resting his chin on a curled fist. I had caught him at a slow moment, and I had his full attention. "I wasn't there," he began, responding to my question, "but I have some co-workers who say that once, on a rotation at a different hospital, they saw patient files marked with crosses to denote how many abortions they had undergone. And there were women with up to *ten crosses*. The professor said that there is a zone nearby where there is a lot of prostitution. So more than anything, they are women who work as prostitutes. At the ILE clinic they come and say, 'I'm a housewife,' but our professor told us that you can see them out there working the streets."

I never met a commercial sex worker in the ILE program, but Tony was not the only provider to assert that they formed part of the ILE clientele. A few months earlier, Dr. Rios had explained to me over lunch in the counseling office that sex workers sometimes visited her clinic. She was once performing an EVA abortion on a patient, she elaborated, when she accidentally stuck herself with a needle after injecting the anesthesia. The patient's chart revealed that she had undergone several abortions, an indication, for Dr. Rios, that she might have sold sex for a living. Dr. Rios panicked. She couldn't eat or sleep for the next week. When she contacted the patient to ask about her HIV status, the woman said she was negative, but Dr. Rios was not convinced. She initiated a taxing month-long course of postexposure prophylaxis antiretrovirals as a precautionary measure. On one hand, Dr. Rios's anxieties and subsequent actions are understandable. As a health worker her job exposed her to blood, vaginal secretions, and other bodily fluids, putting her at risk of contamination. At the same time, her fears, and the hasty conclusions to which she jumped, distilled a constellation of assumptions that circulated in the clinic about the kinds of women who might avail themselves of multiple abortions through the public sector, even in the absence of concrete evidence. For Dr. Rios and others, seeking multiple abortions through the state system was evidence of a low-class and morally dubious status. The needle incident crystallized a sense of endangerment, a threat of contamination from patients to providers in medical and moral terms. The repeat abortion patient embodied many of the anxieties that clinicians brought to abortion, confronting them with questions about their professional role.

Despite their efforts to impart to their patients an understanding of abortion as a singular event, personnel sometimes perceived patients to be exploiting the ILE program through repetitive access. I had been observing in the Santa Marta counseling office one afternoon with Carolina and Roberta when a young patient named Nargas entered to ask if she could take the abortifacient pills home rather than swallowing them at the clinic. She was unsure about interrupting her pregnancy, she told the providers, and wanted more time to reflect. Having the pills on hand would afford her some time while leaving the option of abortion on the table. This way, if she did settle on interrupting her pregnancy, she could avoid the long journey back to the clinic.

"Abortion is something you have to be sure about," Carolina told Nargas. "There is no regret. There is no what if. Why did you come here today? You came here today, didn't you?" Nargas clearly had not anticipated resistance from the providers. She needed more time to mull things over. When she left the clinic to join her aunt on the cement stoop out front, I followed her to ensure that she was okay. The three of us sat together for a while in silence looking out at the neighborhood. We watched as a teenage boy poured grease over a metal grill nearby, and then as a stray dog sauntered past.

Eventually Nargas broke the silence to lay out the facts of her situation. She was twenty years old and pregnant by her boyfriend of five months. He had offered to drop out of school and find work to support her and the baby. Nargas' aunt interjected to emphasize how she had struggled as a young mother herself. Nargas was conflicted. She knew that there was "life inside of her," she said, but also that something, a gut feeling maybe, had led her to the clinic that morning. I reminded her that she was just seven weeks pregnant, early in the first trimester, and therefore had time to think before coming up against the twelve-week limit. But she had traveled over an hour from Mexico State. And she had been waiting at the clinic for several hours. I let her know, as gently as I could, that she had thirty minutes to make up her mind before the clinic would close for the day. And then I left her to arrive at a conclusion with her aunt.

Back inside, Carolina and Roberta were entering patient data into the computer in the counseling office. Before long, we noticed that Nargas and her aunt were no longer on the front stoop. "Oh, she's so young, she should have the abortion, of course," Dr. Alexa said. Roberta and Carolina objected. "No, no!" They recognized the patient's aunt, they claimed. She had been a patient at the clinic. Nargas was not pregnant at all, they insisted. Her aunt had brought her to the clinic to obtain abortifacient pills for *herself*. She must have been too ashamed, the personnel concluded, to admit that she came back for a repeat abortion. I was not convinced. Though their conjecture was impossible to confirm, its presence betrayed their general suspicion about patient motives and their inflated fears that patients would exploit the ILE program, their labor, and the precious health resources on offer. Public health monies, providers often emphasized, were to be rationed and protected for the benefit of all.

COLLECTIVE RESOURCES, COMMUNAL OBLIGATIONS

In the ILE program, like the MOH at large, medical supplies were limited. The providers had to juggle unremitting patient demand with an insufficient supply of resources. These occupational stressors were complicated by the fact that many midlevel providers had unstable labor contracts. Occupational pressures compounded providers' frustrations with patients, whom they begrudged for taking the ILE program for granted. Many providers were aware that the care they were able to offer was inferior to that available in the resource-rich private sector, but there was little they could do to change that. "There are resource shortages at all levels of public health care in Mexico," Tony told me. "We see shortages in IMSS, ISSSTE, the MOH, but in private hospitals patients get their own room. Here in the MOH, sometimes there are six patients to a room." While ILE personnel were quick to recognize the deficiencies with which they had to contend, they were also proud of their role as public health servants. "We aren't as bad as people say!" Dr. Rios once asserted defensively when I asked her why a wealthy woman might choose the ILE program over a private abortion clinic. "There are a lot of people who say that the public sector is bad, that they're terrified to come here and so they use the private sector instead. I've seen that it's not true. Here in the public sector, we are resourceful."

Dr. Rios helped me to appreciate the ways in which time bore down on the personnel as they juggled relentless patient demand. She was well aware of the inconveniences that waiting posed for patients, and she held her staff accountable. "As the boss," she told me, "I pull the reins a bit. Because I've always told my staff to treat [the patients] the way they'd like to be treated. When we provide a public service, we always want to leave quickly. If we don't work, we don't get paid. It's the same with the patients. If they don't go to work [because they are at the ILE clinic], they don't earn an income, and only they and God know the family dynamic, the economic issues, everything they have to sort through to get here. So the quicker we attend to them, the better." The conflicting pressures entailed in appeasing patients, ceding to the dictates of the boss, and managing the extraordinary demand for ILE sometimes led personnel to arrive at hurried judgments of patients, casting them as "lazy." Time weighed on patients, personnel, and clinic administrators, straining relationships between these groups.

Dr. Iberro and I were seated in the small ultrasound room of Reina María Clinic on a weekday afternoon when she began to complain about how resource shortages tied her hands as a doctor. "The supply of abortifacient drugs is not assured. There have been times when there are no more pills and we are pleading for more. Right now, for instance, we've had a problem with the contraceptive methods because we have not had a single IUD to give the patients." Clinicians at Santa Marta faced similar conditions. "The ILE program should have a sufficient supply of materials," Dr. Rios asserted, when I asked her about how the ILE program could be improved. "Those of us who are on the front lines of battle are the ones who run into conflicts due to a lack of supplies. Those of us who work in the clinics, we have discussed how the program would be more sustainable if there were a reserve fund in the MOH to cover abortifacient drugs and supplies." Providers sometimes grew frustrated when supplies ran out, but there was little they could do until the delivery arrived. When this happened the ILE personnel was still required to show up for work from 7:00 a.m. until 4:00 p.m. every day. Occasionally, during a medicine shortage, I arrived at the otherwise empty clinic to find the clinicians reading magazines and novels to occupy themselves until their shift was over.

It was not only supply shortages that made the ILE program a challenging place to work. The program had been short on personnel since its inception, as many health workers invoked their right to conscientious objection and refused to participate. Tony told me, "Yesterday there were something like twenty-three patients--so one is running around. We don't know if everything is going well in the operating theater. It's not the same thing attending to two or three people as twenty. Here [at Reina María] there is one gynecologist and one general practitioner, when there should be two gynecologists. With twenty-three patients, the nurse is not going to sit down and explain everything." This situation is distinct, Tony explained to me, from the private sector, where money buys patients top-notch care, abundant supplies, and also a degree of legal latitude. "[In private clinics] the attention is always going to be [better]—they are going to attend to you *en bandeja de plata* [with silver bandages]. They are going to treat you really well. Why? Because you are paying. You give the orders. In contrast, here at the MOH, you get what is available. Sometimes there are not materials, there is not personnel. If you go to a private clinic maybe they will give you an aspiration abortion up until eighteen or twenty weeks [past the twelve-week legal limit] because you are paying."

ILE personnel also worried about their own economic security. Unless providers were able to secure *una base* (a permanent position) in the MOH, their contracts had to be renegotiated and renewed each year. Temporary posts did not include health insurance, vacation time, or a right to join the labor union. Dr. Rios had worked hard to ensure that her personnel at Santa Marta clinic were content, yet the situation was not entirely in her control. "It doesn't make sense to demand that someone work without a vacation. [My staff] have worked for five years straight without a single vacation period, it's exhausting," she told me. "Nevertheless, they have the best attitude, they are ready to work." At the time of my research only two of the personnel at Santa Marta, Dr. Rios and a nurse named Lourdes, had permanent positions.

Carolina had worked at the clinic for five years on a renewable contract until she was finally given a permanent position a few years after I concluded my study. Before that she had no vacation time and relied on the Seguro Popular for health insurance. While today she is covered by ISSSTE like other state workers, for years she had sought health services through the MOH. Although she made it clear that she would never consider abortion as an option for herself, it is safe to assume that she would have struggled to pay for an abortion through the private sector. To mitigate low wages, Carolina and some of the other midlevel providers at Santa Marta had developed a *tanda*—which functioned like a communal savings account that relied on mutual trust—to pool and stretch their incomes. Everyone donated an equal share of money to the pot each week, and participants took turns drawing the entire sum of funds when they needed money for special events or unexpected costs that they could not assume alone. It was the *tanda* system that had helped Carolina save for her daughter's quinceañera party, to which she invited many of us from the clinic.

If the issue of their own economic insecurity troubled the ILE personnel in private, more central to their public work were concerns about resource scarcity within the clinic. When providers expressed these concerns, they frequently focused on the "freeloading patients" whom they saw as exploiting the program by returning for multiple free abortions. Dr. Iberro described the ILE program as self-defeating in this regard. "Patients know that they now have a place to turn, they have a path to follow," she said. "That's what I mean when I say they use ILE like a contraceptive method. In a way, today they are *less responsible* because they know that nowadays they have the possibility of coming for ILE services that don't cost them a cent. They can come again and again without acquiring any responsibility over their person, over their health." By providing the procedure without cost, in other words, clinicians worried about cultivating a "culture of dependency" among women.

Even though the ILE personnel occasionally cited the constitutional right to health when discussing their work, they often focused on what they saw as the *limits* of that right. Repeat abortion fell under this category. "If you look at the cost for the state, [ILE] is really expensive," a doctor named Lucia, hired at Santa Marta toward the end of my research, told me in an interview. "I've never done the math, but just think, it's the place, the personnel, the supplies. So when you look at that aspect it is frustrating that patients come three, four, five times and don't learn." During a conversation in the counseling office one afternoon, Carolina proposed what she thought to be a practical solution to the "problem" of repeat abortion and the drain in resources it created for the ILE program.

> I think one abortion is valid, but when a woman comes two or three times, we should charge her for the procedure, to *conscientizarla* [awaken her], and in these cases we shouldn't just charge for the second abortion but for the first one too. This way she will think hard before coming back, and here in the clinic we can recuperate some of the money spent on her. Because really an abortion is extremely expensive. From the first consultation it is about 10,000 pesos [$520 USD] if you count the abortifacient drugs, the ultrasound, the clinical history, the gynecologist, the general practitioner, the nurse, refer-

rals, counseling, that's what the MOH invests in each patient. ILE is very expensive!

Do you think that if the MOH charged for ILE, fewer women would come? I asked.

"Of course," Carolina exclaimed. "I think they would have a bigger consequence. Not everyone, but the majority would think harder about coming for an ILE."

"I agree." Dr. Alexa added from across the room. "After the second time, the MOH should charge for ILE services because they think it's a family planning method and it's not."

So why *doesn't* the MOH charge for a second ILE? I asked, hoping to better understand their concerns.

"I think because they never imagined the magnitude of the demand," Carolina replied. "I think they thought that women were going to become more aware and protect themselves after one ILE. They didn't take repeat abortion into consideration when outlining the rules of the program. What's happening is that the demand has shot up and obviously the medicine runs out. I don't think anyone imagined that after six or seven years—because that's how old the ILE program is—the demand would continue. Demand has been growing at an exponential rate. It's getting out of control."

In a separate conversation Dr. Rios had registered her frustration over patients whom she felt did not recognize the broader social value of the ILE program. "They come and ask for a service that is a right," she said.

> In Mexico, there is a right to health, and not just reproductive health, but general health too. It's a constitutional right that we have, a right to free health care, and the state has to guarantee it to the population. The ILE service is public, and it is excellent because the few resources that they give us are used for the women and they are never channeled to any other end. Yet patients underestimate our capacity as health workers. We offer them the implant and they don't accept it. That's what I mean when I say they don't value what they have and what we are offering them.

For personnel, the fact that health services such as ILE were free activated a set of corresponding obligations among those who accessed these services. As recipients of free health services, ILE patients bore a responsibility to care for their health and avoid tapping into the program's limited resources again.

Program administrators had different ideas about how to address the demand that overwhelmed the clinics. Maria Puerto, the assistant director of the ILE program, observed that the demand could be redistributed if abortion were made legal and available across the country. She also raised the issue of the MOH bearing sole responsibility for the delivery of ILE since the Mexican social security institutions and other arms of the state health system refused to offer these services. "A pipe dream I have is that abortion would be provided not just here in the MOH, but that women could access ILE through the ISSSTE, IMSS, that [these institutions] would involve themselves in this question of abortion." To date, Maria Puerto's pipe dream has not been realized.

In their daily work providers like Dr. Rios, Roberta, Carolina, and Dr. Iberro were responsible for distributing limited public health supplies to an overwhelming number of patients. They carried out this job for limited pay even as their medical colleagues and the broader public maligned their work. The most important aspect of the job, as they saw it, was not to embolden women to exercise their right to an abortion. It was, rather, to instill in their patients a sense of concern for their health and a sense of moral responsibility to others. ILE providers felt discouraged when they perceived women to be gambling on their sexual health at the expense of the collective. The providers shouldered the responsibility for fixing a broken social body marked by poverty, gendered violence, and abuse. They sought to create a more utopian society by transmitting their vision of responsibilized citizenship to their patients, citizens whom they hoped after their abortion would henceforth embody the qualities that providers wanted for the broader social whole. An idealized vision of what Mexico ought to be thus motivated these public providers who strove, day after day, to protect their patients and the wider collective.

CHAPTER FIVE

AT THE LIMIT OF RIGHTS
Abortion in the Extralegal Sphere

ISA ARRIVED FOR ABORTION CARE at Reina María Clinic on a
busy Monday morning in the spring of 2015. She was nineteen years old and
accompanied by her partner, who waited in the large health center that houses
the ILE wing. I had stationed myself in the ultrasound room that day to observe
as Dr. Iberro and Dr. Cruz scanned each woman's abdomen to measure the
gestational age of her pregnancy. Patient after patient filed in and out unevent-
fully, until Isa entered. Unlike the others before her, Isa was visibly pregnant.
Her distended abdomen protruded under her T-shirt. Dr. Cruz asked her to lie
down on the exam table and lower her pants just enough to run the ultrasound
probe along her middle. As she peeled back her shirt to expose her abdomen,
his eyes widened. He shook his head while smearing a dollop of blue gel over
her skin. "No young lady, this can't be," Dr. Cruz said as the scan materialized
before us. "You're eighteen weeks pregnant, *estás enorme* [your pregnancy is
very advanced]. You have fallen outside the program." The scan, a mediation
of her body, posed a limit. Without uttering a word, Isa pulled up her jeans
and returned to the waiting room to gather her belongings. She seemed to understand that there was nothing to be done.

When I approached Isa in the waiting room a few minutes later, she was eager to talk. She had a high school degree and a two-year-old daughter, and she worked in a small cosmetics store in downtown Mexico City. When she and her partner had learned of the second pregnancy, they were excited. The couple had been trying for another baby. But as the weeks passed, Isa developed unrelenting nausea. "I don't want the doctors to say it's me or the baby, or maybe they save the baby, but they can't save me," she said. "I don't want to leave my daughter behind." She feared for the safety of her pregnancy: "What if I can't eat and the baby dies inside of me?" After weeks of insufferable illness, they searched online for options. By the time the couple arrived at Reina María Clinic, Isa had dropped ten pounds. Though she didn't admit it to Dr. Cruz, Isa was surprised by the ultrasound scan results. "According to my last period, I thought I was just over ten weeks pregnant," she told me, "because I calculated the date. That's what I did with my daughter [too]." But in the ILE clinic, the scan results were definitive. After she left that day, I never saw or heard from Isa again. No one knew what became of her or her pregnancy.

Isa is one of dozens of women turned away from the ILE program during the months I spent there because their pregnancies fell outside of the twelve-week gestational limit on ILE services. The ILE program keeps no record of how many women it has turned away, what prevented them from arriving earlier to the clinic, or what became of their pregnancies. Women in Isa's situation have limited options. Some may attempt to induce an abortion on their own using over-the-counter pharmaceuticals or other means, and if they lack the proper information on how to do so safely they may suffer injuries, or even death, because of it. Others likely bear the pregnancy to term against their will. Those who are able to scrape together the funds may opt to purchase second-trimester abortion care through a private clinic, where the procedure can cost up to 12,000 pesos ($600 USD). Although everyone working in the ILE program on the day Isa arrived knew about this last option, technically they were not allowed to offer this information to their patients unless there was a medical necessity for the procedure. Even if Isa had had the money to purchase private second-trimester abortion care, which was unlikely given her low-wage work, she would have had to find a private clinic on her own.

At eighteen weeks gestation, Isa's pregnancy was clearly outside program limits. Yet measuring the gestational age of a pregnancy through sonogram was not always so straightforward. In the ILE clinic a gestational age was assigned according to the size of the embryo/fetus rendered through the scan, which might or might not correspond with the date of conception or the woman's calculation of her pregnancy. Rather than simply visualizing the contents of the womb, in other words, sonograms are mediations that are open to interpretation. In the ILE program this interpretive process was fraught. The 2007 law was just seven years old at the time of my research, and the MOH had not yet specified how the "twelve-week" gestational limit on abortion should be implemented in practice. A number of questions thus emerged for clinicians in their daily work: Were the last six days of the twelfth week included? What happened when a scan measured a pregnancy of twelve weeks and three days? Should women in this situation be turned away? And with what information?

I never observed an ILE provider offering an abortion beyond the strictest interpretation of the 12.0–week limit. But it was common knowledge in the ILE program that providers had different ways of interpreting and acting on the discursive ambiguity embedded in the law. Many providers sent women away when their pregnancies measured just one day beyond twelve weeks. Others read the twelve-week limit differently, offering the procedure to women whose pregnancies measured anywhere up to twelve weeks and six days gestation. The interpretive work that ILE clinicians engaged in to address the gap between legal directives and medical care underlines what Mara Buchbinder describes as "laws as written and laws as practiced."[1] In this murky space where legal and medical realms converged, ILE providers made complicated decisions about translating legal directives into clinical practice. "The meaning of law is not inscribed, a priori, in legislative texts," Buchbinder writes.[2] "Instead, law is made through interpretive processes when social actors put law into practice at various institutional sites and stages of implementation."

To understand how the ILE clinicians navigated the uncertainties that surrounded their work, I sometimes asked them about their own approach. One day at Reina María Clinic I proposed a hypothetical scenario to Dr. Jimenez: What if the sonogram measured a woman's pregnancy at twelve weeks and one day gestation, would she fall outside of the ILE program? "Yes," he said, unequivocally. "Because, given the reform, the laws of Mexico, in the capital, abortion is permitted up to twelve weeks, outside this time frame it's forbidden. With that, no one can break the rule because—I think in that sense one has to be conscious of the benefit to the patient versus the risk to our own juridical security." When I pressed him about the ambiguity written into the law, he defended his interpretation.

"Let's suppose we provided abortion care to a patient after twelve weeks and she had a complication. After the twelfth week, that would be the responsibility of the doctor, so it doesn't really make sense to [risk our livelihood] in order to help someone who requires it. I would fear that my team might not support and defend me, they might leave me hanging in such a case." Of all of the ILE personnel I met, Dr. Jimenez was the most vocal about protecting women's reproductive rights. "In the ILE program, doctors can be useful by giving women their rights to reproductive health, giving them their rights as human beings, as legal persons, as social beings, and not merely as producers of children," he had told me in our first conversation at Reina María Clinic. If he expressed reluctance to harness the ambiguity of the law and stretch the limits of the ILE program to meet women's needs, I imagined most other ILE providers would feel similarly. As health care providers navigating a new arena of medical practice within the public sector, the ILE clinicians had to weigh their own legal security and occupational stability against the needs of their patients. While some providers were willing to assume the risk, there was limited latitude within the MOH for public clinicians to interpret the murkiness of the law.

In 2017, a couple years after I wrapped up my resident fieldwork, I contacted Dr. Carmen, the director of reproductive health at the MOH who oversaw the ILE program, to request permission for a follow-up study I was developing with a local public health researcher. We were troubled by the lack of transparency about what happened to women who fell outside ILE program limits and were turned away. With permission, we wanted to understand what, if any, counseling or referrals they received in the ILE clinic and what, ultimately, became of their pregnancies. Dr. Carmen refused our request almost immediately, pointing to the negative media coverage that such a study might bring to the ILE program. Maria Puerto, who worked alongside Dr. Carmen, had warned me on other occasions about the *amarillismo* (yellow journalism) that slandered the ILE program through sensational accounts of botched abortions and un-founded accusations of criminal activity among its personnel. One article was published that year—not coincidentally the ten-year anniversary of the 2007 reform—in a local tabloid called *Diario Basta!* The story related the experience of a patient who had arrived at an ILE clinic with a pregnancy of sixteen weeks. Because her pregnancy surpassed the twelve-week limit, the personnel allegedly referred her to a private clinic where she could access a second-trimester abor-tion for 4,500 Mexican pesos (roughly $230 USD). After the abortion, according to the author, she suffered severe depression, guilt, and regret. Her mother was quoted in *Diario Basta!* faulting the ILE personnel for her daughter's distress and speculating about financial kickbacks they had received for guiding her daughter to the private sector for a costly second-trimester abortion.

Although there was no evidence to support the mother's speculation, and although the accusations of financial gain were likely false, the publication nevertheless stirred public suspicion, disparaged the ILE program, and left program administrators and personnel on guard. It was precisely the wrong moment for my colleague and me to propose a study on gestational limits. We abandoned the project. Researching abortion, like obtaining the procedure, entailed many limits.

This chapter takes the notion of limits—legal, temporal, geographic, moral—as a starting place to consider the gaps between abortion rights and access. I consider the experiences of women for whom abortion rights remain elusive, as well as the sympathetic doctors who help them and the activist net-works that have emerged to patch over the rough edges where abortion rights drop off. In her edited volume *Gender and Culture at the Limit of Rights*, an-thropologist Dorothy Hodgson explores the "social life" of the notion that *women's rights are human rights*, tracking the deployment of this claim in global struggles for gender justice.[3] "What," Hodgson asks, does a "'rights frame' en-able and what does it ignore, dismiss, or proscribe?"[4] Here I take up a related set of questions around abortion rights, which Mounia El Kotni and I have ex-plored elsewhere:[5] Toward what ends do Mexican abortion rights advocates and sympathizers deploy the human rights strategy, and with what success? What possibilities, experiences, and subjectivities does a rights approach to abortion give rise to, and what does it preclude?

My sense of abortion *at the limit of rights* is twofold. On the one hand, I am interested here in the practical limits of abortion rights for women who are unable to access the procedure because of legal, geographic, economic and other constraints. At the same time, I consider the approaches of individuals dedicated to "working the limits" of abortion rights by bending, stretching, overlooking, and at times knowingly violating the law to expand abortion access. Studying these limits entailed a good deal of digging and cross-checking information, as the strategies people developed to circumvent existing confines were, in some cases, in direct violation of the law. Aside from gaps in what people were willing to say, the convoluted web of strategies themselves at times made it hard to understand anything definitive about the extralegal sphere of Mexican abortion. As such, the geographically dispersed scenes collected in this chapter mirror the varied methods used to realize abortion rights in a landscape of uneven legality.

Even though I could not systematically study what happened to women like Isa who are turned away from the ILE program, my research took me into the private sector of abortion care, where clinicians are less subject to government oversight and thus have more leeway to perform abortions and more liberty to speak openly about what happens to women who fall through the cracks of the ILE program.

PRIVATE MEDICINE AND THE ELASTICITY OF LAW

"After twelve weeks women no longer have rights?" Dr. Mendez asked rhetorically from within a small office at a private reproductive health care clinic on the border between Mexico City and Mexico State, where he worked a few times a week. I had traveled to interview him after we met a few weeks earlier through my volunteer work as an accompanier for Conéctame, an organization based in Mexico City that offers financial, emotional, and logistical support to women traveling to the capital for an abortion from other Mexican states.[6] The vast majority of Conéctame clients obtain first-trimester abortions through the ILE program, where an assigned accompanier stays with them throughout the process to provide logistical and moral support. At the time I volunteered for the organization in 2014, Conéctame had facilitated thousands of accompaniments. In certain cases, when a woman's pregnancy exceeds the twelve-week limit, the organization arranges for second-trimester abortions through the private sector and helps cover the associated costs. When this is necessary Conéctame often turns to Dr. Mendez.

As a devoted advocate of reproductive rights, Dr. Mendez was vocal in his critique of the twelve-week limit on abortion within the ILE program. "Changing the definition of abortion to make it less offensive was politically expedient, but not in terms of women's rights," he told me. His critique centered on a seldom-discussed dimension of the 2007 reform that transformed elective first-trimester abortion into a legal right of women by redefining abortion up to twelve weeks as legal interruption of pregnancy (ILE): the reform left intact the crime of abortion *beyond* twelve weeks of gestation, an infraction that can carry penalties of three to six months in prison, or a fine of up to $600 USD.[7]

Feminist activists and women's health advocates worked diligently in the years leading up to the 2007 reform to reposition first-trimester abortion from a religious or moral issue to one of women's human rights, public health, and democratic citizenship. They demonstrated the high cost of abortion-related complications for the Mexican health system and generated public support to pave the way for legal change. Yet second-trimester abortion did not figure into this advocacy work. The religious and bioethical debates over when "life" begins, and at which point a developing fetus can feel pain, are particularly charged in Mexico with regard to abortion after the first trimester. At the time of my research second-trimester abortion was legal only under exceptional circumstances, such as when the pregnancy resulted from rape or posed a grave risk to the woman's life. Even in these severe circumstances, however, the procedure was extremely difficult to obtain.

Dr. Mendez is a respected leader in the abortion advocacy community. He holds a variety of prestigious posts in the local reproductive health world and was one of few doctors in the country who provides second-trimester abortion care. Dr. Mendez serves as the national medical director of Hope, an international chain of private abortion clinics, in addition to his private gynecological practice on the border with Mexico State. As a Conéctame volunteer, I sometimes accompanied women for second-trimester abortions to his private practice. Those visits entailed several hours of waiting as a woman's cervix dilated in preparation for the procedure, and I used the opportunity to ask questions.

How, I asked him once, did he avoid legal trouble when providing second-trimester abortions? "My work is *not* outside the law," Dr. Mendez insisted. "I have worked so that women can access abortion, and I would say that [these cases fall under the legal exception of] mortal danger, based on their age, or an illness they might have. This is the medical argument that we use in order to provide women with abortion access. Abortion should be elective, but since the law doesn't permit it—" Dr. Mendez interrupted his own sentence. In his silence I inferred the unmentionable reality of which we were both aware: the interpretive work or "legal play" he and other clinicians carried out to expand abortion access. As a physician working in the private sector, Dr. Mendez holds the medical authority to make determinations about when a pregnancy poses a "mortal danger" to a woman's life—a space of uncertainty he leverages to align with his moral and political convictions as a doctor and an advocate of reproductive rights.

Because he often attended to women turned away from the ILE program on account of gestational restrictions, his position afforded him a unique perspective on the program's limits. I prompted him to share his reflections one evening in his private practice, where I had accompanied a woman named Rosalia for a second-trimester abortion.[8] At fourteen weeks pregnant, Rosalia could not seek abortion care through the ILE program, and Conéctame had arranged for her procedure with Dr. Mendez. Earlier that evening I met her at a bus stop beside a congested thoroughfare that hugged the border with Mexico State. Leaving behind the busy city highways, we crossed into Mexico State by foot, walking a couple blocks to Dr. Mendez's clinic. Through tears, Rosalia divulged that she did not want to interrupt her pregnancy but felt she had no other option given that the man involved was married. Despite his promises, she feared he would never leave his wife, and it would be too difficult to support the baby alone. She had contacted Conéctame for assistance after learning about their services online. I sat in the clinic waiting room during Rosalia's procedure. Dr. Mendez walked in and out of the procedure room, checking on Rosalia and engaging me in an interrupted conversation.

"My main issue with the ILE program is that they made a program in the first place," he said, before detailing a set of concrete critiques. His criticisms cohered around three aspects of the program. First, he regretted that the creation of an ILE program designed specifically to provide abortion services was unnecessarily expensive for the MOH. "The moment you create a program you have to designate certain resources. When you already have hospitals, why waste double? And you have to hire new personnel, so you waste more. It's pricier to have a special program than to manage abortion patients as they arrive [to the hospital on a case-by-case basis]." For Dr. Mendez, the ILE program was an economically wasteful undertaking for an already strapped public health system. The ILE clinics frequently run out of supplies, he observed, including abortifacient pills and contraceptive methods. Because the MOH operates on a fixed budget that is unable to respond to the vast demand for ILE services, the program relies on medical supplies and other forms of assistance from nongovernmental organizations such as those where Dr. Mendez works.

The second part of Dr. Mendez's critique related to what he described as the discriminatory character of the program. Cordoning off abortion care from the broader medical establishment, he argued, further stigmatized the procedure among medical personnel, patients, and the broader public. His critique echoed those made in the US context, where in the aftermath of *Roe v. Wade* abortions have been performed primarily in freestanding clinics that are separated from mainstream medical care.[9] Critics note that separating abortion from medical institutions has afforded prolife activists easier access to the clinics and to the women seeking its services. "Historically we had leprosaria where they confined people with leprosy in one place," Dr. Mendez told me. "Today we have AIDS sanitoria, where they confine people with AIDS. These are public health problems. To create an ILE program in a few clinics is to [similarly] confine women. We are generating stigma. A gynecologist *has* to perform abortions and must be trained as an expert in the procedure. But to change this ideology [in Mexico] is tough. [Here] we critique gynecologists because they perform abortions. Of course, a neurosurgeon opens the skull, an orthopedist cuts legs. Abortion is part of being a good obstetrician." For Dr. Mendez, the creation of the ILE program further stigmatized abortion by segregating it from the broader field of women's health and detaching it from general gynecological training. The institutional separation of abortion care has had iatrogenic effects, generating stigma among medical personnel, many of whom are unwilling to perform the procedure, and producing gynecologists who are technically unprepared to perform abortions. Dr. Mendez had worked to remedy this systemic problem for years by seeking to establish mandatory abortion training as part of the reproductive health specialty in the medical school of the UNAM.

Dr. Mendez's final critique centered on the twelve-week limit on abortion in the ILE program, which, he argued, stigmatized second-trimester abortion—a procedure that was legal in the capital and available through the MOH under certain, very restrictive circumstances. By offering abortion services only within the first twelve weeks of pregnancy, he argued, the ILE program thus obscured the rare legal circumstances in which second-trimester abortion was lawful. "The MOH erects barriers," he told me. "It erects barriers because in their minds it is not possible for women to have access to abortion. The law says that when, in the judgment of the doctor assisting a woman, abortion is medically necessary, it should be provided, even beyond twelve weeks."

Years earlier, when Dr. Mendez served as the clinical adviser to a major reproductive rights organization in Mexico City that works closely with the MOH, he had suggested that the organization advocate for the provision of second-trimester abortion within the ILE program. His colleagues dismissed his recommendations, fearful of political backlash.

> They didn't want to touch the topic then. I don't know about now, I'm not there anymore. But [I ask myself,] what lies ahead? Where are we going? What is the mission of the ILE program, the vision? What will happen in the next few years? Are we going to continue to provide abortion services exclusively in the first trimester? What about the second trimester? The women who die from unsafe abortions are in their second trimester or third trimester, and no one will provide them with abortion services. They reject them, they neglect them. These are the women that I attend to.

Here he disappeared again to check on Rosalia. "These are the women that I see," he called out from the other room.

Like Rosalia, many of Dr. Mendez's patients traveled to his private practice from states where abortion is heavily restricted, often with the support of Conéctame and other organizations engaged in similar work. Harsh abortion laws outside the capital prevented many of these women from seeking abortion care earlier in their pregnancies, pushing them into the second trimester when abortion was even more difficult to access. At least some portion of Dr. Mendez's work at his private practice in Mexico State entailed, paradoxically, attending to women living in the capital who could not access ILE services because their pregnancies exceeded program limits. The irony of the latter situation—that MOH restrictions prompted women to travel from Mexico City (home to the country's most progressive abortion law) to Mexico State (where abortion laws are more stringent)—was not lost on Dr. Mendez. "They go from Mexico City to Mexico State when one would assume that it's the reverse!"

If some women are able to subvert state laws to obtain second-trimester abortions with the assistance of advocacy organizations like Conéctame and sympathetic physicians like Dr. Mendez, many more must work around the legal restrictions in their home states by traveling to the capital. Around seventy thousand of the abortion procedures performed through the ILE program at the time of this writing were among women who had traveled to the capital from elsewhere in the country. Their experiences of what I have come to think of "abortion exile" form an important part of the extralegal sphere of Mexican abortion.

ABORTION EXILE

When Celeste arrived at Santa Marta Clinic I had been conducting research there for several months. Pale and weary, she pushed her way into a rather full waiting room. At twenty-four years old, Celeste was pregnant for the first time. Unlike the others seated around her, she was originally from Brazil and had traveled several hours to the capital by bus from the state of Querétaro, where she lived with her husband, José. In the counseling office Celeste disclosed to Roberta and Carolina that the man involved in the pregnancy was not her husband. Although she had been pushing for a divorce, José refused to sign the papers. Celeste had moved out and was renting a small apartment nearby on her own. The pregnancy was the unexpected result of a casual evening out. She had no feelings for the man involved and no desire to keep the pregnancy, particularly in light of her fraught marital situation. Celeste had been open with José about the affair and the pregnancy, and he knew she had traveled to the capital for an abortion. Even though José had promised to support Celeste with the baby to preserve their marriage, she had refused his offers. She was resolute in her decision to interrupt the pregnancy, but she worried that José would report her to the Querétaro authorities for seeking an abortion, which is illegal in their state, putting her visa in jeopardy. She had nothing to go back to in Brazil.

Because she lives outside the capital, Carolina and Roberta recommended that Celeste undergo an EVA procedure not being offered at Santa Marta at the time. According to the ultrasound scan her pregnancy was 9.2 weeks—well within the 12-week limit—but the aspiration would be safer given that she lived out of state and could not easily return for a follow-up scan. Celeste was to arrive at a different ILE clinic to obtain the EVA procedure the following morning, no later than 7:00 a.m. The social workers contacted Conéctame, which covered Celeste's hotel fees and transportation costs and arranged for in-person accompaniment to the clinic. I offered to meet her at the hotel later that afternoon to check on her.

When I approached a midcentury bathhouse-turned-hotel a few hours later, I assumed I was in the wrong place. Up a wide stairwell on a landing was a Virgin of Guadalupe statue encased in a glass box. At the end of a narrow hallway a young man sat at a wide desk behind a plexiglass barrier. "In room 407," he said, when I asked for Celeste. She greeted me with an apprehensive smile, relieved, perhaps, to see a familiar face, if also discomfited by the circumstances of our meeting. The hotel room was furnished only with a wooden table and a twin bed, where Celeste and I sat together discussing her situation. She insisted that having a baby would lock her into a life of unhappiness. She had left Brazil for Mexico two and a half years earlier after an amorous online relationship evolved into a hasty marriage proposal. At the time, she had been eager to leave Brazil, where her family struggled to get by on the meager wages her father earned as a taxi driver. Celeste's brother was addicted to crack cocaine, and her mother suffered from compulsive hoarding. Marriage to José, a devout Christian with a stable family life, seemed to offer a world of opportunity and a way out.

Celeste's fantasy of a new life shattered upon arrival to Mexico. "Everything about Mexico annoys me, even the food," she said, as if seeking agreement from another foreigner. She felt suffocated by her husband. During our conversation she pulled up the cascade of text messages José had sent her that day alone. But their lives were fully enmeshed; the two worked together in her father-in-law's company in Querétaro, and the boundaries between their domestic life and that of her in-laws were blurry. When Celeste redecorated the house where she lived with José, her mother-in-law quickly switched out the paintings without asking. Celeste replaced them for those she had chosen, but her mother-in-law snatched them down once more when she was out. For Celeste, the passive dance with her mother-in-law was emblematic of her broader struggle for power within her new family and in the new country she called home. She reiterated that the abortion was the best way forward. I offered to meet Celeste at the ILE clinic the following morning, even though a different accompanier had been arranged. She agreed and we said goodnight before I walked back down the narrow hallway, past the young man in his glass box and the Virgin in hers.

Celeste is one of tens of thousands of women living in states across the country who have traveled to the capital to seek abortion care that is unavailable or outlawed at home.[10] According to MOH data from December 2020, around 30 percent of the abortions performed through the ILE program were among women who had arrived from outside the capital. While most in this group traveled from neighboring Mexico State, around six thousand women traveled longer distances from more remote states. Some have traveled to the capital from as far away as Baja California, in the northwest corner of the country, and Quintana Roo, in the southeast corner of the country.

In the past two decades, a growing number of anthropologists have explored the domestic and international journeys of women and couples in search of reproductive services that are inaccessible in their own communities.[11] Much of the research to date has centered on travel for assisted fertility services. Researchers have struggled to develop terminology that accurately captures the experiences of reproductive "travelers" as well as the global power relations that give rise to this unique kind of movement.[12] While debates on terminology abound, Marcia Inhorn and Pasquale Patrizio have drawn on Roberto Matorras's notion of "reproductive exile" to critique the romance and leisure implied in dominant frameworks that characterize reproductive travel as a variety of medical tourism.[13] *Reproductive exile*, they suggest, is a more appropriate descriptor that conveys the emotional and economic burdens so often incurred in the process of relocating for fertility assistance. The

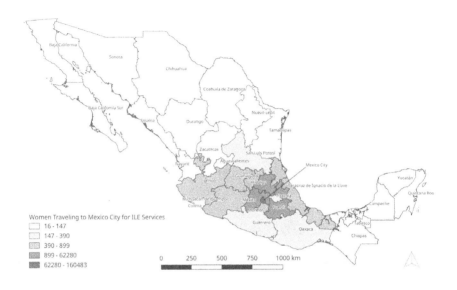

Women Traveling to Mexico City for ILE Services
- 16 - 147
- 147 - 390
- 390 - 899
- 899 - 62280
- 62280 - 160483

0   250   500   750   1000 km

FIGURE 6. Women who have accessed ILE services in Mexico City according to state of residence, 2007–20. Heat map created by Eric Seymour.

abundance of anthropological literature tracking global fertility journeys signals the significance of this phenomenon for contemporary anthropological inquiries into globalization, technology, and kinship. Despite this trend in the literature, however, ethnographic accounts of the situations of women forced to relocate, not to conceive a pregnancy, but rather to safely interrupt one that they cannot continue, are remarkably scarce.

A small but growing body of work explores abortion travel in Canada, Australia, and the United States, and more recently, throughout Europe.[14] The literature that does exist shows that women undertake abortion travel to circumvent restrictive abortion laws as well as extralegal obstacles such as prohibitive costs, complex referral and reimbursement procedures, harassment from anti-abortion activists outside clinics, lack of nearby clinics, a dearth of nonobjecting physicians, and fear or shame about being seen at an abortion clinic within one's community.[15] Studies indicate that traveling to access abortion disproportionately burdens low-income women, for whom time off work and other costs of travel can pose serious economic disadvantages. Nevertheless, within anthropological discussions of reproductive mobility a focus on abortion has been marginal; a recent annual review paper on "reproductive tourism" does not mention abortion once.[16]

I see compulsory abortion travel, like forced movement for fertility assistance, as a form of "exile." Indeed, we might classify women like Celeste—those confronted with untenable pregnancies yet without recourse to address them at home—as exiles more readily than their childless counterparts who struggle to become pregnant. These women must resolve their pregnancies independently, sometimes with perilous physical and legal consequences, or else accept obligatory motherhood even when ill prepared to do so. "Abortion exile" captures the forced movement that women must endure to access indispensable reproductive health care, as well as the biopolitical exclusion and state abandonment that its criminalization at home represents. State denial of abortion rights and care forces many women into compulsory maternity, saddling them with social and biological labor against their will. The concept can elucidate the forced movement, political status, and subjective experiences of women in many parts of the world where abortion rights are limited or under threat, and for whom reproductive citizenship remains elusive.

In the end, Celeste was able to interrupt her pregnancy through the ILE program. By 2:00 p.m. she emerged from the recovery room of the clinic, where we spent most of the day together with her Conéctame accompanier. As we walked toward the bus station that afternoon to say goodbye, Celeste told us that she had been anxious when boarding the bus that brought her across state lines and into the heart of the expansive capital. A few hours later, she made the journey in reverse, eventually arriving back home to Querétaro. She had plans to keep pursuing the divorce the last time we spoke, a few months after her abortion. Celeste's experience captures some of the logistical and interpersonal circumstances that freight abortion decisions in contexts where the procedure is geographically restricted. Her anxieties about seeking a criminalized procedure added to her concerns that her husband would use the illegality of abortion against her to put her visa in jeopardy, underlining the gendered dimensions of "exile" as it intersects with citizenship status and criminalized reproductive health care.

A different patient named Clara was seeking her second abortion when I met her at Santa Marta Clinic in the summer of 2014. Although she had been born in the capital, by the time we met she was living in neighboring Mexico State with her parents and attending college to become a veterinarian. At the time she became pregnant Clara had recently removed her hormonal implant because it was causing spontaneous bleeding, she told me, and the pregnancy came as a surprise. Her relationship with her boyfriend was rocky, and his failure to meet her at the ILE clinic that day as he promised left her deeply hurt. Like Celeste, Clara knew of women who had paid for an abortion outside the capital. But as a student in her early twenties, she couldn't afford it. For her, going to an ILE clinic in Mexico City felt like a safer option. "If I seek an abortion in Mexico State, they'll put me in jail," she told me. Her first experience at Santa Marta had been positive. She explained that her mother and cousin had also sought abortions there two years earlier. "A lot of people come here from outside the capital. There are a lot of girls in the waiting room that come from far away," she said. As Clara saw it, abortion was a better alternative to a life of suffering: "I say that it's better that people seek abortion than—think of all of the homeless kids, people suffering from hunger, people who have ten kids . . . it's better like this. As the population grows, we are worse off." Clara made it to the ILE clinic a few days after learning she was pregnant. Her geographic proximity to the capital made for a relatively short trip. But it was too late. Although by her own calculations she was only around 8 weeks pregnant, the clinical ultrasound measured her pregnancy at 12.5 weeks, five days beyond the gestational limit in the ILE program. The last I knew, Clara had plans to seek an abortion through a private clinic in the capital with financial help from her boyfriend. Because she lived in nearby Mexico State, and because she already had experience accessing an ILE procedure, Clara was able to cross into the capital and arrive at Santa Marta with relative ease, even if it was too late by the time she arrived. It is not entirely clear whether Clara would have arrived at the ILE clinic in time had she lived in Mexico City and closer to the clinic, but her story nevertheless draws attention to the ramifying geographic and gestational constraints on abortion that leave many women with few options but to bear a pregnancy to term against their will.

Even as tens of thousands of women have traveled to the capital to obtain ILE care from states where the procedure is forbidden, many more are unable to get there. Conéctame represents a model of abortion accompaniment that works by facilitating mobility between the capital and parts of the country where abortion is legally proscribed. The model thus circumvents restrictive abortion laws in the states without directly breaking them. Below I consider the work of Las Fuertes, an organization that has developed an alternative model of abortion accompaniment that works not by circumventing abortion laws but by openly undermining them in a context of near-total criminalization.

REALIZING ABORTION RIGHTS AT THE MARGINS OF LEGALITY

Las Fuertes en Red, a Mexican human rights organization that has garnered international attention for its abortion advocacy work, sits on a remote bend in the colonial city of San Pedro, Guanajuato. The organization is removed from the city center and the winding *callejones* (alleyways) that draw thousands of international tourists each year. From the outside, the stucco house is indistinguishable from others throughout the city, which is better known in the national imaginary as a stronghold of Catholic conservatism than as a hub of feminist activity. Inside, Maria Hernandez and her younger sister Eugenia spend their days arranging abortions for women across the state. The organization's "Modelo Integral de Acompañamiento para un Aborto Seguro" (holistic model of accompaniment for safe abortion), or MIAAS, includes the provision of emotional and logistical support for inducing abortion at home with misoprostol in contexts of criminalization. The Hernandez sisters carry out this work by collaborating with a network of doctors, psychologists, journalists, and lawyers who provide voluntary assistance on an as-needed basis.

Along with providing misoprostol for free to clients who cannot afford to purchase it over the counter, Las Fuertes offers tailored instruction and emotional support to minimize physical harm and legal risks and to diminish abortion stigma. When I flew to Mexico to meet the siblings in 2016, they estimated that they had already accompanied nearly six thousand women using the MIAAS. "We always say that while abortion is a crime here according to the law, the law was written by those who want it to be criminalized," Maria said, capturing Las Fuertes's driving philosophy. "For us, abortion is the exercise of a human right." Although the group's tactics are controversial, particularly in the conservative environment of Guanajuato, the global nongovernmental organization Human Rights Watch recently honored Maria Hernandez as a "key defender of human rights."

Spending time in the city of San Pedro was an experience quite apart from my time in Mexico City. Five hours north of the capital, Guanajuato sits in the heart of the Bajío, a region governed by the conservative PAN. As part of the "Rosary Belt," the Bajío has long been a bastion of Catholic conservatism.[17] As *la cuna de independenia* (the cradle of the revolutionary war for independence from Spain), the region is infused with nationalistic pride. Activists there have been subjected to extraordinary violence in recent years, making Las Fuertes's work particularly noteworthy. Despite the area's historical significance and its contemporary status as a major center of tourism, the Bajío is considered by many Mexico City residents to be *la provincia*—a term connoting cultural and geographic distance from the capital. Affirming its political divergence from Mexico City, Guanajuato was the tenth state to modify its constitution to redefine life as beginning from the moment of conception in response to the 2007 reform. In Guanajuato abortion is almost entirely criminalized and can carry a prison sentence of up to six years.[18] Maria and Eugenia explained to me some of the less visible consequences of the Mexico City reform, which, according to Maria, "has made our work here more difficult."

Las Fuertes first began to implement the MIAAS locally as early as 2004, three years before abortion became legal in the capital. After the Mexico City reform, the Hernandez sisters had to contend with increased criminal prosecution of women in their state. The rapid tightening of abortion laws across several states in response to the Mexico City reform generated mass confusion. With increasing frequency, hospital workers reported women to the authorities when they suspected them of having illegally induced abortions.[19]

While abortion rights groups across the country have leveraged human rights as a platform for their advocacy work in recent years, Las Fuertes stands out for its unique approach. Most groups use human rights arguments as a lobbying tool to pressure local governments to reform restrictive abortion laws, a strategy that bore fruit in Mexico City. Las Fuertes's approach diverges from that of mainstream feminist organizations in the capital in important ways. The group has mobilized human rights concepts to realize abortion rights rather than waiting for the state to grant them. Like its peer organizations in Mexico City, Las Fuertes's members support abortion legalization in the capital and elsewhere across the country, and they hope to see Mexico's restrictive abortion laws change. Because the group sees abortion as a human right, however, the organization is committed to offering women *immediate* abortion assistance in spite of existing laws that prohibit the procedure.

The perspective of the Hernandez sisters echoes the work of legal anthropologists who argue that the law can serve as a mechanism of social control.[20] Research into "illegalized" populations reveals that in some cases "ignoring the law and its demands . . . [is] experienced as [a form] of political resistance, protest, or struggle for political visibility."[21] This is especially true in contexts where the state is perceived to be an oppressive force, such as Mexico. By mobilizing the human rights strategy to challenge normative legal definitions of abortion, Las Fuertes effectively resists local laws that criminalize women. While the organization's work unfolds outside the legal system, it is not in actuality forbidden in the law.

Guanajuato's penal code does not explicitly prohibit "abortion accompaniment"—a legal loophole that Las Fuertes exploits in the event that its members encounter legal trouble. Abortion accompaniment in Guanajuato thus exists in a legal gray zone. Las Fuertes works to fulfill women's rights at the margins of legality, without technically violating the law. I have come to think of its approach to realizing abortion rights as "alegal."[22] Alegal approaches to abortion require some conceptual explanation. Human rights, inasmuch as they are used to bring national laws in line with global standards, are a quintessentially legal concept. Las Fuertes, however, draws on human rights as a moral idiom with global purchase not primarily to effect legal change but rather to repudiate state control over the procedure. The group's work exists in dialogue with global notions of human rights but ultimately takes place in an alegal sphere.

Las Fuertes's organizational history is one of political resistance. The group formed in August 2000 in response to a political move to undermine the limited abortion rights that were in place in Guanajuato at the time. A month after the presidential elections that toppled the PRI regime, Guanajuato approved a bill penalizing abortion after rape with up to three years' imprisonment.[23] By negating the rape exception, the bill eliminated the one legal circumstance for abortion in place across the country and the only legal exception for abortion in Guanajuato. The new president, Vincente Fox, originally from Guanajuato, had been vocal in his opposition to abortion. Feminist actors and sympathetic allies within the PRD saw the move as a harbinger of things to come. Some suspected that the newly elected president had personally coordinated the measure.

To resist the erosion of abortion rights in Guanajuato, feminist groups mobilized in different parts of the country. Activists congregated outside the PAN offices in Mexico City and before the local congress in Guanajuato, demanding a veto of the bill. As Marta Lamas and Sharon Bissel write about that time, "Opinion leaders—medical doctors, public servants from all parties including the PAN, civic leaders and NGOs—expressed their opposition based on religious freedom, the need to strengthen the separation of church and state, democracy, social justice and the right to decide."[24] The Guanajuato governor surveyed state residents about the bill through an opinion poll. When the poll results ostensibly showed that *Guanajuatenses* did not want to eliminate the bill, GIRE, a Mexico City reproductive rights organization, hired a statistician to evaluate the poll questions and results for bias and manipulation. A careful evaluation of the poll showed the questions to be biased. Eventually, the governor of Guanajuato scrapped the bill.[25]

In the aftermath of these events, Maria Hernandez and a group of Guanajuato residents with different professional backgrounds were galvanized to form a local organization to defend women's rights, and specifically abortion. "Ever since then," Eugenia told me, "struggling for women's rights, and especially sexual and reproductive rights, has been our political banner. We believe that all women should be guaranteed the right to decide. This is what we do every day, struggle to make it a reality." Her sister echoed these sentiments: "Abortion is an issue that has to do with the bodies and therefore the lives of women, with the domination of women. The imposition of maternity exercises control over the life of women, not only biological reproduction but [also] social reproduction." For the Hernandez sisters, social conditions of compulsory motherhood were a means for the state to exploit the unremunerated biological and cultural labor of women. State denial to women of control over their reproductive lives represented for these activists a clear statement of women's inferior status in society. From its inception, Las Fuertes adopted a human rights platform as a framework to conduct its local abortion advocacy work. The group's unique model of accompaniment was central to its mission.

MODELING ABORTION ACCOMPANIMENT

I cannot forget the Guanajuato summer rains. Every afternoon rain came gushing down, forming little pools along the cobblestone *callejones*. At night I used to lie awake listening to it drum the roof of the house where I rented a room that summer in the center of San Pedro. Sandra, a local university student, and her friend José had barely escaped the daily downpour when they arrived at the Las Fuertes office on a weekday afternoon. "We got lost," Sandra announced, breathless from scurrying to escape the storm. "We weren't sure if this was the right place." It was a running joke between Maria and Eugenia that people often got turned around on their way to the Las Fuertes office. "Everyone looks for a clinic, but there is no clinic," Maria said, underlining an important aspect of their accompaniment model, which unfolds outside the medical sphere.

I looked on as Eugenia began the accompaniment process with Sandra, who had discovered that she was pregnant a week earlier after taking a blood test when she missed her period. "It looks like you are about seven weeks along," Eugenia said from her seat on one of the sofas in the living room of the house, which doubled as a reception area for clients. Eugenia had used a chart to calculate the gestational age of Sandra's pregnancy by counting backwards from the first day of her last menstrual cycle. "Your pregnancy is early enough that you can induce it with medication at home with no issue. If for some reason it doesn't work, we'll have to try again. But there shouldn't be a problem," she continued.

Sandra told us that the pregnancy was unplanned. She had recently split up with her boyfriend, the man involved, and she didn't have the economic means or desire to become a parent at this point in her life. She wanted to finish college before thinking about having a family. She seemed overwhelmed by the idea of bearing the pregnancy to term. "And the only reason I ask about your circumstances," Eugenia interjected, "is that you are the one that will carry out the procedure, but we need a bit of information to know if there might be any issues afterwards that we should be prepared for. At the end of the day this process happens in your body. We at Las Fuertes are convinced that abortion is a valid option. But we need to know, when we are accompanying someone, which resources we might need on hand in case of any subsequent emotional issues, so that the person, in this case you, is calm and confident in her choice."

Eugenia walked Sandra through the process of inducing a medical abortion in the MIAAS model, which the sisters call the "4 x 4 x 4 method." She explained that the misoprostol pills could be administered sublingually (under the tongue), bucally (between the gum and cheek), or vaginally (placed manually near the cervix). For the first dose, a woman would take four 200 mg misoprostol pills through either of the three administration pathways. She would wait four hours, during which cramps and other side effects including nausea, dizziness, diarrhea, and vomiting usually begin. If bleeding occurred, it meant the abortion was under way. If there was no bleeding after four hours, the woman would take another dose of four 200 mg pills in the same pathway she used the first time. The process could be repeated up to three times—hence the 4 x 4 x 4 method—until all twelve pills were used. Two weeks after the abortion all clients visited the organization's volunteer gynecologist for a sonogram scan to ensure that no embryonic tissue remained in the uterus. She emphasized that there had been very few complications among their clients. Eugenia assured Sandra that she would be available by phone throughout the entire process, at any time of day or night, in case she had questions or doubts. "We want you to feel accompanied and safe, that nothing bad is going to happen and that what you are doing is exercising your right and the decision you made," Eugenia affirmed, handing Sandra a packet of misoprostol pills.

Las Fuertes provided women with abortifacient pills at no cost. Since the group operated on a limited and fluctuating budget, however, this could be challenging. "There is a brutal load [of stigma] in terms of clandestine abortion," Maria told me. "Typically, clandestine abortion is very expensive if you hire a doctor. So we have found that when it's free it diminishes women's anxiety a lot." At the time of my research, a packet of misoprostol containing twenty-eight pills cost roughly $100 USD. For some women an abortion was induced with just four pills, but for others it could take as many as twelve pills. To preserve the organization's limited funds, Las Fuertes asked women to return any unused pills so they could be passed on to future clients.

Along with review of potential medical risks and warning signs to watch for, an essential component of the MIAAS involved educating women on how to proceed in the rare event of a medical emergency so that they could seek help while avoiding legal repercussions. "If a [hemorrhage] occurs," Maria explained, "we always tell the women, don't even stop and think, just go to a hospital or another clinic near you. If for any reason you end up at a public hospital, even if you inserted the misoprostol vaginally and [the doctor] removes the pills from your vagina and holds them in front of you, you must say, 'I don't know, I don't know, I didn't do it.'" Las Fuertes's model relies on the ambiguities of misoprostol—what Silvia De Zordo calls the drug's "double life."[26] Often sold under the generic name Cytotec, misoprostol is officially indicated for treatment of gastric ulcers but is widely used off-label in gynecological care.[27] The drug works to stimulate labor, manage post-partum bleeding, produce contractions to clean out the uterus after miscarriage, and to induce medical abortions.[28] In contexts of restrictive abortion law, the drug offers a convenient way for women to induce abortions while evading legal trouble. For the Hernandez sisters, the legal and medical opacity embedded in the materiality of the drug itself was central to their approach to abortion accompaniment. "As long as you do not incriminate yourself," Maria said, "there is no way [for the authorities to prove that you took the drug to induce an abortion and prosecute you]. The doctors can't say that you took the pills with the intention of aborting. Everyone knows that that's what the pills are for, but there's no way to prove it."

By the time Eugenia finished explaining the process to Sandra the rain had stopped and the clouds had cleared. Brightly colored houses studded the hills in every direction, a palette of purple, magenta, yellow, and red. Sandra and José thanked us and left the office by foot, winding their way up a steep bend and out onto the main street. I wondered if I would run into them again, in town or on the university steps where young people sometimes congregated on cool evenings. Before long, Sandra and José were two faint dots on the horizon, their secret lost to the *callejones* that cut like veins throughout the city.

The path they took that day was the same one I walked each morning to arrive at the office. The scenes were unimaginably beautiful. Every direction I turned was like a travel brochure: rolling hills, cacti, colorful homes. But uglier realities lurked behind all that beauty. The corpses of two young women had been found in the hills near the Las Fuertes office that summer. One had been badly burned before being discarded among the cacti and low shrubs. The Hernandez sisters kept careful track of these murders and were sometimes called upon to help families solve them as another aspect of their work. Rates of femicide in Guanajuato are among the highest in the country. I wasn't prepared for this reality when I made plans to spend the summer of 2016 there, and I found myself overcome with paranoia. The Hernandez sisters had said I could move into one of the rooms on the second floor of their office, but I was too scared to sleep there alone. I thought I would feel better staying in the guesthouse behind a family home closer to the center of town, but there were only a couple other guests that summer. Once they left, the mother of the household invited me to sleep in a spare room inside the main house. She said she felt more comfortable with me inside. Though in another context I might have felt stifled by her concern, I was grateful for her protectiveness. Yet even the proximity of her and her husband did not diminish my fear. Even when the temperatures soared above ninety degrees, I slept with the window closed every night.

Accompaniment, in this context, had a particular significance. It was about providing social support and connection in the face of uncertainty. When it came to abortion, accompaniment was a means to information on how to induce an abortion, but also, and perhaps more importantly, a means for women to avoid physical and legal danger. For the Hernandez sisters, abortion accompaniment works on three different levels. The MIAAS is grounded in three mutually reinforcing dimensions that operate across different scales to "socially decriminalize" abortion: the emotional-affective, the communicational-relational, and the sociopolitical. The first component entails the provision of in-person support to address potential emotional concerns or misgivings among women seeking to interrupt their pregnancies. Clients experiencing internal conflict, guilt, or shame have the opportunity to work with Las Fuertes's volunteer psychologist to reconcile these issues or take more time to reflect on whether they want to proceed with an abortion. It is critical, the Hernandez sisters told me, that the accompanier believe firmly that women have a right to make decisions about their own bodies so she can convey this understanding to women seeking abortion.

The communicational-relational dimension is achieved through the establishment of informational networks on safe self-managed abortion with misoprostol. Las Fuertes disseminates information through an organizational Facebook page and website, public speaking events, media interviews for which its members are regularly solicited, and above all, word of mouth beginning with the women they accompanied. Women who undergo abortion accompaniment in the MIAAS have the option to serve as accompaniers themselves afterward. Drawing on their own experience, accompaniers are able to empower their peers to feel assured in the abortion process. Information on how to safely induce abortion with misoprostol is therefore diffused through social networks that expand as more women undergo the accompaniment process, communicate their experience, and guide others to do the same.

Finally, the sociopolitical component reflects Las Fuertes's view that undergoing abortion accompaniment in and of itself is a transformative process with the power to reconfigure women's sense of themselves as political subjects entitled to abortion rights. Las Fuertes's members described their work as fostering individual and collective processes of "citizenship," whereby women come to internalize and claim abortion as their right. In the context of Guanajuato, the group's work counters the social and legal definition of abortion as a crime, a religious offense, and an abnegation of women's divine obligation to privilege reproduction over other life projects.

Maria and Eugenia detailed some of the transformations they had observed in San Pedro since they founded the organization sixteen years earlier. Whereas early on most clients had arrived at their office alone, in more recent years most women were accompanied by a friend, family member, or partner. For Las Fuertes, this was evidence of a slow but steady process of "social decriminalization" of abortion, as women were more inclined to share their abortion decisions and seek social support. The sisters had also noticed that over time women arrived for abortion services earlier in their pregnancies, at six weeks versus later in the first trimester—evidence for Maria and Eugenia that the informational networks they nurtured had stretched across the city. Over the years the scope of Las Fuertes's work had extended beyond state and, in some cases, national borders. I once attended an event in Mexico City where Maria had been invited to train a group of women in the MIAAS so they might replicate the model in the capital as a more accessible alternative to the ILE program. On the last day of my research in Guanajuato that summer, Eugenia was conducting an abortion accompaniment over the phone with a young woman in Colombia who had found Las Fuertes's Facebook page online.

REPUDIATING STATE CONTROL OVER REPRODUCTION

As the human rights strategy has gained traction in Mexico, abortion advocacy organizations across the country have adopted the framework as a platform in their work, calling on local and national leaders to reform restrictive abortion laws to protect women's human rights. For social psychologist Camila Gianella, this kind of "legal mobilization" is a strategy of abortion activism "that [uses] rights and the law as central tools for advancing a contested political goal."[29] In recent decades, legal mobilization has been an important strategy in the struggle for abortion rights across Latin America, where "the promotion of the rule of law was perceived as a necessary step toward democratization" in a region long marked by undemocratic governance.[30] Legal mobilization can take different forms, unfolding at the grassroots level, in courtrooms, and even outside the machineries of the state.

It was not until I met the Hernandez sisters that I understood some of the differences in *how* activists conduct "legal mobilization" in abortion advocacy work. The pair distinguish their organization's approach from that of mainstream feminist organizations in the Mexican capital. Departing from legalistic styles of abortion advocacy that position the state as the guarantor of reproductive rights and the law as the arbiter of moral life, Las Fuertes dismisses the legal system, which its members describe as working against women. Unlike the advocacy groups in Mexico City that urged the Mexican government to enforce existing legal exceptions for abortion, expand the circumstances under which the procedure was exempt from punishment, and decriminalize of the procedure altogether, Las Fuertes draws on human rights concepts to openly flout punishing abortion laws in Guanajuato as an act of political resistance. Divergences in these styles of legal mobilization reflect divisions that cleaved the Mexican feminist movement in the 1990s, as "radical" and "state" feminists advanced distinct visions for achieving gender equality by condemning versus engaging the political apparatus, respectively.

One afternoon later that summer, Eugenia and I chatted as we waited for clients to arrive at the office. I asked her to clarify what she saw as the central differences between her organization's approach and that of abortion advocacy groups in the capital, whose approach she and her sister often critiqued. "Of course, we celebrate that abortion has been legalized there," she said. "But if we could critique one thing, it would be that [those activists] never thought about the negative political effects that the reform would have here in the states, which we have to contend with. To think that legalizing abortion in Mexico City would be a magic wand so that the whole country would work as we want it to was delusional on their part, and a little irresponsible." Eugenia was referencing the cascade of constitutional amendments that swept across the country in the aftermath of the 2007 reform. In 2009, Guanajuato became the tenth state to amend its constitution to protect life from conception, in addition to Quintana Roo, Baja California, Sonora, Morelos, Jalisco, Puebla, Colima, Durango, and Nayarit.

Las Fuertes's grievances were not restricted to the legislative repercussions that followed the abortion reform. The Hernandez sisters also bemoaned what they perceived to be an unfair concentration of resources and power among feminist organizations in Mexico City as compared to those working elsewhere across the country. "Because abortion is now legal in Mexico City," Eugenia said, "and because that is where all the big, international organizations are located, all the abortion funding is channeled there, and we don't have a right to resources. Meanwhile, we are the ones carrying out the local work, we are the ones directly serving women while the organizations in Mexico City negotiate with politicians about Guanajuato's abortion laws."

Unlike abortion advocacy organizations in Mexico City, which were connected to international flows of capital, including private monies from major international donors, Las Fuertes operates almost entirely on grant money, honoraria, donations, and above all, volunteer work. The money is insufficient to hire a steady team of salaried staff. The professionalization, or "NGO-ization," of feminist activism throughout the 1990s established hierarchies of funding and other forms of capital from which Las Fuertes has been largely excluded.[31] Even though financial shortages are an impediment to Las Fuertes's work, the Hernandez sisters acknowledged that their economic situation also affords them a degree of autonomy that is beneficial. The Mexico City organizations are bound by the conditions of their private donors, including abiding by state law, terms that considerably hamper their work in Las Fuertes's view. "Don't put conditions on me," Maria once said, as if in response to a private donor. "[Feminists in the capital] are going to keep administering the problem in order to have private funding and political power. When I started this work, I told them that we operate in two separate worlds. Here at Las Fuertes, we want to *resolve* the problem. That is different from *managing* the problem in order to continue surviving off the issue."

For Maria and her colleagues there was a difference between negotiating for incremental legal reform and "resolving the problem" by offering abortion care in spite of the law. By accusing other organizations of failing to resolve the issue of limited abortion access, Maria questioned the ethics of prioritizing fundraising and organizational survival above helping women to exercise their rights. Las Fuertes's members are well acquainted with many of the feminists who make up the abortion advocacy community in the capital, with whom they have attended a range of interorganizational meetings and events in the previous sixteen years. "Sitting through these meetings is extremely frustrating," Maria told me. "I have to listen to them fighting for *causales* [legal exceptions for abortion]." She was confounded by the narrow focus on legal change, when Mexican law, as she sees it, has always worked against women. "Those feminists feel criminalized. They fear they will get put in jail," she stressed. "How can you empower women when you are playing into the fears generated by the state?"

Las Fuertes's critiques of feminist groups in the capital must be read through the lens of entrenched historical and economic chasms between Mexico City and the rest of the country, which have led to persistent anti–Mexico City sentiments. Today this rift is largely related to the centralization of power and resources in the capital at the expense of other regions of the country. But these divisions can be traced to the anticlerical character of the Revolution. At the time, Mexico City was associated with Mexico's new revolutionary citizenry, which was linked first to the official party of the Revolution (today the PRI), and in more recent decades to the PRD. By contrast, Guanajuato, and the Bajío more broadly, have long been a cradle of antirevolutionary Catholic conservatism. The animus with which Las Fuertes discussed feminist groups in the capital despite their shared convictions reflects these deep-seated schisms, economic disparities, and political resentments that have been etched into the political geography of the country.

Despite Las Fuertes's disavowal of state authority over reproduction, the Hernandez sisters are not naive about the potential risks of their approach. Nor do they advocate a wholesale dismissal of the law. The group keeps a team of volunteer lawyers on staff to defend their clients in the event that they encounter legal trouble. "We have experience and a support structure in place and a critical route that must be followed in the case that a woman is criminalized," Eugenia explained. "But this is part of our work—first believing that abortion is the exercise of a right and then transmitting that understanding to women. We are not telling them that they should violate all laws, but we believe that the crime of abortion should not be a crime, and we try to modify that understanding among the women who live here." Both Maria and Eugenia emphasized that they seek to minimize discussions of the potential for criminalization in their conversations with clients so as to communicate their belief that abortion is a universal right of women. When I asked about the risks of their work in terms of their own legal safety, they articulated the following position. "Many people tell us we have to take security measures, but we don't want to spend our energies on that," Eugenia told me. "Maria and I trust what we are doing is right. We have talked a lot about not being afraid because if we're afraid, it's better we do nothing. It is impossible to work with fear."

When spending time with the Hernandez sisters, I sometimes wondered why they had not developed a model of accompaniment that facilitated travel to the capital, like Conéctame. Maria seemed offended by the question. "The women who come to us do not need to go to Mexico City because we are resolving the problem *here*," she asserted. "We know what women's needs are. We know how to accompany them for abortions. It would be so sad if we just threw our hands up and said, 'Our work here is done. All women should go get abortions in the capital.'" The existence of the organization, I eventually came to understand, disproved the notion that abortion advocacy work could not be conducted outside the capital. For the Hernandez sisters, sending women to

Mexico City would entail yielding to the legal system and validating the notion that abortion was a criminal act—concessions that belied their convictions.

Today, many women in and beyond Guanajuato have the opportunity to interrupt their pregnancies safely in spite of local laws that criminalize the procedure. By openly defying restrictive abortion laws to defend women's human rights, Las Fuertes has conducted a symbolic intervention into dominant constructions of abortion as a legal and moral transgression. The group has been able to avoid legal repercussions for their work, which the Hernandez sisters attribute to the fact that they have built up enough of a national reputation that local politicians and law enforcement leave them alone. Although Guanajuato's penal code continues to prohibit abortion in all but a few extreme circumstances, Las Fuertes offers a practical means for women to access abortion at the margins of the law.

As human rights concepts have gained traction across Mexico, the approaches of abortion rights advocates in different regions of the country suggest that activists do not engage the framework uniformly to resist the forces of Mexican reproductive governance. While some groups leverage human rights concepts in the pursuit of legal reform, others seize the rights framework to prioritize the immediate expansion of abortion access even when it subverts the law.

ABORTION AT THE LIMIT OF RIGHTS

As we have seen, Mexico's unequal legal landscape has pushed many women across state lines in the pursuit of abortion care, paradoxically driving them both toward and away from Mexico City. Yet many women arrive at an abortion clinic too late and are left to resolve their pregnancies on their own or else carry an untenable pregnancy to term. Though bureaucratic limits prevented me from systematically exploring the experiences of women turned away from the ILE program because their pregnancies exceeded gestational limits, the glimpses I could access suggest that very few options are available to them.

If the notion of limits, as I have used it here, illuminates the experiences of women for whom abortion rights go unrealized, it also offers a window onto the work of prochoice doctors and activists who have dedicated themselves to pushing back against legal, moral, and geographic boundaries to expand abortion access. Indeed, the picture of extralegal abortion offered here unsettles

popular and scholarly assumptions that equate illegal abortion with dangerous conditions and disempowering outcomes, revealing instead how it can be
a thoughtful site of political resistance. With the help of sympathetic physicians and feminist accompaniment networks, some women today are able to
circumvent Mexico's punitive laws. Regrettably, many more are less fortunate.
For these women, the stakes of abortion criminalization could not be higher.

CONCLUSION

IF THE EXTENSION OF ABORTION RIGHTS in the Mexican capital has afforded more agency and choice to women in their reproductive lives, it has also expanded processes of reproductive governance whereby the state, and other actors, work to regulate women's bodies. This paradox—that abortion rights promise emancipation from the same systems of power from which they stem—is one that I have grappled with throughout this project. Political theorist Wendy Brown has observed that "although rights may attenuate the subordination and violation to which women are vulnerable in a masculinist social, political, and economic regime, they vanquish neither the regime nor its mechanism of reproduction."[1] Rights, in other words, insofar as they are channeled through inequitable legal and state systems, can soften injustice in reproductive and other realms, but they cannot eradicate it. By virtue of their collusion with the political apparatus, rights inevitably extend the regulatory capacity of the state.

On September 7, 2021, while I was finalizing the copyedits on these pages, the Mexican Supreme Court determined in a momentous decision that criminal penalties for abortion are unconstitutional. The ruling responded to a case brought before the court from the northern state of Coahuila, where abortion had been punishable with three years' jail time. Prior to the determination, voluntary abortion had been allowed in just four of Mexico's thirty-two federal entities, Mexico City, Oaxaca, Hidalgo, and Veracruz. The decree establishes a significant precedent that will undoubtedly transform the national and regional panorama of abortion law in the coming years. However, there is still work to be done. Activists will need to challenge abortion laws at the state level for the ruling to apply outside Coahuila. In other words, while there is cause for celebration, and the future of Mexican reproductive governance appears bright, the struggle for abortion justice in Mexico and across North America is far from over.

As we have seen in these pages, abortion legalization does not guarantee its access. Even in Mexico City, the first state to legalize voluntary abortion and inaugurate new institutional spaces for public abortion care, access to the procedure remains limited and fraught. Many women are unable to meet the bureaucratic and temporal demands of the public ILE clinics. Those who can must then confront an intractable health bureaucracy marked by resource scarcity and overwhelming demand in which abortion rights are tethered to corresponding obligations and responsibilities. If abortion legalization in Mexico City is more troubled than prevailing advocacy narratives admit, this right still remains heavily circumscribed outside the capital, and in some places access to the procedure has become more encumbered since passage of the Mexico City reform.

When I embarked on this international project, I never would have guessed that by its completion abortion rights would be more fragile than ever in my home country. Not a week before the historic Mexican Supreme Court ruling, the United States Supreme Court clamped down on abortion rights by condoning passage of the most extreme antiabortion law in the country. The bill, passed in Texas, bans abortion after six weeks of gestation, so early in pregnancy that many women are unaware they are pregnant. The architects of the carefully crafted bill took pains to work around the constitutional protection of abortion established with *Roe vs. Wade* by endowing individual citizens with the authority to sue those who assist a woman in obtaining an abortion, including clinicians, clinic escorts, drivers, and so on. The following week, international media outlets drew attention to the fact that women in Texas may soon have an easier time accessing an abortion south of the border in Coahuila. The right to abortion in the US is more precarious today than at any other point in my lifetime.

There has been a certain discomfort while finishing this book in knowing that any academic critique I advance about abortion rights, in Mexico and in general, must be weighed against the fact that I have never known a world in which I did not hold that right. I have had to reckon—now more than ever—with a nagging concern that I might be taking abortion rights for granted, even if only on the abstract level of theoretical critique. As *Roe v. Wade* hangs in the balance, it seems there is no theoretical remove, no space or time for academic conjecture. To question abortion rights at this moment can feel particularly inappropriate, or, in the words of Wendy Brown and Janet Halley, "impractical, merely critical, unattuned to the political exigencies at hand, intellectually indulgent, easier than fixing things or saying what is to be done—in short, either ultraleftist or ultratheoretical but in either case without purchase on or in the Real World."[2] Yet critique, I've resolved, may also offer a path ahead, a way through the impasse.

If at the start of this project I didn't expect that *Roe v. Wade* would one day be in peril, there is also no way I could have known that by the time this project drew to a close I would be living in a US state with "the most pro-life governor."[3] Teaching reproductive politics in Oklahoma has made it impossible to ignore the pitfalls of legalistic approaches to reproductive equity, as abortion rights here are constantly under attack. On my way to class these days I sometimes pass campus protesters waving the same grisly fetal images that I remember from my time as an abortion counselor at Hope Clinic in Granite City, Illinois.

Recently, I visited that clinic while driving east from Oklahoma. Part of me wanted visual proof that the clinic had not capitulated to legislative and regulatory assaults like so many other abortion clinics across the country in recent years. Another part of me, I realized only as I turned off the highway and back into that forlorn industrial city, didn't know how to say goodbye to this project without returning. It was there on the eastern banks of the Mississippi River, after all, that the seeds of this international work had first taken hold. Rolling past the old steel factory, a tangle of metal pipes suspended in the air like a postmodern sculpture, unleashed a rush of dispersed memories.

I recalled the stories that the director of counseling had once told me about firebombs and kidnappings at the clinic in the early seventies, and the wall of picketers that continued to assemble daily outside by the time I arrived nearly forty years later; how different the protesters who prayed peacefully at Santa Marta Clinic had seemed by comparison; all of those afternoons in the Santa Marta counseling office; and Mexico City, incomprehensible in its vast scale, its energy and verve. I thought, too, of the ten years that had elapsed since I first traveled that route through Granite City. How this project had taken me so far from home, and how different my life had become. After a few smoky miles, there it was: a cement fortress in an otherwise empty lot. I could make out some movement through the tinted windows, hazy shapes that danced from left to right, yet most of the staff I knew from my graduate school days had left in the intervening years.

While Hope Clinic is still standing, the lessons I learned in Mexico are remarkably pertinent at home today. Even before the Texas abortion ban was implemented in September 2021, the United States Supreme Court had been preparing to hear a case that directly challenges *Roe v. Wade*.[4] If the court strikes down *Roe,* adjudication of abortion law will return to the states for the first time in nearly half a century. Analysts predict that in such a scenario at least twenty states would immediately ban abortion, leaving access to the procedure badly splintered. According to one recent analysis, the repeal of *Roe* would force nearly half of US women to travel as many as 279 miles to access the nearest abortion clinic, whereas they currently must travel 35 miles.[5] The preceding pages about Mexican abortion capture a picture of such a scenario. The experiences of women like Celeste and Clara, who traveled several hours to reach the Mexican capital in search of legal and safe abortion care, with mixed success, are powerful auguries of the legal situation that might await us in a post-*Roe* United States.

After all of this research and reflection, I remain convinced that abortion should be a legal option for women, *a right* of women. But today I am more ambivalent about the political potential of abortion rights in guaranteeing reproductive equity. At its core, my ethnographic material emphasizes the shortcomings of a feminist vision focused narrowly on securing legal options for fertility limitation. In Mexico, as elsewhere around the world, it is women who bear the moral and practical responsibility of a state that has failed to provide them with the conditions to keep all of their desired pregnancies and to care for their children in circumstances of dignity. Without options for formal employment, affordable child care, and freedom from everyday violence, the implementation of abortion rights cannot resolve the struggles that women face. What is urgently needed is a reproductive justice framework that fuses the push for safe and accessible abortion with social and institutional supports that facilitate reproduction and parenting among women who desire to sustain their pregnancies to term.

At this anxious moment global calls for reproductive justice are more urgent than ever. As feminists have long argued, abortion will remain among the reproductive options that women around the world pursue, regardless of legal or religious prohibitions. The lessons in this book about the limits of the rights framework can be of value at this critical juncture. While reproductive rights have the potential to expand opportunities for choice, channeling political aspirations toward the legal realm can delimit the reach and scope of struggles for reproductive justice, reinstating what Wendy Brown and Janet Halley have called "normativizing deployments of state power."[6] The Mexican abortion accompaniment organizations that we learned about here have long had to contend with a landscape of uneven abortion legality. Groups like Conéctame and Las Fuertes present a powerful alternative to legalism in the quest for reproductive justice. By circumventing legal restrictions on abortion through facilitating the arrival of women to the capital, and by openly defying abortion laws through provision of the procedure in a context of criminalization, respectively, these organizations have worked to challenge regimes of Mexican reproductive governance. The methods of these groups, whose work unfolds at the interstices of Mexican abortion law, suggest that reproductive freedom does not, ultimately, depend on authorization by the state. This point, it seems, holds relevance for us all.

CODA

COMING TO THE END of this project on reproduction, which has put my own desires for a family on hold for so long, has made me think harder about generational time and the sacrifices that the women in my family have made, wittingly or not, to structure the possibilities of my life. I recently had a phone call with my ninety-year-old maternal grandmother. She told me that she was proud of me for getting the book done and then mused about the paradoxes of life and time, of children growing up. As a child I used to feel annoyed when my grandmother told me endlessly that I needed to learn how to type, that it was a skill that would secure my future. My mother explained to me years later that secretarial work was one of the only remunerated jobs that would become available to my grandmother in her life, despite her extraordinary artistic talents. Typing, for her, was a means to some limited measure of economic independence, something she needed desperately when she found herself alone without formal work and with three children by the time she was my age. Her insistence, I can see now, was an act of care. And I suppose on some level my grandmother was right.

My mother read this book as I typed the final edits. She took issue with one portion of the Introduction, the part about the argument on fetal personhood that we had during my college years. She insisted I had gotten the story wrong. She was never concerned about whether the fetuses she gestated constituted "life" in some abstract sense; during her pregnancies these academic and political questions were beside the point. For her *what grew within her was human*, even if she did support a woman's right to abortion. As she uttered those words, I thought of what Teresa had told me seven years earlier during one of the first interviews I conducted for this book at Santa Marta Clinic. I have no way of knowing how Teresa is now, though her son must have recently turned twelve. Anthropologists have imperfect ways of accounting for the time lapses that transpire as we write up our findings, but my mother reminded me with that comment of how long this project has been with me in some form or another.

By the time my mother and I initiated that old debate, she had already lost a fallopian tube to an ectopic pregnancy and learned that she might never conceive again. She had nonetheless gone on to deliver two healthy babies and terminate a fourth pregnancy after coming to the painful recognition, together with my father, that raising three children was at odds with her budding career and their economic means. She and my father had seen two children through infancy, childhood, adolescence, and young adulthood, first as a married couple and later apart. And, as my mother neared her fifth decade, she had experienced new burdens at the other end of the reproductive cycle in caring for her own aging mother. Though I couldn't have fully understood what it entailed at the time, my mother had also conducted doctoral research on reproductive illness. I know now that by that point she had read much of the same literature that my college professors were assigning me.

After years of thinking about reproduction, now as a woman academic working to reconcile the different schedules to which I am subject, I have new perspective on the experience my mother brought to that debate. I also have a different sense, after all this work, of what she meant when she critiqued feminist perspectives on fetal personhood, how they flattened out her own moral experience of pregnancy and the affective attachments she had to her fetuses, even the one she opted to part with. The research for this book, ultimately, has led me to appreciate what she was gesturing to all those years ago.

Somewhere in between raising my brother and me and working full-time, my mother made the hard decision to abandon her doctoral dissertation. I like to think of this book, in a way, as the culmination of the project she set down for my sake roughly thirty years ago. This project, and the different phases of life it has seen me through, have led me to grasp the chronic nature of reproduction, a capaciousness that exceeds any one reproductive event, like abortion or birth. Ultimately, these pages about pregnancy interruption capture a mere moment in an ongoing cycle.

I wonder whether, if I have a child one day, I will insist that she learn to type.

ACKNOWLEDGMENTS

If one is lucky, as I have been, writing a book is a collective process. This book is the result of years of support from my moral and intellectual community. The research for this study was made possible by the Mexico City Ministry of Health, and in particular its former director of reproductive health. I benefited enormously from the generosity of several health workers within the ILE program who opened their workplace to me and answered my questions with patience and good humor. I am also grateful to feminist activists in and outside Mexico City, whose work is inspiring beyond measure. My deepest appreciation, however, goes to the women who form the core of my research sample, who revealed intimate dimensions of their reproductive lives so I could write this book. I hope that my account fairly represents your stories. Vanessa Cravioto was an amazing research assistant during formative stages of the research process. To my friends in Mexico City, Mario Viveros Barragán y Luciana Bandoli (y las nenas), Enrique Alejandro Furlani, Dayvid Ruben Garces Villalobos, Emma Bolos, Jose María Ibarro Castro (Chema), Emir Olivares, Juan Espindola Mata, Lorena Ibarro Castro, Juan Carlos Narváez Guttiérez (Juanis), and Efrén Ordóñez Garza, you have given me a home away from home. It was in Lina Rosa Berrio's anthropology seminar at el Ciesas that I began some of the early writing on this project.

Mentors and friends at a variety of institutions have offered invaluable help and inspiration for this project. Lynn M. Morgan and Elizabeth F. S. Roberts—the architects of "reproductive governance"—are a formidable intellectual force. I am grateful for Lynn's brilliant feedback at every stage, and for her encouragement to get the book done. I thank Liz for consistently and productively pushing my ideas in unexpected directions. For reading and commenting on pieces of this manuscript in various forms, thanks to Bayla Ostrach, Carole Browner, Ana Amuchástegui, Joanna Mishtal, Mounia El Kotni, Lydia Zacher-Dixon, Adrienne Strong, Mara Buchbinder, Iván Sandoval-Cervantes, Elise Andaya, and Joanna Mishtal. I first became interested in anthropology, the body, and reproduction as an undergraduate at Bard College, where a few inspiring professors made these topics exciting. Megan Callaghan continues to inspire me as much as she did when I took my first anthropology class with her so many years ago.

A range of institutions has supported this project, enabling me to continue at various stages. The research and writing were made possible by funding from a National Science Foundation Graduate Research Fellowship, a grant from the Wenner-Gren Foundation for Anthropological Research, and a fellowship from the American Association for University Women, as well as smaller grants from Washington University in St. Louis and the University of Oklahoma. A manuscript development workshop hosted by the OU Humanities Forum, directed first by Janet Ward and now by Kimberly Marshall, provided a venue for feedback at a critical moment. Thank you to Elizabeth Roberts, Megan Crowley-Matoka, Misha Klein, and Lucas Bessire for reading an earlier draft of this manuscript in the workshop and for pushing me to think harder about its stakes. Writing can be isolating at times. A virtual Abortion Writing Group made my process less lonely and more inspiring. Thank you to Siri Suh, Jessica Newman, Julia McReynolds-Pérez, and Seda Saluk.

At Washington University in St. Louis, I am grateful for Rebecca Lester's thoughtful engagement with this project from early on, and for her reassurance and compassion when my confidence faltered. Deep thanks go to Kedron Thomas for her intelligent engagement with this project from beginning to end. Other faculty at Washington University made my time there stimulating and memorable: Peter Benson, Ignacio Sanchez-Prado, Carolyn Sargent, Shanti Parikh, Linda Nicholson, Mary Ann Dzuback, Talia Dan-Cohen, Aria Nakissa, Priscilla Song, and John Bowen. My graduate student cohort in cultural anthropology offered companionship, solidarity, and impressive academic standards to live up to: Jenny Heipp, Andrea Bolivar, Adrienne Strong, Andrew Flachs, Colleen Walsh Lang, and Chaoxiong Zhang. Other friends in St. Louis also sustained over the years of graduate school: Nikhil Kothegal, Arielle

Wright, Daniella Farah, Jarot Guerra, Sherria Ayuandini, Livia Stone, Katie Rynkiewich, Ali Heller, Jacob Labendz, Anita Charry, and Chelsey Carter. Amanda Scott, thanks for much laughter from the first moments of graduate school to today. Susanna Williams and Eric Perley (and Arthur and Theo) made my last year of graduate school unforgettable and have continued to be the best of friends.

A Postdoctoral Fellowship at the Population and Studies Training Center at Brown University provided the essential time and space to mold this book. At Brown, special thanks go to Jessaca Leinaweaver, Daniel Jordan Smith, Isaac Mbiti, Matthew Gutmann, Susan Short, Almita Miranda, Whitney Arey, Eric Seymour (who made the heat map in chapter 5), and members of the PSTC Postdoctoral Writing Group.

At the University of Oklahoma I have found a circle of friends and interlocuters for whom I am very grateful. My colleagues in the Anthropology Department and in the Department of Women's and Gender Studies have made this a great place to be. Thanks, in particular, to Asa Randall, the chair of anthropology, for guiding me on innumerable questions of navigating life as a junior faculty member. Thanks also go to Misty Wilson for helping me on a daily basis as a faculty member. Lucas Bessire has pushed me to abandon the disciplinary conventions that imprisoned my writing and thinking on this project. So many other people at OU have made life in Norman bright, but a few deserve special thanks here: Tess Catalano, Ronnie Grinberg, Courtney Hoffman, Jennifer Holland, Erin Duncan-O'Neil, Marc Levine, Adam Malka, and Traci Brynne Voyles. Matt Pailes and Amy Clark (and Inez and Julius) have been family to me. Sarah Hines (and Maia and Nina) also fall into the family category; thank you for being there.

At Stanford University Press thank you to Michelle Lipinski for seeing potential in this project before it was a book, and to Margo Irvin for seamlessly guiding it through production. At the press, I am grateful as well for assistance from Cindy Lim and Emily Smith. Finally, thank you to Emily Wentzell and two anonymous reviewers for your helpful feedback on different stages of this manuscript.

Friends and family in far-off places have offered fellowship and laughter over the years. I am lucky to call Madeline Gottlieb, Katy Nally, Caitlin Steckler,

Bronwyn Cunningham, and Kimberly Moynihan my oldest friends. Maddie, in particular, is one of the most cherished and constant sources of emotional support in my life. Thank you to Pam Erickson for taking such good care of my dad. My brother Jake Singer, and his partner, Susan Blasi, always encourage me. Thanks to you all for prying me away from the screen now and again, and for reminding me of what really matters.

It is my parents who deserve my deepest thanks. My father has inspired this project in too many ways to count. I hope to make him as proud of me as I am of him. My mom, who makes appearances in these pages, provided immeasurable emotional and editorial support, particularly in the final stages of the writing. Mom, Dad, I wrote this book for you.

APPENDIX

Formal Interviews with ILE Patients

Pseudonym	Gestational age	Procedure	Age	Residence	Children	Education	Occupation	Marital status	Religion	Reason for abortion
Margarita	10.3	Medical	23	Mexico State	1	Elementary school	Store clerk	Single	Catholic	Economic reasons
Mariana	5.6	Medical	32	Mexico City	0	In college	Student	Partnered	Atheist	Life project, college
Luz	5.5	Medical	35	Mexico City	3	Middle school	Factory	Partnered	Catholic	Unstable relationship, economic reasons
Lucinda	10.2	Medical	26	Mexico City	0	College	Company	Partnered	Catholic	Life project
Emma	6	Medical	32	Mexico State	2	in college	NA	Partnered	Catholic	Already has two children
Yasmin	11	Aspiration	27	Mexico City	3	Elementary school	Home	Partnered	Catholic	Economic reasons
Gaby	8.5	Medical	22	Mexico State	0	In college	Student	Partnered	None	Life project
Karen	5.3	Medical	23	Mexico City	0	Middle school	Family Store	Single	Catholic	Relationship status
Yesenia	7.5	Medical	29	Mexico City	1	Middle school	NA	Single	Catholic	Relationship Status
Ines	7.2	Medical	32	Mexico City	3	Elementary school	Informal economy	Single	Catholic	Economic reasons, already has kids

Maricel	8	Medical	40	Mexico City	2	Elementary school	Self-employed	Partnered	Catholic	Medical reasons
Clara	12.5	Denied ILE	22	Mexico State	0	High school	Student	Single	None	Relationship status, life project
Naomi	7.6	Medical	24	Mexico City	0	College	NA	Single	Catholic	Career plans, life project
Elsa	7.2	Medical	34	Mexico City	3	Middle school	Factory	Separated	Catholic	Economic reasons
Adela	7	Medical	19	Mexico City	1	Middle school	NA	Partnered	None	Relationship status
Esther	6.4	Medical	22	Puebla	0	High school	Student	Partnered	Catholic	Life project
Lupe	Not Pregnant	NA	18	Mexico City	0	High school	NA	Partnered	Other	Life project
Carmen	6.4	Medical	18	Mexico City	0	In college	Student	Partnered	Catholic	Unstable relationship
Teresa	6	Medical	23	Mexico City	1	Middle school	Self-employed	Separated	Catholic	Life project
Mercedes	6	Medical	24	Mexico City	3	Middle school	House painter	Partnered	Catholic	Economic reasons
Araceli	11	Aspiration	21	Mexico City	1	High School	NA	Partnered	Atheist	Medical reasons

Pseudonym	Gestational age	Procedure	Age	Residence	Children	Education	Occupation	Marital status	Religion	Reason for abortion
Edna	6	Medical	23	Mexico City	0	In college	Student	Partnered	Atheist	Economic reasons, life project
Claudia	6.5	Medical	31	Mexico State	1	High school	Secretary	Partnered	Catholic	Medical reasons
Dulce	7.5	Medical	25	Veracruz	2	High school	Stylist	Single	Other	Life project, relationship status
Dani	6	Medical	23	Hidalgo	0	College	Masseuse	Partnered	None	Life project
Itzel	7	Medical	20	Mexico City	0	High school	Student	Partnered	Other	Life project
Frida	5	Medical	30	Mexico City	1	in college	Student	Partnered	Catholic	Life project, college
Beatriz	10.2	Aspiration	23	Mexico City	1	High school	NA	Single	Catholic	Medical reasons
Erika	6.5	Medical	22	Mexico City	1	High school	Student	Single	Christian	Life project, relationship status
Lisset	8	Medical	27	Mexico State	2	Middle school	NA	Partnered	Other	Economic reasons
Nadia	7	Medical	29	Mexico City	1	High school	Student	Single	Christian	Unstable relationship

Areli	5	Medical	27	Mexico City	2	Elementary school	NA	Partnered	Catholic	Done having kids
Flor	9.5	Medical	19	Mexico City	1	Middle school	Store clerk	Partnered	Christian	Relationship status
Ofelia	5.2	Medical	41	Mexico State	4	Middle school	Sewing workshop	Partnered	Catholic	Economic reasons
Nayely	5	Medical	25	Mexico City	0	College	NA	Single	Catholic	Life projects
Fernanda	8.6	Medical	23	Mexico City	0	In college	Student	Partnered	Catholic	Life project, unstable relationship
Graciela	10	Aspiration	39	Mexico City	2	Middle school	NA	Married	Christian	Medical reasons
Giselle	8	Medical	18	Mexico State	0	In college	Student	Partnered	Atheist	Life project
Amalia	6	Medical	27	Mexico City	2	In college	Student	Separated	Atheist	Economic reasons, already has kids
Viane	10.6	Aspiration	20	Guanajuato	1	Middle school	Store clerk	Single	Catholic	Unstable relationship, economic reasons
Adriana	7.1	Medical	23	Mexico City	0	In college	Student	Partnered	None	Medical reasons, economic reasons
Bianca	6	Medical	21	Mexico State	0	In college	Student	Partnered	Catholic	Economic reasons, life project

Pseudonym	Gestational age	Procedure	Age	Residence	Children	Education	Occupation	Marital status	Religion	Reason for abortion
Sandra	5.6	Medical	26	Mexico City	0	In college	Student	Partnered	Catholic	Economic reasons, life project
Paloma	8.9	Medical	19	Mexico City	0	High School	Student	Partnered	Catholic	Life project
Isa	18	Denied ILE	19	Mexico City	1	High School	Domestic worker	Partnered	Catholic	Medical reasons
Sari	6.5	Medical	30	Mexico City	3	Cosmetology school	Home	Partnered	Catholic	economic reasons
Ximena	6	Medical	25	Mexico City	2	High School	Office worker	Separated	Christian	Economic reasons, relationship status, life project
Yolanda	6.1	Medical	28	Mexico City	2	Magisterial Technician	Office worker	Separated	Catholic	Done having kids
Aurelia	5.2	Medical	34	Mexico City	2	High School	NA	Divorced	Atheist	Done having kids, relationship status
Blanca	5.3	Medical	33	Mexico State	2	Elementary school	Waitress	Separated	Catholic	Relationship status
Abril	7.4	Medical	25	Mexico City	0	In college	Student	Partnered	None	Life project, school

Name			Age	Location		Education	Occupation	Relationship	Religion	Reasons
Norma	7.5	Medical	25	Mexico State	2	Middle school	Domestic worker	Partnered	Catholic	Done having kids
Paula	8	Medical	23	Mexico State	1	Middle school	Self-employed	Single	Catholic	Relationship status, economic reasons
Sofía	5.2	Medical	25	Mexico City	0	College	Self-employed	Partnered	Atheist	life project
Zaira	5.2	Medical	22	Mexico City	0	High School	NA	Partnered	Catholic	Life project, relationship status
Lety	7.5	Medical	32	Mexico City	1	In college	Student	Partnered	Atheist	Economic reasons, life project
Iris	6	Medical	22	Mexico State	0	In college	Student	Single	Atheist	Life project
Alejandra	6	Medical	21	Mexico City	0	High School	Student	Partnered	None	Life project
Monserrat	7.6	Medical	28	Mexico City	0	College	Office worker	Partnered	Catholic	economic reasons, unstable relationship
Ángeles	7.2	Medical	35	Mexico City	3	Technical school	NA	Partnered	Catholic	Economic reasons, medical reasons

NOTES

INTRODUCTION

1. When I refer to the ILE program and its clinics throughout this book, I am referencing the public health sector unless I specify otherwise.

2. Kulczycki 2003.

3. Pou Jiménez 2009.

4. Mason 1999.

5. Murillo 2016; Reagan 1997.

6. Ojeda 2006.

7. Andaya and Mishtal 2016, 54.

8. Mccammon 2019.

9. Misoprostol, sold under the generic name Cytotec, is useful in contexts with restrictive abortion laws and in low-resource settings where abortion services may be legal but prohibitively costly.

10. Barot 2018.

11. Rocca et al. 2020.

12. Andaya 2014; Gammeltoft 2002; Kimport 2012.

13. Ginsburg 1989; Mishtal 2015; Morgan 2009; Rapp 1999.

14. Andaya and Mishtal 2016, 42.

15. Caivano and Marcus-Delgado 2012, 6.

16. Kulczycki 2003.

17. This figure is drawn from the Guttmacher Institute (2018). While Latin American abortion laws are extremely strict, a few notable exceptions include Cuba, where abortion up to ten weeks has been legal and available through the public health system since 1965; Uruguay, which legalized abortion up to twelve weeks in 2012; and Argentina, which legalized abortion up to fourteen weeks in 2020.

18. Guttmacher Institute 2018.

19. Paxman et al. 1993.

20. Kulczycki 2007, 62.

21. Jaffary 2016; Ortiz-Millán and Kissling 2020.

22. All of Mexico's thirty-two federal entities (the capital plus thirty-one states) have their own penal codes, and abortion laws vary by state.

23. Abortion is permitted in twenty-four Mexican states when necessary to save a woman's life; in sixteen states when the pregnancy poses a grave danger to women's health; in sixteen states in cases of fetal anomaly; and in two states for economic reasons (Ortiz-Millán and Kissing 2020).

24. Sánchez-Fuentes et al. 2008.

25. Sousa, Lozano, and Gakidou 2010.

26. Petryna and Karolina Follis 2015.

27. Paine, Noriega, and Beltrán y Puga 2014, 63.

28. Amuchástegui et al. 2010, 989.

29. Lamas 1997.

30. Maier 2012.

31. Lamas 1997, 2014.

32. Amuchástegui and Flores 2013.

33. Amuchástegui and Flores 2013; E. Singer 2016.

34. Morgan and Roberts 2012.

35. Roseneil et al. 2013, 901.

36. Rabinow and Rose 2006, 208.

37. Gammeltoft and Wahlberg 2014.

38. El Kotni and Singer 2019, 119.

39. Colen 2006.

40. Marchesi 2012; Krause 2012.

41. Marchesi 2012, 173.

42. Browner and Sargent 2011; Ginsburg and Rapp 1991.

43. Stepan 1991; Morgan and Roberts 2012.

44. Petchesky 1995; Zampas and Gher 2008.

45. Grimes 1998.

46. Amuchástegui et al. 2010; Lamas 1997.

47. Sánchez Fuentes, Paine, and Elliott-Buettner 2008.

48. Lamas 1997.

49. For this history, see Lamas 1997; Lamas and Bissel 2000; Sánchez Fuentes, Paine, and Elliott-Buettner 2008.

50. The first legislative reform, the Ley Robles, was passed in 2000. The law expanded allowable reasons for abortion to include a grave risk to the woman's health, the presence of fetal anomaly, and forcible artificial insemination without the woman's consent. The Ley Robles also eliminated a section of the abortion law that decreased legal consequences when a woman's pregnancy occurred within the confines of a marital partnership (Madrazo 2009). In 2004, another reform established that women's consent was necessary to undergo an abortion. With this iteration of the law, the punishment for coerced abortion was expanded from three to six years in prison to five to eight years.

51. Mexico City's 2007 abortion reform also redefined "pregnancy" as the implantation of an embryo in the uterus, thereby condoning emergency contraception, in vitro fertilization, and stem-cell research. Additionally, the law decreased the punishment for obtaining an illegal abortion (after twelve weeks of gestation) and increased the punishment for forc-

ing a woman to undergo an abortion against her will. Finally, the law emphasized sexual and reproductive health services as a means to prevent untenable pregnancy and promote reproductive and sexual health (Sánchez Fuentes, Paine, and Elliott-Buettner 2008).

52. Sánchez Fuentes, Paine, and Elliott-Buettner 2008.

53. Paine, Noriega, and Beltrán y Puga 2014. Moreover, the Information Group on Reproductive Choice (GIRE), a leading abortion advocacy NGO in the capital that was essential in paving the way for the 2007 reform, estimates that between the years of 2007 and 2016, as many as fifty-three people were imprisoned for procuring or providing abortions, and eighty-three more were detained awaiting trial (GIRE 2018).

54. Billings et al. 2009; Lara, Garcia, Wilson, and Paz 2011.

55. Ortiz-Ortega 2005; Schiavon, Troncoso, and Polo 2012.

56. Berer 2009, 154.

57. Richard Wilson (2006) coined this term.

58. Goodale 2006b, 491.

59. In the aftermath of World War II, members of the American Anthropological Association refused to offer support for a draft of the Universal Declaration of Human Rights, asserting that a universal set of values produced by Western elites and visited on the rest of the world would be tantamount to moral imperialism (Goodale 2006b).

60. See Merry 2006; Speed 2006, 2008; Willen 2011.

61. Wilson 2006, 108. Also see Hale 2002.

62. Levitt and Merry 2011, 83. Also see Shweder (2000).

63. Gerber Fried 1990; Hartmann 1995; Petchesky 1995.

64. Rapp 2001.

65. L. Ross and Solinger 2017.

66. Gammeltoft 2014; Rapp 1999; Williamson 2020.

67. Roberts 2012.

68. Bastian Duarte 2012; Roberts 2012; Williamson 2020.

69. Gammeltoft 2014.

70. Ostrach 2017.

71. Suh 2021.

72. Wilson 2006, 78

73. Morgan and Roberts 2012, 243.

74. Luna 2009; Price 2010; Spade 2013; L. Ross 2017; Zavella 2016.

75. Briggs 2002.

76. L. Ross and Solinger 2017.

77. Davis 2019.

78. Luna and Luker 2013.

79. Kierans and Bell 2017.

80. Buchbinder 2021, 21.

81. Amuchástegui, Flores, and Aldaz 2015.

82. Berlin 2015, 111.

83. J. Ross 2009, 15.

84. Luiselli 2014, 28.

85. Villoro 2021.

86. Villoro 2021, 11.

87. Andrés Manuel López Obrador was elected to the presidency in 2018, representing his new party, Morena.

88. Sánchez Fuentes, Paine, and Elliott-Buettner 2008.

89. Bessire 2014, xii.

90. Lester 2019; E. Martin 2007, 1987; Rapp 1999; L. Ross and Solinger 2017; Zavella 2020.

91. Here I am grateful to Megan Crowley-Matoka for pushing me to think about the temporalities of abortion and how it is and is not "chronic."

92. Because most of my research was conducted at Santa Marta, this clinic features more prominently in the descriptive account of daily life in the ILE program, but interviews and data are drawn from both the Santa Marta and Reina María clinics.

93. While living in Mexico City I spent most of my time in two public ILE clinics, where I interviewed sixty patients, fifteen providers, and one program administrator. Outside formal interviews, I conducted hundreds of hours of observation and informal conversation with patients and their accompaniers, clinicians and other ILE staff, and to a lesser extent, the protesters who regularly gathered outside. My research also led me to a handful of private abortion clinics throughout the capital, where I spoke with a smaller sample of patients and providers for comparative purposes. Once I immersed myself in the local abortion community and learned to identify its important actors, I began to spend time in some of the numerous advocacy organizations and feminist abortion networks based in and outside Mexico City.

94. I was clear, from the beginning, that participation in interviews was voluntary and would have no bearing on the care women received in the clinic. I obtained informed consent and conducted interviews in a private room in the back of the clinic. Interviews generally lasted an hour, and with women's consent I recorded them all. During the first three months of the study I hired a research assistant, Vanessa María Cravioto Fierro, to help design and conduct interviews and to offer feedback on patterns emerging in the data.

95. I am indebted again here to Megan Crowley-Matoka for prompting me to meditate on the layered meanings of "interruption."

96. Hannig 2017.

97. For an in-depth account of feminist accompaniment networks, see also Krauss 2018a.

98. Kimball 2020.

99. Unnithan and de Zordo 2018, 2.

CHAPTER 1

1. I have altered the location of the clinic to protect the privacy of clinicians and patients.

2. Eventually the clinic placed a sign out front to clarify for confused patients that the antiabortion stands and storefronts did not belong to the MOH.

3. Here I draw on the ideas of anthropologist Iván Sandoval Cervantes (2017), who, in a brilliant article about migration, connects the materiality of unfinished homes in Mexico to aspirations for better futures.

4. I use the Spanish translation of this prayer from Vatican News, https://www.vatican-

news.va/es/oraciones/ave-maria.html, and Aaron Green's 2018 English translation at https://www.liveabout.com/ave-maria-text-and-english-translation-724041

5. Kaufman and Morgan 2005, 329.

6. Guadalupe is a powerful icon, but she should not be read as an overdetermined symbol of "Mexican femininity." Gender, of course, is never fixed. Gendered norms and expressions are quickly shifting in Mexico, even as motherhood is widely cherished (Hirsch 2008; Wentzell 2013). Moreover, notions of "macho" masculinities, as problematic and as invocations of the concept can be, find vocal critique today as feminist principles have gained traction (Gutmann 2007; Inhorn and Wentzell 2011).

7. Maier 2012, 158.

8. Ginsburg 1989, 7.

9. Peterson 1992.

10. There are many versions of this story, but I rely on Eric Wolf's 1958 account and Alyshia Gálvez's 2010 account.

11. Poole 2017.

12. Nesvig 2006.

13. Wolf 1958, 37.

14. Peterson 1992.

15. Peterson 1992.

16. Wolf 1958, 38.

17. Jaffary 2016.

18. Roberts 2012.

19. Jaffary 2016.

20. Jaffary 2016.

21. Blancarte 2000.

22. Ortiz-Ortega 2005, 165.

23. Olson 2020.

24. Amuchástegui, Cruz, Aldaz, and Mejía 2010.

25. Morgan 2019.

26. Urías Horcasitas 2003.

27. Stepan 1991.

28. Stern 1999.

29. McCaa 2003.

30. Cabrera 1994.

31. Sanders 2009, 1543.

32. Gutmann 2011.

33. Stepan 1991.

34. Stepan 1991.

35. Prominent twentieth-century Mexican anthropologist Manuel Gamio also participated in the promulgation of mestizaje. Gamio had studied under Franz Boas at Columbia University in New York and, like his renowned mentor, embraced cultural relativism as a guiding approach to the study of culture. Rather than evolving in hierarchical stages from "barbarism" to "civilization," Boas held, culture was subject to historical influences

and processes of exchange. Despite his relativist training, Gamio was not immune to the postrevolutionary climate in his home country. Mestizaje, for Gamio, spelled progress for the nation. In his edited translation of Gamio's 1916 text *Forjando patria: Pro-nacionalismo*, Fernando Armstrong-Fumero (2010, 10–12) observes, "[Gamio's] work involved the markedly non-relativistic assumption that national progress hinged on the assimilation of indigenous people into a homogeneous Hispanic culture. . . . [Yet] for Gamio, the pinnacle of Mexican Revolution would not be a carbon copy of the most 'civilized' nations of Europe but the development of a mixed or intermediate culture that was better suited to its times and its environment than either the European or indigenous."

36. Coffey 2012.

37. Greeley 2012, 2.

38. Bakewell 1993.

39. Bakewell 1993, 168.

40. Zetterman 2010, 230.

41. Zetterman 2010, 230.

42. For a critical account of the place of Mexican muralism in twentieth-century politics, see Anreus, Folgarait, and Greeley 2012.

43. Bartra 1992.

44. Manrique 2016; Smith-Oka 2013b.

45. Stern 1999.

46. Lester 2005, 285–86.

47. Cházaro and Kersey 2005.

48. Cházaro and Kersey 2005, 101.

49. Sanders 2009.

50. Stern 1999, 375.

51. Maier 2012.

52. CONAPO 2016.

53. Braff 2013; Cabrera 1994.

54. Soto Laveaga 2007.

55. Gutiérrez 2008.

56. Cited in Gutiérrez 2008, 18.

57. Bourbonnais 2019.

58. Gutiérrez 2008.

59. Soto Laveaga 2009.

60. Soto Laveaga 2009, 3.

61. Cabrera 1994.

62. US National Security Council 1974.

63. Gutmann 2011.

64. Guttmann 2011.

65. Cited in Soto Laveaga 2007, 23.

66. Cabrera 1994; Soto Laveaga 2007.

67. Folch-Lyon, de la Macorra, and Schearer 1981.

68. Braff 2013; A. Castro 2004.

69. Soto Laveaga 2007, 19.

70. Soto Laveaga 2007.

71. Cabrera 1994.

72. CONAPO 2016.

73. Lawson 2000.

74. Fox 1994, 159.

75. Lamas 2011.

76. Lamas 2011.

77. Ortiz-Ortega 2005.

78. Lamas 1997.

79. Lamas 2011.

80. Lamas 2011.

81. Lamas 2011.

82. Levy, Bruhn, and Zebadúa 2001.

83. Lawson 2000.

84. Lamas 1997.

85. Sánchez Fuentes, Paine, and Elliott-Buettner 2008.

86. Lamas 2011.

87. Lamas 2011.

88. Lamas 2011.

89. GIRE 2008.

90. Lamas and Bissel 2000.

91. GIRE 2008.

92. Morgan 2019.

93. Sánchez Fuentes, Paine, and Elliott-Buettner 2008.

94. Ortiz-Millán 2018.

95. Ortiz-Millán 2018, 2.

96. Contreras et al. 2011.

97. Ortiz-Millán 2018.

98. In the first few months of the ILE program surgical abortions were performed using sharp curettage, but protocols quickly evolved to eliminate this method, replacing it with medical abortion or vacuum aspiration abortion, both manual and electric.

99. Mifepristone causes the placenta to separate from the endometrium and softens the cervix, and misoprostol induces uterine contractions and facilitates expulsion of the products of conception to produce an abortion.

100. Moreno-Ruiz et al. 2007; World Health Organization 2018.

101. For updated information on ILE statistics, see Gobierno de la Ciudad de México, Secretaría de Salud, "Interrupción Legal del Embarazo (ILE), Estadísticas," http://ile.salud. cdmx.gob.mx/estadisticas-interrupcion-legal-embarazo-df/.

102. Gobierno de la Ciudad de México, Secretaría de Salud, "Interrupción Legal del Embarazo (ILE): Estadísticas," April 2007–March 2021, http://ile.salud.cdmx.gob.mx/ estadisticas-interrupcion-legal-embarazo-df/.

103. Smith-Oka 2012, 2013b.

104. Basave 2011.

105. Braff 2013, 126.

106. Amuchástegui and Flores 2013, 916.

107. Faulkner 2011, 73.

108. Carrillo 2002; Wentzell 2013.

109. Lester 2005.

110. While writing this historical chapter I benefited enormously from the breathtaking style of Amy Moran-Thomas (2019) in *Traveling with Sugar: Chronicles of a Global Epidemic*.

CHAPTER 2

1. Since she could not identify a clinician in Mexico who would perform the procedure, her doctor had suggested a US specialist.

2. Crowley-Matoka 2016, 43.

3. Lipka 2016.

4. Even though there is no explicit mention of abortion in the New Testament, religious scholars maintain that prohibitions against abortion can be inferred (Noonan 1967). Curiously, Christian teachings against abortion appeared in opposition to a cultural milieu in which infant and fetal life were scarcely valued (Noonan 1967). It was not until the nineteenth century, alongside developments in embryology, that Catholic dogma began to emphasize life as beginning from conception (Roberts 2012).

5. Povoledo and Stack 2016.

6. I concluded my fieldwork before Pope Francis determined in 2016 that priests had the power to pardon women for the din of abortion. My data therefore do not reflect his determination or its impact on women's experiences with abortion.

7. San Martín 2020.

8. Mishtal and Dannefer 2010; Roberts 2012.

9. Maier 2012, 160.

10. Pew Research Center 2014.

11. Chowning 2013.

12. Chowning 2013, 197.

13. Voekel 2002.

14. Blancarte 2000, 599.

15. Historian Pamela Voekel (2002) argues that Mexico's reform war, which historians describe as a battle between secular revolutionaries and religious forces, can more aptly be described as a "religious war" over styles of Catholic piety. Against the prevailing style of Baroque Catholicism in late eighteenth-century Mexico, a group of reformist clergy, together with members of the laity, sought to establish their vision of an "enlightened" Catholicism. Fashioning their faith in part on Protestantism, Enlightened Catholics rejected Baroque Catholicism for its extravagance, rigid hierarchy, and emphasis on clerical intervention, promoting instead moderation, disciplined internalization of church rules, and more egalitarian social arrangements. Historian Matthew Butler (2009) argues that a similar tendency to conflate anticlericalism with secularism has prevailed in historical accounts of twentieth-century

Mexico. Butler complicates reigning understandings of a dichotomous postrevolutionary struggle between religious forces and secular liberals, describing a movement to reform the Catholic Church from within that crystallized after the Mexican Revolution of 1910.

16. For a discussion of the story in the Ecuadorian context, see Roberts 2006.

17. Ebert 2002.

18. Henriquez and Montaño 2002.

19. Shepard 2000.

20. In the aftermath of the 2007 reform, at least thirty-six pro-prolife organizations have incorporated across the country (Flores 2019).

21. Mishtal 2015; Inhorn 2011; Sargent 2006; Kahn 2000; Roberts 2006; Thompson 2006.

22. Hirsch 2008, 94.

23. Hirsch 2008, 95.

24. Georges 1996.

25. Mishtal and Dannefer 2010.

26. Hirsch 2008, 99.

27. Hartmann 1995.

28. Braff 2013, 132.

29. Nehring, Esteinou, and Alvarado 2016.

30. L. Ross and Solinger 2017.

CHAPTER 3

1. Soto Laveaga 2016.

2. Soto Laveaga 2016, 277.

3. Since he assumed the presidency in 2018, Andrés Manuel López Obrador (AMLO) has undertaken a massive reformation of the national health system, a process that anthropological doctoral student Mary Bugbee is exploring. The reforms are designed to establish a centralized system that roots out corruption and decreases out-of-pocket expenses. AMLO has eliminated Seguro Popular, which he publicly critiqued for years as a neoliberal system that was, in his pithy phrase, "ni seguro, ni popular" (neither safe nor popular) (Reich 2020). My account of the national health system thus reflects an earlier moment in time.

4. Puig, Pagán, and Wong 2009.

5. Doubova et al. 2018.

6. It bears repeating that wealthy women have the option of purchasing abortion care in one of the various private clinics and reproductive health care chains that have opened throughout the capital since 2007. Although abortion was available for purchase even before it became legal, the law triggered the inauguration of a range of private ILE clinics. In the private sector, abortion can cost up to $600 USD, which is prohibitively costly for many people. While the current president has recently raised the national minimum wage by a small percentage, at the time of my study it was just five dollars a day. Private abortion clinics are generally quiet, well stocked, and well staffed as compared to the ILE clinics. Instead of arriving before dawn to wait outside the clinic in the hopes of securing an appointment, women are scheduled for procedures. Patients find an assortment of magazines as well as

couches and coffee in the waiting room. Women have the option, whenever safe and appropriate, of choosing a medical or an aspiration procedure, and all medical provisions are included in the purchased package of care. In some private clinics, patients can purchase additional analgesics to reduce pain. Extensive abortion counseling is generally available to women and their romantic partners. With the sympathetic perspective of a prochoice counselor, women and couples can sift through any emotional or spiritual misgivings around the abortion decision for as much time as they need. As we might expect, the women who visited private abortion clinics, by and large, were considerably wealthier than those who depended on the free services offered through the ILE program. Extremely high patient demand and insufficient personnel precluded this kind of painstaking emotional care within the public ILE clinics.

7. Fisk 2000, 64.

8. Laurell 2007.

9. Laurell 2007.

10. Laurell 2001, 294.

11. Crowley-Matoka 2016.

12. AlJazeera 2014.

13. F. Martínez 2014.

14. My translation.

15. Lomnitz 2014.

16. Semple, Villegas, and Kitroeff 2020.

17. Laurell 2015, 261.

18. Wright 2011.

19. Crowley-Matoka 2016.

20. Wentzell 2015, 654.

21. Amuchástegui and Flores 2013.

22. Amuchástegui and Flores 2013, 920.

23. Bourdieu 1997, 228.

24. Andaya 2019; Heller 2019; Lee, James, and Hunleth 2020.

25. Auyero 2012, 2.

26. Mulcahy, Perry, and Glover 2010.

27. Crowley-Matoka 2016, 123.

28. Minors arriving at the ILE program had to bring with them a birth certificate, proof of residence in both original and copied forms, and a formal ID with a photo. They also had to come accompanied by a parent or legal representative with an official ID and proof of residence in original and copied forms. Women arriving at an ILE clinic from outside the capital were required to bring an ID in original and copied forms as well as proof of residence, and were to be accompanied by someone with an original and copied form of ID.

29. Biehl 2013; Petryna 2013.

30. Sánchez 2011, 197. See also De León 2015; Willen 2007.

31. Abadia and Oviedo 2009; Auyero 2012.

32. Castro and Erviti 2014; D'Gregorio 2010; Quattrocchi and Magnone 2020.

33. Sesia 2020b, 8.

34. R. Castro and Frías 2020.

35. Dixon 2015.

36. Castro and Erviti 2014; Erviti, Castro, and Sánchez 2006; Dixon 2015; Smith-Oka 2015.

37. R. Castro and Frías 2020.

38. Sesia 2020a.

39. Erviti, Castro, and Sánchez 2006; Suh 2020.

40. Stevenson 2012.

41. A. Martin, Myers, and Viseu 2015, 267.

42. A. Garcia 2015; Sufrin 2017.

43. Stevenson 2012; Strong 2020.

44. Williamson 2020, 8.

45. Amuchástegui and Flores 2013; R. Castro 2014a; Roseneil et al. 2013.

CHAPTER 4

1. As institutions in which core societal values inhere, hospitals are key site for processes of subjectification (Livingston 2012).

2. M. Singer 1989; M. Singer et al. 2010; Petryna 2013; Willen 2019.

3. Brotherton 2012; R. Martínez 2018.

4. Cooper 2015, 461.

5. Buchbinder 2016, 774.

6. Buchbinder 2016; Joffe, Weitz, and Stacey 2004; Joffe 1995; E. Singer and Ostrach 2017.

7. Here I draw inspiration from Tine Gammeltoft's groundbreaking 2014 account of reproductive politics in Vietnam, where public health workers were passionately engaged with their patients, in many cases steering their reproductive decisions as a way to protect them.

8. Ortiz-Millán 2018.

9. Joffe 1995.

10. Willen 2012.

11. Smith-Oka 2013b.

12. Smith-Oka 2013b, 76.

13. Taracena 2002.

14. Kelley 2014, 317.

15. During my prior work in a private US abortion clinic, I almost never heard personnel discuss the risks of abortion outside of reading medical consent forms to patients. There was an implicit recognition among the providers that abortion, when performed in an adequate setting, was minimally risky. US providers were transparent with patients about the risks entailed in an abortion procedure, but they strove to relay the information in neutral terms while emphasizing the technical skill and competency of the doctor and to reassure patients of the general safety of the procedure they would undergo. ILE providers took a very different approach, exaggerating the risks of abortion to their patients in the context of emotional appeals to avoid recourse to the procedure.

16. Raymond and Grimes 2012.

17. Fordyce and Maraesa 2012; Howes-Mischel 2012; Lupton 2012; R. Martínez 2018; Oaks 2000; Smith-Oka 2012.

18. Oaks 2003, 80.

19. Andaya and Mishtal 2016, 50.

20. Raymond and Grimes 2012.

21. Nelson 2019.

22. Uterine perforation during aspiration abortion is rare but can be extremely dangerous if left untreated. Data from the US indicate that 9 percent of cases of uterine perforation from abortion result in hysterectomy (Shakir and Diab 2013).

23. Shakir and Diab 2013, 258.

24. Bazelon 2007; Kelly 2014.

25. Dadlez and Andrews 2009.

26. Holland 2020.

27. Major et al. 2009.

28. Andaya and Mishtal 2016, 42.

29. Biggs et al. 2017.

30. Kumar, Hessini, and Mitchell 2009, 628.

31. Kumar, Hessini, and Mitchell 2009.

32. Sorhaindo et al. 2014.

33. López et al. 2019.

34. Rapp 1999, 3.

35. Rapp 1999, 3.

36. Morgan and Roberts 2012, 244. A genealogy of responsibility in Mexican reproductive governance reveals that what it means to be responsible has shifted dramatically over time. The concept was first mobilized in the aftermath of the Revolution of 1910. Medical and educational campaigns called upon women to contribute to the project of revolutionary nationalism through bountiful reproduction under the banner of "responsible motherhood." As the leaders of the new republic charted a path for national success, women, and their reproductive bodies, proved central to the consolidation of the modern state. Responsibility had taken on new meanings by the closing decades of the century, when political leaders and intellectual elites began to fear that national fertility rates had climbed too high. If these were left unchecked, leaders feared, the growing population could spell national collapse. Being responsible in Cold War–era Mexico, therefore, unlike in decades past, entailed the adoption of modern family-planning methods to limit fertility, create smaller families, and, ultimately, secure the viability of the nation-state. Political anxieties about "overpopulation" waned as national fertility rates fell steadily from the 1970s onward, eventually hovering around replacement levels. While the projected devastation of the "population bomb" never came to pass, state emphasis on responsibility as a guiding ethos in reproductive life endured.

37. Decreto por el que se Reforma el Código Penal para el Distrito Federal y se Adiciona la Ley de Salud para el Distrito Federal, Gaceta Oficial del Distrito Federal, April 26, 2007, 3.

38. My translation.

39. Rose 2000, 34.

40. Rose 2000, 324.

41. Rose 2000, 334–35.

42. Wentzell 2015, 2021.

43. Gammeltoft 2014.

44. CONAPO 2016.

45. Johnson-Hanks 2002; Krause 2012; Ruhl 2002.

46. Fordyce 2012.

47. Andaya 2014.

48. Paxson 2002.

49. Ginsburg and Rapp 1995; Greenhalgh 1994; Kligman 1998.

50. Ciudad de México, Secretaría de Salud 2017.

CHAPTER 5

1. Buchbinder 2021, 23.

2. Buchbinder 2021, 23.

3. Hodgson 2011.

4. Hodgson 2011, 5.

5. El Kotni and Singer 2019.

6. As part of the organization's work, Conéctame trains a cohort of around ten volunteers each year to accompany women to and from abortion clinics. The vast majority of the organization's work involves assisting women with bus transport and other logistical costs and barriers that might otherwise prevent them from arriving to Mexico City for abortion. Once a woman arrives to the city, a volunteer accompanier meets her outside the ILE clinic or at an agreed-upon location and stays with her throughout the day until the abortion procedure is over. Many of these women have never visited Mexico City before, and navigating the city can be overwhelming.

7. Madrazo 2009.

8. Rosalia's story is a composite account that blends the stories of real patients without referencing any individual in particular. I use the composite format here because I made a point not to mix my role as an abortion accompanier with my role as a researcher. While I could never "turn off" my researcher subject position entirely, I want to respect the anonymity and experiences of those for whom I served as an accompanier, even though that work informs my analysis here.

9. Joffe 1995.

10. Gobierno de la Ciudad de México, Secretaría de Salud, "Interrupción Legal del Embarazo (ILE): Estadísticas," April 2007–December 2020, http://ile.salud.cdmx.gob.mx/estadisticas-interrupcion-legal-embarazo-df/. The data at this site is regularly updated.

11. Bergmann 2011; Deomampo 2016; Inhorn 2012, 2015.

12. Pennings 2002; Whittaker and Speier 2010.

13. Inhorn and Patrizio 2009; Matorras 2005.

14. Bloomer and O'Dowd 2014; De Zordo et al. 2020; Gerdts et al. 2016; Sethna and Davis 2019.

15. Gilmartin and White 2011; Mishtal 2015; Ostrach 2017; Sethna and Doull 2012, 2013.

16. Nahman 2016.

17. Fallow 2013.

18. The Guanajuato penal code defines abortion as a crime, yet the procedure is not punishable when the pregnancy results from rape or when the abortion results from "imprudence," defined as an accident. Outside these two circumstances, women who undergo abortion can face a jail sentence of anywhere from three months to six years, and anyone assisting her in terminating her pregnancy can face charges of one to three years' imprisonment.

19. Paine, Noriega, and Beltrán y Puga 2014.

20. Thomas and Galemba 2013.

21. Panella and Thomas 2015, 6. See also Willen 2007; De Genova 2004.

22. My categorization of Las Fuertes's style of abortion advocacy builds on Davis-Floyd and Johnson's (2008, 9) discussion of "alegal" practices of direct-entry midwifery in the United States, where midwifery is not expressly prohibited in all state statutes but is often understood to be illegal. Other models of "alegal" abortion advocacy exist in contemporary Mexico, but these have achieved far less visibility than Las Fuertes, and a full discussion of the range of existing activist strategies is beyond the scope of this chapter. My decision to juxtapose Las Fuertes's approach with that of activist groups in the capital reflects the organization's own conception of the landscape of Mexico's abortion advocacy world.

23. Lamas and Bissel 2000.

24. Lamas and Bissel 2000, 18.

25. Lamas and Bissel 2000.

26. De Zordo 2016.

27. Lara et al. 2011; MacDonald 2020; Solheim et al. 2020.

28. R. Allen and O'Brien 2009.

29. Gianella 2017, 134.

30. Gianella 2017, 133.

31. Alvarez 1999.

CONCLUSION

1. Brown and Halley 2002, 422.

2. Brown and Halley 2002, 25.

3. Dillon 2021.

4. Totenberg 2021.

5. Quoctrung, Miller, and Sanger-Katz 2021.

6. Brown and Halley 2002, 14.

BIBLIOGRAPHY

Abadia, César Ernest, and Diana G. Oviedo. 2009. "Bureaucratic Itineraries in Colombia: A Theoretical and Methodological Tool to Assess Managed-Care Health Systems." *Social Science and Medicine* 68 (6): 1153–60.

AlJazeera. 2014. "Mexico Cartel Member Held in Organ Theft Case." March 18. https:// www.aljazeera.com/news/2014/3/18/mexico-cartel-member-held-in-organ-theft-case.

Allen, Lori. 2013. *The Rise and Fall of Human Rights: Cynicism and Politics in Occupied Palestine.* Stanford, CA: Stanford University Press.

Allen, Rebecca, and Barbara M. O'Brien. 2009. "Uses of Misoprostol in Obstetrics and Gynecology." *Reviews in Obstetrics and Gynecology* 2 (3): 159–68.

Alvarez, S. E. 1999. "Advocating Feminism: The Latin American Feminist NGO 'Boom.'" *International Feminist Journal of Politics* 1 (2): 181–209.

Amuchástegui, Ana, and Edith Flores. 2013. "Women's Interpretations of the Right to Legal Abortion in Mexico City: Citizenship, Experience and Clientelism." *Citizenship Studies* 17 (8): 912–27.

Amuchástegui, Ana, Edith Flores, and Evelyn Aldaz. 2015. "Disputa social y disputa subjetiva. Religión, género y discursos sociales en la legalización del aborto en México." *Revista de Estudios de Género* 5 (41): 153–95.

Amuchástegui, Ana, Guadalupe Cruz, Evelyn Aldaz, and María Consuelo Mejía. 2010. "Politics, Religion and Gender Equality in Contemporary Mexico: Women's Sexuality and Reproductive Rights in a Contested Secular State." *Third World Quarterly* 31 (6): 989–1005.

Andaya, Elise. 2014. *Conceiving Cuba: Reproduction, Women, and the State in the Post-Soviet Era.* New Brunswick, NJ: Rutgers University Press.

Andaya, Elise. 2019. "Race-ing Time: Clinical Temporalities and Inequality in Public Prenatal Care." *Medical Anthropology* 38 (8): 651–63.

Andaya, Elise, and Joana Mishtal. 2016. "The Erosion of Rights to Abortion Care in the United States: A Call for Renewed Anthropological Engagement with the Politics of Abortion." *Medical Anthropology Quarterly* 31 (1): 40–59.

Anreus, Alejandro, Leonard Folgarait, and Robin Adèle Greeley, eds. 2012. *Mexican Muralism: A Critical History.* Oakland: University of California Press.

Armstrong-Fumero, Fernando. 2010. Introduction to *Forjando patria: Pro-nacionalismo,* by Manuel Gamio, edited and translated by Fernando Armstrong-Fumero. Boulder: University of Colorado Press.

Auyero, Javier. 2011. "Ethnographic Account of Poor People's Waiting." *Latin American Research Review* 46 (1): 5–29.

Auyero, Javier. 2012. *Patients of the State: The Politics of Waiting in Argentina*. Durham, NC: Duke University Press.

Bakewell, Liza. 1993. "Frida Kahlo: A Contemporary Feminist Reading." *Frontiers: A Journal of Women's Studies* 13 (3): 165–89.

Barot, Sneha. 2018. "The Roadmap to Safe Abortion Worldwide: Lessons from New Global Trends on Incidence, Legality and Safety." *Guttmacher Policy Review* 21:17–22.

Bartra, Roger. 1992. *The Cage of Melancholy: Identity and Metamorphosis in the Mexican Character*. New Brunswick, NJ: Rutgers University Press.

Basave, Agostín. 1992. *México mestizo: Análisis del nacionalismo mexicano en torno a la mestizofilia*. Mexico City: Fondo de Cultural Económica.

Bastian Duarte, Ángela Ixkic. 2012. "From the Margins of Latin American Feminism: Indigenous and Lesbian Feminisms." *Signs* 38 (1): 153–78.

Bazelon, Emily. 2007. "Is There a Post-abortion Syndrome?" *New York Times Magazine*, January 21.

Bearak, J., K. Burke, and R. Jones. 2017. "Disparities and Change over Time in Distance Women Would Need to Travel to Have an Abortion in the USA: A Spatial Analysis." *Lancet Public Health* 2 (11): 493–500.

Berer, Marge. 2009. "The Cairo 'Compromise' on Abortion and Its Consequences for Making Abortion Safe and Legal." In *Reproductive Health and Human Rights: The Way Forward*, edited by Laura Reichenbach and Mindy Jane Roseman, chap. 11. Philadelphia: University of Pennsylvania Press.

Bergmann, Sven. 2011. "Fertility Tourism: Circumventive Routes That Enable Access to Reproductive Technologies and Substances." *Signs* 36 (2): 280–89.

Berlin, Lucia. 2015. *A Manual for Cleaning Women*. Edited by Stephen Emerson. New York: Picador.

Bessire, Lucas. 2014. *Behold the Black Caiman: A Chronicle of Ayoreo Life*. Chicago: University of Chicago Press.

Biehl, João. 2013. *Vita: Life in a Zone of Social Abandonment*. Berkeley: University of California Press.

Biggs, Antonia, Ushma D. Upadhyay, Charles E. McCulloch, and Diana Foster. 2017. "Women's Mental Health and Well-Being 5 Years after Receiving or Being Denied an Abortion: A Prospective, Longitudinal Cohort Study." *JAMA Psychiatry* 74 (2): 169–78.

Billings, Deborah, Dilys Walker, Guadalupe Mainero del Paso, Kathryn Andersen Clark, and Ila Dayananda. 2009. "Pharmacy Worker Practices Related to Use of Misoprostol for Abortion in One Mexican State." *Contraception* 79 (6): 445–51.

Blancarte, Roberto. 2000. "Popular Religion, Catholicism, and Socioreligious Dissent in Latin America: Facing the Modernity Paradigm." *International Sociology* 15 (4): 591–603.

Blofield, Merike, and Christina Ewig. 2017. "The Left Turn and Abortion Politics in Latin America." *Social Politics* 24 (4): 481–510.

Bloomer, Fiona, and Kellie O'Dowd. 2014. "Restricted Access to Abortion in the Republic of Ireland and Northern Ireland: Exploring Abortion Tourism and Barriers to Legal Reform." *Culture, Health and Sexuality* 16 (4): 366–80.

Bourbonnais, Nicole C. 2019. "Population Control, Family Planning, and Maternal Health Networks in the 1960s/70s: Diary of an International Consultant." *Bulletin of the History of Medicine* 93 (3): 353–64.

Bourdieu, Pierre. 1997. *Pascalian Meditations.* Stanford, CA: Stanford University Press.

Braff, Lara. 2013. "*Somos Muchos* (We Are So Many): Population Politics and 'Reproductive Othering' in Mexican Fertility Clinics." *Medical Anthropology Quarterly* 27 (1): 121–38.

Briggs, Laura. 2002. *Reproducing Empire: Race, Sex, Science, and U.S. Imperialism in Puerto Rico.* Berkeley: University of California Press, 2002.

Brotherton, Sean P. 2012. *Revolutionary Medicine: Health and The Body in Post-Soviet Cuba.* Durham, NC: Duke University Press.

Brown, Wendy, and Janet Halley. 2002. *Left Legalism/Left Critique.* Durham, NC: Duke University Press.

Browner, Carole. 2000. "Situating Women's Reproductive Activities." *American Anthropologist* 102 (4): 773–88.

Browner, Carole, and Carolyn Sargent. 2011. *Reproduction, Globalization, and the State: New Theoretical and Ethnographic Perspectives.* Durham, NC: Duke University Press.

Buch, Elana D. 2015. "Anthropology of Aging and Care." *Annual Review of Anthropology* 44:277–93.

Buchbinder, Mara. 2016. "Scripting Dissent: US Abortion Laws, State Power, and the Politics of Scripted Speech." *American Anthropologist* 118 (4): 772–83.

Buchbinder, Mara. 2021. *Scripting Death: Stories of Assisted Dying in America.* Oakland: University of California Press.

Bui, Quoctrung, Claire Cain Miller, and Margot Sanger-Katz. 2021. "Where Abortion Access Would Decline if Roe vs. Wade Were Overturned." *New York Times*, May 18. https://www.nytimes.com/interactive/2021/05/18/upshot/abortion-laws-roe-wade-states.html.

Burden, B. C., D. T. Canon, K. R. Mayer, and D. P. Moynihan. 2012. "The Effect of Administrative Burden on Bureaucratic Perception of Policies: Evidence from Election Administration." *Public Administration Review* 72:741–51.

Butler, Matthew. 2009. "Sontanas Rojinegras: Catholic Anticlericalism and Mexico's Revolutionary Schism." *The Americas* 65 (4): 535–58.

Cabrera, Gustavo. 1994. "Demographic Dynamics and Development: The Role of Population Policy in Mexico." *Population and Development Review* 20:105–20.

Caivano, Joan, and Jane Marcus-Delgado. 2012. "Time for Change: Reproductive Rights in Latin America in the 21st Century." Reproductive Laws for the 21st Century Papers. Center for Women Policy Studies, May. https://www.thedialogue.org/wp-content/uploads/2020/02/Time_for_Change_Reproductive_Rights_in_L-1.pdf.

Carrillo, Héctor. 2002. *The Night Is Young: Sexuality in Mexico in the Time of AIDS.* Chicago: University of Chicago Press, 2002.

Castro, Arachu. 2004. "Contracepting at Childbirth: The Integration of Reproductive Health and Population Polices in Mexico." In *Unhealthy Health Policy: A Critical Anthropological*

Examination, edited by A. Castro and M. Singer, 133–44. Walnut Creek, CA: AltaMira, 2004.

Castro, Arachu. 2019. "Witnessing Obstetric Violence during Fieldwork: Notes from Latin America." *Health and Human Rights Journal* 21 (1): 103–11.

Castro, Roberto. 2014a. "Génesis y práctica del habitus médico autoritario en México." *Revista Mexicana de Sociología* 76 (2): 167–97.

Castro, Roberto, and Joaquina Erviti. 2014. "25 años de investigación sobre violencia obstétrica en México." *Conamed* 19 (1): 37–42.

Castro, Roberto, and Sonia M. Frías. 2020. "Obstetric Violence in Mexico: Results from a 2016 National Household Survey." *Violence against Women* 26 (6–7): 555–72.

Cházaro, Laura, and Paul Kersey. 2005. "Mexican Women's Pelves and Obstetrical Procedures: Interventions with Forceps in Late 19th-Century Medicine." *Feminist Review* 79:100–115.

Chowning, Margaret. 2013. "The Catholic Church and the Ladies of the Vela Perpetua: Gender and Devotional Change in Nineteenth Century Mexico." *Past and Present* 221 (1): 197–237.

Ciudad de México, Secretaría de Salud. 2017. Sistema de Acceso a la Información Pública: Infomex: Consulta sobre el Programa de Interrupción Legal del Embarazo. http://www.infomexdf.org.mx/InfomexDF/default.aspx.

Coffey, Mary K. 2012. *How a Revolutionary Art Became Official Culture: Murals, Museums, and the Mexican State*. Durham, NC: Duke University Press.

Colen, Shellee. 2006. "Stratified Reproduction and West Indian Childcare Workers and Employers in New York." In *Feminist Anthropology: A Reader*, edited by Ellen Lewin, 380–96. Malden, MA: Blackwell.

CONAPO (Consejo Nacional de Población). 2016. *Situación de la salud sexual y reproductiva, República Mexicana, 2016*. Mexico City: CONAPO.

Connelly, Matthew. 2003. "Seeing beyond the State: The Population Control Movement and the Problem of Sovereignty." *Past and Present* 193:197–233.

Contreras, Xipatl, Marieke G. van Dijk, Tahilin Sanchez, and Patricio Sanhueza Smith. 2011. "Experiences and Opinions of Health-Care Professionals regarding Legal Abortion in Mexico City: A Qualitative Study." *Studies in Family Planning* 42 (3): 183–90.

Cooper, Amy. 2015. "The Doctor's Political Body: Doctor-Patient Interactions and Sociopolitical Belonging in Venezuelan State Clinics." *American Ethnologist* 42 (3): 459–74.

Crowley-Matoka, Megan. 2016. *Domesticating Organ Transplant: Familial Sacrifice and National Aspiration in Mexico*. Durham, NC: Duke University Press.

Cuddhe, Mary. 2012. "Mexico's Anti-abortion Backlash." *The Nation*, January 4. https://www.thenation.com/article/archive/mexicos-anti-abortion-backlash/.

Dadlez, E. M., and William L. Andrews. 2009. "Post-abortion Syndrome: Creating an Affliction." *Bioethics* 24 (9): 445–52.

Darney, B., P. Saavedra-Avendano, P. Sanhueza, and R. Schiavon. 2016. "Disparities in Access to First-Trimester Legal Abortion in the Public Sector in Mexico City: Who Presents past the Gestational Age Limit?" *Contraception* 94 (4): 400–401.

Davis, Dana-Ain. 2019. *Reproductive Injustice: Racism, Pregnancy, and Premature Birth*. New York: New York University Press.

Davis-Floyd, R., and C. B. Johnson. 2008. *Mainstreaming Midwives: The Politics of Change.* New York: Routledge.

De Genova, Nicholas. 2004. "The Legal Production of Mexican/Migrant 'Illegality.'" *Latino Studies* 2:160–85.

De León, Jason. 2015. *The Land of Open Graves: Living and Dying on the Migrant Trail.* Oakland: University of California Press.

Deomampo, Daisy. 2016. *Transnational Reproduction: Race, Kinship, and Commercial Surrogacy in India.* New York: New York University Press.

De Zordo, Silvia. 2016. "The Biomedicalisation of Illegal Abortion: The Double Life of Misoprostol in Brazil." *História, Ciências, Saúde-Manguinhos* 23 (1): 19–35.

De Zordo, Silvia, Giulia Zanini, Joanna Mishtal, Camille Garnsey, Ann-Kathrin Ziegler, and Caitlin Gerdts. 2020. "Gestational Age Limits for Abortion and Cross-border Reproductive Care in Europe: A Mixed-Methods Study." *BJOG: An International Journal of Obstetrics and Gynaecology* 128 (5): 838–45.

D'Gregorio, Pérez. 2010. "Obstetric Violence: A New Legal Term Introduced in Venezuela." *International Journal of Gynecology and Obstetrics* 111:201–2.

Dillon, Richard. 2021. "'Proud to Be Called the Most Pro-life Governor': Gov. Stitt Signs Another Abortion-Related Bill." KOCO News 5, April 27. https://www.koco.com/article/proud-to-be-called-the-most-pro-life-governor-gov-stitt-signs-another-abortion-related-bill/36267627.

Dixon, Lydia. 2015. "Obstetrics in a Time of Violence: Mexican Midwives Critique Routine Hospital Practices." *Medical Anthropology Quarterly* 29 (4): 437–.

Doubova, Svetlana, Sebastiían García-Saiso, Ricardo Pérez-Cuevas, Odet Sarabia-González, Paulina Pacheco-Estrello, Claudia Infante-Castañeda, Carmen Santamaría, Laura Del Pilar Torres-Arreola, and Hannah H. Leslie. 2018. "Quality Governance in a Pluralistic Health System: Mexican Experience and Challenges." *Lancet Global Health* 6 (11): E1149–E1152.

Ebert, Roger. 2002. "The Crime of Father Amaro." RogerEbert.com, November 15. https://www.rogerebert.com/reviews/the-crime-of-father-amaro-2002.

El Kotni, Mounia, and Elyse Ona Singer. 2019. Introduction to "Human Rights and Reproductive Governance in Transnational Perspective," edited by Mounia el Kotni and Elyse Ona Singer. Special issue, *Cross-Cultural Studies in Health and Illness* 38 (2): 118–22.

Ellner, Steve. 2020. "Introduction: Salient Characteristics of Mexico's Neoliberal Turn and Andrés Manuel López Obrador's Critique." *Latin American Perspectives* 235 (476): 4–19.

Erlich, Paul. 1968. *The Population Bomb.* New York: Ballantine Books, 1968.

Erviti, Joaquina, Roberto Castro, and Itzel A. Sosa Sánchez. 2006. "Las luchas clasificatorias en torno al aborto: El caso de los médicos en hospitales públicos de México." *Estudios Sociológicos* 24 (72): 637–65.

Fallow, Ben. 2013. *Religion and State Formation in Postrevolutionary Mexico.* Durham, NC: Duke University Press, 2013.

Faulkner, William. 2011. *Requiem for a Nun.* New York: Vintage Books, 2011.

Febrero, Eduardo. 2014. "La historia negra de Juan Pablo II, encubridor de pedófilos, canonizado junto a Juan XXII." *La Jornada*, April 28, 2014. https://www.jornada.com. mx/2014/04/28/politica/005a1pol.

Fine, Johanna B., Katherine Mayall, and Lilian Sepúlveda. 2017. "The Role of International Human Rights Norms in the Liberalization of Abortion Laws Globally." *Health and Human Rights* 19 (1): 69–80.

Fisk, Milton. 2000. "Neoliberalism and the Slow Death of Public Healthcare in Mexico." *Socialism and Democracy* 14 (1): 63–84.

Flores, Linaloe R. 2019. "Los grupos anti aborto del País captaron en el 12 años 857 millones de la IP . . . y del gobierno federal." Sinembargo.mx, April 24. https://www.sinembargo. mx/24-04-2019/3569837.

Folch-Lyon, Evelyn, Luise de la Macorra, and S. Bruce Schearer. 1981. "Focus Group and Survey Research on Family Planning in Mexico." *Studies in Family Planning* 12 (12): 409–32.

Fordyce, Lauren. 2012. "Responsible Choices: Situating Pregnancy Intention among Haitians in South Florida." *Medical Anthropology Quarterly* 26 (1): 116–35.

Fordyce, Lauren, and Amínata Maraesa. 2012. *Risk, Reproduction, and Narratives of Experience*. Nashville, TN: Vanderbilt University Press.

Fox, Jonathan. 1994. "The Difficult Transition from Clientelism to Citizenship." *World Politics* 46 (2): 151–84.

Gaceta Oficial del Distrito Federal. 2007. "Decreto por el que se Reforma el Código Penal para el Distrito Federal y se Adiciona la Ley de Salud para el Distrito Federal." Marcelo Luis Ebrard Casaubon, jefe de Gobierno del Distrito federal, April 26. https://www. ddeser.org/wp-content/uploads/2016/05/Gaceta-ILE-DF.pdf.

Gálvez, Alyshia. 2010. *Guadalupe in New York: Devotion and the Struggle for Citizenship Rights among Mexican Immigrants*. New York: New York University Press.

Gammeltoft, Tine. 2002. "Between 'Science' and 'Superstition': Moral Perceptions of Induced Abortion among Young Adults in Vietnam." *Culture, Medicine and Psychiatry* 26:313–38.

Gammeltoft, Tine. 2014. *Haunting Images: A Cultural Account of Selective Reproduction in Vietnam*. Oakland: University of California Press.

Gammeltoft, Tine, and Ayo Wahlberg. 2014. "Selective Reproductive Technologies." *Annual Review of Anthropology* 43:201–16.

Garcia, Angela. 2015. "Serenity: Violence, Inequality, and Recovery on the Edge of Mexico City." *Medical Anthropology Quarterly* 29 (4): 455–72.

García, Sandra, Diana Lara, and Lisa Goldman. 2003. "Conocimientos, actitudes, y prácticas de los médicos mexicanos sobre el aborto: Resultados de una encuesta nacional." *Gaceta Médica de México* 139 (1): 91–102.

Georges, Eugenia. 1996. "Abortion Policy and Practice in Greece." *Social Science and Medicine* 42 (2): 509–19.

Gerber Fried, Marlene. 1990. *From Abortion to Reproductive Freedom: Transforming a Movement*. Boston: South End Press.

Gerdts, C., S. De Zordo, J. Mishtal, J. Barr-Walker, and P. Lhor. 2016. "Experiences of Women Who Travel to England for Abortions: An Exploratory Pilot Study." *European Journal of Contraception and Reproductive Health Care* 31 (5): 401–7.

Gianella, Camila. 2017. "Abortion Rights Legal Mobilization in the Peruvian Media, 1990–2015." *Health and Human Rights* 19 (1): 133–48.

Gilbert, Joseph M., and Jurgen Buchenau. 2013. *Mexico's Once and Future Revolution: Social Upheaval and the Challenge of Rule since the Late Nineteenth Century*. Durham, NC: Duke University Press.

Gilmartin, M., and A. White. 2011. "Interrogating Medical Tourism: Ireland, Abortion, and Mobility Rights." *Signs* 36 (2): 275–80.

Ginsburg, Faye. 1989. *Contested Lives: The Abortion Debate in an American Community*. Oakland: University of California Press.

Ginsburg, Faye, and Rayna Rapp. 1991. "The Politics of Reproduction." *Annual Review of Anthropology* 20:311–43.

Ginsburg, Faye, and Rayna Rapp. 1995. *Conceiving the New World Order: The Global Politics of Reproduction*. Oakland: University of California Press.

GIRE (Grupo de Información en Reproducción Elegida). 2018. "Motherhood or Punishment: Criminalizing Abortion in Mexico." http://criminalizacionporaborto.gire.org.mx/assets/pdf/GIRE_Motherhood_or_Punishment.pdf.

GIRE (Grupo de Información en Reproducción Elegida). 2019. "La pieza faltante: Justicia reproductiva." November. https://gire.org.mx/wp-content/uploads/2019/11/JusticiaReproductiva.pdf.

González de León Aguirre, Deyanira, and Deborah Billings. 2001. "Attitudes towards Abortion among Medical Trainees in Mexico City Public Hospitals." *Gender and Development* 9 (2): 87–94.

Goodale, Mark. 2006a. Introduction to "Anthropology and Human Rights in a New Key," edited by Mark Goodale. Special issue, *American Anthropologist* 108:1–8.

Goodale, Mark. 2006b. "Toward a Critical Anthropology of Human Rights." *Current Anthropology* 47 (3): 485–511.

Goodale, Mark. 2013. Foreword to *The Rise and Fall of Human Rights: Cynicism and Politics in Occupied Palestine*, edited by L. Allen, xi–xii. Stanford, CA: Stanford University Press.

Greeley, Robin Adèle. 2012. Introduction to *Mexican Muralism: A Critical History*, edited by Alejandro Anreus, Leonard Folgarait, and Robin Adèle Greeley, 1–10. Oakland: University of California Press.

Greenhalgh, Susan. 1994. "Controlling Births and Bodies in Village China." *American Ethnologist: Journals of the American Ethnological Society* 21 (1): 3–30.

Grimes, Seamus. 1998. "From Population Control to 'Reproductive Rights': Ideological Influences in Population Policy." *Third World Quarterly* 19 (3): 375–94.

Gutiérrez, Elena R. 2008. *Fertile Matters: The Politics of Mexican-Origin Women's Reproduction*. Austin: University of Texas Press.

Gutierrez-Romine, Alicia. 2018. "Abortion and Intimate Borderlands." In *Beyond the Borders of the Law: Critical Legal Histories of the North American West*, edited by Katrina Jagodinsky and Pablo Mitchell, 101–31. Lawrence: University Press of Kansas.

Guttmacher Institute. 2018. "Abortion in Latin America and the Caribbean." Fact sheet, July. https://www.guttmacher.org/fact-sheet/abortion-latin-america-and-caribbean.

Gutmann, Matthew C. 2002. *The Romance of Democracy: Compliant Defiance in Contemporary Mexico*. Berkeley: University of California Press.

Gutmann, Matthew C. 2007. *The Meanings of Macho: Being a Man in Mexico City*. Berkeley: University of California Press.

Gutmann, Matthew C. 2011. "Planning Men Out of Family Planning: A Case Study from Mexico." In *Reproduction, Globalization, and the State*, edited by Carole H. Browner and Carolyn F. Sargent, 53–67. Durham, NC: Duke University Press.

Hale, Charles R. 2002. "Does Multiculturalism Menace? Governance, Cultural Rights and the Politics of Identity in Guatemala." *Journal of Latin American Studies* 34 (3): 485–524.

Hamdy, Sherine. 2008. "When the State and Your Kidneys Fail: Political Etiologies in an Egyptian Dialysis Ward." *American Ethnologist* 35 (4): 553–69.

Hamdy, Sherine. 2012. *Our Bodies Belong to God: Organ Transplants, Islam, and the Struggle for Human Dignity*. Berkeley: University of California Press.

Hannig, Anita. 2017. *Beyond Surgery: Injury, Healing, and Religion at an Ethiopian Hospital*. Chicago: University of Chicago Press.

Harris, Hope Lisa, Michelle Debbink, Lisa Martin, and Jann Hassinger. 2011. "Dynamics of Stigma in Abortion Work: Findings from a Pilot Study of the Providers Share Workshop." *Social Science and Medicine* 73 (7): 1062–70.

Hartmann, Betsy. 1995. *Reproductive Rights and Wrongs: The Global Politics of Population Control*. Boston: South End Press.

Heller, Alison. 2019. *Fistula Politics: Birthing Injuries and the Quest for Continence in Niger*. New Brunswick, NJ: Rutgers University Press.

Henriquez, Elio, and Ericka Montaño. 2002. "El crimen del padre Amarro desprestigia a la Iglesia Católica: Felipe Arizmendi." *Las Jornada*, August 11. https://www.jornada.com. mx/2002/08/11/06an1esp.php?origen=espectaculos.html.

Hirsch, Jennifer S. 2008. "Catholics Using Contraceptives: Religion, Family Planning, and Interpretive Agency in Rural Mexico." *Studies in Family Planning* 39 (2): 93–104.

Hodgson, Dorothy. 2011. *Gender and Culture at the Limit of Rights*. Philadelphia: University of Pennsylvania Press.

Holland, Jennifer L. 2020. *Tiny You: A Western History of the Anti-abortion Movement*. Oakland: University of California Press.

Howes-Mischel, Rebecca. 2012. "Local Contours of Reproductive Risk and Responsibility in Oaxaca." In *Risk, Reproduction, and Narratives of Experience*, edited by Lauren Fordyce and Amínata Maraesa, 123–40. Nashville, TN: Vanderbilt University Press.

Hull, Matthew S. 2012. "Documents and Bureaucracy." *Annual Review of Anthropology* 41:251–67.

Inhorn, Marcia C. 2011. "Globalization and Gametes: Reproductive 'Tourism,' 'Islamic Bioethics,' and Middle Eastern Modernity." *Anthropology and Medicine* 18 (1): 87–103.

Inhorn, Marcia C. 2012. "Rethinking Reproductive Tourism as Reproductive Exile." *Cultural Politics* 8 (2): 283–306.

Inhorn, Marcia C. 2015. *Cosmopolitan Conceptions: IVF Sojourns in Global Dubai*. Durham, NC: Duke University Press.

Inhorn, Marcia C., and Pasquale Patrizio. 2009. "Rethinking Reproductive 'Tourism' as Reproductive Exile." *Fertility and Sterility* 92 (3): 904–6.

Inhorn, Marcia, and Emily Wentzell. 2011. "Embodying Emergent Masculinities: Men Engaging with Reproductive and Sexual Health Technologies in the Middle East and Mexico." *American Ethnologist* 38 (4): 801–15.

Instituto Federal Electoral. 2010. "2006 Elección de Presidente de los Estados Unidos Mexicanos." January 9. https://web.archive.org/web/20100109163113/http://www.ife.org.mx/documentos/Estadisticas2006/presidente/nac.html.

Jaffary, Nora E. 2016. *Reproduction and Its Discontents in Mexico: Childbirth and Contraception from 1750 to 1905.* Chapel Hill: University of North Carolina Press.

Joffe, Carole. 1995. *Doctors of Conscience: The Struggle to Provide Abortion before and after Roe v. Wade.* Boston: Beacon Press.

Joffe, Carole, T. A. Weitz, and C. L. Stacey. 2004. "Uneasy Allies: Pro-choice Physicians, Feminist Health Activists and the Struggle for Abortion Rights." *Sociology of Health and Illness* 26 (6): 775–96.

Johnson-Hanks, Jennifer. 2002. "On the Modernity of Traditional Contraception: Time and the Social Context of Fertility." *Population and Development Review* 28:229–49.

La Jornada. 2016. "Papa hace perenne facultad de curas para absolver abortos." November 22, 2016. https://www.jornada.com.mx/2016/11/22/sociedad/036n1soc.

Kahn, Susan Martha. 2000. *Reproducing Jews: A Cultural Account of Assisted Conception in Israel.* Durham, NC: Duke University Press.

Kaufman, Sharon, and Lynn Morgan. 2005. "The Anthropology of the Beginnings and Ends of Life." *Annual Review of Anthropology* 34:317–41.

Kelley, Lisa M. 2014. "Reckoning with Narratives of Innocent Suffering in Transnational Abortion Litigation." In *Abortion Law in Transnational Perspective: Cases and Controversies*, edited by Rebecca J. Cook, Joanna N. Erdman, and Bernard M. Dickens, 303–26. Philadelphia: University of Pennsylvania Press.

Kelly, Kimberly. 2014. "The Spread of 'Post Abortion Syndrome' as Social Diagnosis." *Social Science and Medicine* 102:18–25.

Kierans, Ciara, and Kirsten Bell. 2017. "Cultivating Ambivalence: Some Methodological Considerations for Anthropology." *HAU: Journal of Ethnographic Theory* 7 (2): 23–44.

Kimball, Natalie. 2020. *An Open Secret: The History of Unwanted Pregnancy and Abortion in Modern Bolivia.* New Brunswick, NJ: Rutgers University Press.

Kimport, Katrina. 2012. "(Mis)Understanding Abortion Regret." *Symbolic Interaction* 35 (2): 105–22.

Kissinger, Henry. 1998. *Report of the National Bipartisan Commission on Central America.* Collingdale, PA: Diane.

Kligman, Gail. 1998. *The Politics of Duplicity: Controlling Reproduction in Ceausescu's Romania.* Berkeley: University of California Press.

Knight, Alan. 2016. *The Mexican Revolution: A Very Short Introduction.* Oxford: Oxford University Press.

Krause, Elizabeth L. 2012. "'They Just Happened': The Curious Case of the Unplanned

Baby, Italian Low Fertility, and the 'End' of Rationality." *Medical Anthropology Quarterly* 26 (3): 361–82.

Krause, Elizabeth L., and Silvia De Zordo. 2012. "Introduction: Ethnography and Biopolitics: Tracing 'Rationalities' of Reproduction across the North–South Divide." *Anthropology and Medicine* 19:137–51.

Krauss, Amy. 2018a. "The Ephemeral Politics of Feminist Accompaniment Networks in Mexico City." *Feminist Theory* 20 (1): 27–54.

Krauss, Amy. 2018b. "Luisa's Ghosts: Haunted Legality and Collective Expressions of Pain." *Medical Anthropology: Cross-cultural Studies in Health and Illness* 37 (8): 688–702.

Kulczycki, Andrej. 2003. "'De eso no se habla': Aceptando el aborto en México." *Estudios Demográficos y Urbanos* 18 (2): 353–86.

Kulczycki, Andrej. 2007. "The Abortion Debate in Mexico: Realities and Stalled Policy Reform." *Bulletin of Latin American Research* 26 (1): 50–68.

Kumar, Anuradha, Leila Hessini, and Ellen M. H. Mitchell. 2009. "Conceptualizing Abortion Stigma." *Culture, Health and Sexuality* 11 (6): 625–39

Lamas, Marta. 1997. "The Feminist Movement and the Development of Political Discourse on Voluntary Motherhood in Mexico." *Reproductive Health Matters* 5 (10): 58–67.

Lamas, Marta. 2001a. "Abortion and Politics." *Voices of Mexico*, no. 55 (April–June): 27–30. http://ru.micisan.unam.mx:8080/bitstream/handle/123456789/18117/VOM-0055-0027. pdf?sequence=1.

Lamas, Marta. 2001b. "Standing Fast in Mexico: Protecting Women's Rights in a Hostile Climate." *NACLA Report on the Americas* 34 (5): 36–40.

Lamas, Marta. 2011. *Feminism: Transmissions and Retransmissions*. New York: Palgrave Macmillan.

Lamas, Marta. 2014. "Entre el estigma y la ley: La interrupción legal del embarazo en DF." *Salúd Publica de México* 56:56–62.

Lamas, Marta, and Sharon Bissel. 2000. "Abortion Politics in Mexico: 'Context Is All.'" *Reproductive Health Matters: An International Journal on Sexual and Reproductive Health and Rights* 8 (16): 10–23.

Lara, Diana, Sandra García, Kate Wilson, and Francisco Paz. 2011. "How Often and under Which Circumstances Do Mexican Pharmacy Vendors Recommend Misoprostol to Induce an Abortion?" *International Perspectives on Reproductive Health* 37 (2): 75–83.

Laurell, Asa Christina. 2001. "Health Reform in Mexico: The Promotion of Inequality." *International Journal of Health Services* 31 (2): 291–321.

Laurell, Asa Christina. 2003. "What Does Latin American Social Medicine Do When It Governs? The Case of the Mexico City Government." *American Journal of Public Health* 93 (12): 2028–31.

Laurell, Asa Christina. 2007. "Health System Reform in Mexico: A Critical Review." *Journal of Health Services* 37 (3): 515–35.

Laurell, Asa Christina. 2015. "Three Decades of Neoliberalism in Mexico: The Destruction of Society." *International Journal of Health Services* 45 (2): 246–64.

Lawson, Chappell. 2000. "Mexico's Unfinished Transition: Democratization and Authoritarian Enclaves in Mexico." *Mexican Studies / Estudios Mexicanos* 16 (2): 267–87.

Lee, Amanda, Aimee James, and Jean Hunleth. 2020. "Waiting for Care: Chronic Illness and Health System Uncertainties in the United States." *Social Science and Medicine* 264:1–8.

Lester, Rebecca J. 2005. *Jesus in Our Wombs: Embodying Modernity in a Mexican Convent.* Berkeley: University of California Press.

Lester, Rebecca J. 2016. "Ground Zero: Ontology, Recognition, and the Elusiveness of Care in American Eating Disorders Treatment." *Transcultural Psychiatry* 55 (4): 516–33.

Lester, Rebecca J. 2019. *Famished: Eating Disorders Treatment and Failed Care in America.* Oakland: University of California Press.

Levitt, Peggy, and Sally Engle Merry. 2011. "Making Women's Human Rights in the Vernacular: Navigating the Culture/Rights Divide." In *Gender and Culture at the Limit of Rights*, edited by Dorothy Hodgson, 81–100. Philadelphia: University of Pennsylvania Press.

Levy, Daniel C., Kathleen Bruhn, and Emilio Zebadúa. 2001. *Mexico: The Struggle for Democratic Development.* Berkeley: University of California Press.

Littlefield, Amy, and Laura Gottesdiener. 2019. "When Abortion after Rape Is Legal—but Nearly Impossible to Obtain." *The Nation*, September 17. https://www.thenation.com/article/archive/abortion-mexico-rape-survivors-green-tide/.

Lipka, Michael. 2016. "A Snapshot of Catholics in Mexico: Pope Francis' Next Stop." Pew Research Center, February 10. https://www.pewresearch.org/fact-tank/2016/02/10/a-snapshot-of-catholics-in-mexico-pope-francis-next-stop/.

Livingston, Julie. 2012. *Improvising Medicine: An African Oncology Ward in an Emerging Cancer Epidemic.* Durham, NC: Duke University Press.

Lomnitz, Claudio. 2001. *Deep Mexico, Silent Mexico: An Anthropology of Nationalism.* Minneapolis: University of Minnesota Press.

Lomnitz, Claudio. 2008. *Death and the Idea of Mexico.* New York: Zone Books.

Lomnitz, Claudio. 2014. "Michoacán, tierra de suposiciones." *La Jornada*, July 30. https://www.jornada.com.mx/2014/07/30/opinion/023a1pol.

Lomnitz-Adler, Claudio. 1992. *Exits from the Labyrinth: Culture and Ideology in the Mexican National Space.* Berkeley: University of California Press.

Lomnitz, Larissa Adler, and Marisol Pérez-Lizaur. 1987. *A Mexican Elite Family, 1820–1980.* Princeton, NJ: Princeton University Press, 1987.

López, Midiam Moreno, Karla Flores Celis, Catalina González-Forteza, María Teresa Saltijeral, Raffaela Schiavon, María Elena Collado, Olivia Ortiz, and Luciana Ramos Lira. 2019. "Relationship between Perceived Stigma and Depressive Symptomology in Women Who Legally Interrupt Pregnancy in Mexico City." *Salud Mental* 42 (1): 25–32.

Luiselli, Valeria. 2014. *Sidewalks.* Translated by Christina MacSweeney. Minneapolis, MN: Coffee House Press.

Luna, Zakiya. 2009. "From Rights to Justice: Women of Color Changing the Face of US Reproductive Rights Organizing." *Societies without Borders* 4 (3): 343–65.

Luna, Zakiya, and Kristin Luker. 2013. "Reproductive Justice." *Annual Review of Law and Social Science* 9:327–52.

Lupton, Deborah. 2012. "'Precious Cargo': Foetal Subjects, Risk and Reproductive Citizenship." *Critical Public Health* 22 (3): 329–40.

MacDonald, Margaret E. 2020. "Misoprostol: The Social Life of a Life-Saving Drug in Global Maternal Health." *Science, Technology and Human Values* 46 (2): 376–401.

Madrazo, Alejandro. 2009. "The Evolution of Mexico City's Abortion Laws: From Public Morality to Women's Autonomy." *International Journal of Gynecology and Obstetrics* 106:266–69.

Maier, Elizabeth. 2012. "Documenting Mexico's Culture War." *Latin American Perspectives* 187 (6): 155–64.

Major, Brenda, Mark Appelbaum, Linda Beckman, Mary Ann Dutton, Nancy Felipe Russo, and Carolyn West. 2009. "Abortion and Mental Health: Evaluating the Evidence." *American Psychologist* 64 (9): 863–90.

Manrique, Linnete. 2016. "Dreaming of a Cosmic Race: José Vasconcelos and the Politics of Race in Mexico, 1920s–1930s." *Cogent Arts and Humanities* 3:1–13.

Marchesi, M. 2012. "Reproducing Italians: Contested Biopolitics in the Age of 'Replacement Anxiety.'" *Anthropology and Medicine* 19 (2): 171–88.

Marcus-Delgado, Jane. 2019. *The Politics of Abortion in Latin America: Public Debates, Private Lives*. Boulder, CO: Lynne Rienner.

Marshall, Patricia, and Barbara Koenig. 2004. "Accounting for Culture in a Globalized Bioethics." *Journal of Law, Medicine and Ethics* 32:252s–66s.

Martin, Aryn, Natasha Myers, and Ana Viseu. 2015. "The Politics of Care in Technoscience." *Social Studies of Science* 45 (5): 625–41.

Martin, Emily. 1987. *The Woman in the Body: A Cultural Analysis of Reproduction*. Boston: Beacon Press.

Martin, Emily. 2007. *Bipolar Expeditions: Mania and Depression in American Culture*. Princeton, NJ: Princeton University Press.

Martínez, Fabiola. 2014. *"Templarios* 'sí extraían órganos a niños': Se investigan ritos de iniciación: Castillo." *La Jornada*, March 19. https://www.jornada.com.mx/2014/03/19/politica/013n1pol.

Martínez, Rebecca C. 2018. *Marked Women: The Cultural Politics of Cervical Cancer in Venezuela*. Stanford, CA: Stanford University Press.

Mason, Carol. 1999. "Minority Unborn." In *Fetal Subjects, Feminist Positions*, edited by Lynn M. Morgan and Meredith W. Michaels, 159–74. Philadelphia: University of Pennsylvania Press.

Matorras, Roberto. 2005. "¿Turismo reproductivo o exilio reproductivo?" Editorial. *Revista Iberoamericana de Fertilidad* 22 (2): 85.

Merry, Sally Engle. 2006. "Transnational Human Rights and Local Activism: Mapping the Middle." *American Anthropologist* 10 (8): 38–51.

Messer, Ellen. 1997. "Pluralist Approaches to Human Rights." *Journal of Anthropological Research* 53 (3): 293–317.

McCaa, Robert. 2003. "Missing Millions: The Demographic Costs of the Mexican Revolution." *Mexican Studies / Estudios Mexicanos* 19 (2): 367–400.

Mccammon, Sarah. 2019. "With Abortion Restrictions on the Rise, Some Women Induce Their Own." *All Things Considered*, September 19, National Public Radio.

https://www.npr.org/2019/09/19/759761114/with-abortion-restrictions-on-the-rise
-some-women-induce-their-own.

Mishtal, Joanna. 2015. *The Politics of Morality: The Church, the State, and Reproductive Rights in Post-socialist Poland.* Athens: Ohio University Press.

Mishtal, Joanna, and Rachel Dannefer. 2010. "Reconciling Religious Identity and Reproductive Practices: The Church and Contraception in Poland." *European Journal of Contraception and Reproductive Health Care* 15 (4): 232–42.

Montes de Ocas, Yessica Paola, José Luis Valdez Medina, Norma Ivonne González-Arratia López Fuentes, and Sergio González Escobar. 2013. "Los roles de género de los hombres y las mujeres en el México contemporáneo." *Enseñanza e Investigación en Psicología* 18 (2): 207–24.

Montgomery, Heather. 2001. "Imposing Rights? A Case Study of Child Prostitution in Thailand." In *Culture and Rights: Anthropological Perspectives*, edited by J. K. Cowan, M. Dembour, and R. Wilson, 80–101. Cambridge: Cambridge University Press.

Moran-Thomas, Amy. 2019. *Traveling with Sugar: Chronicles of a Global Epidemic.* Oakland: University of California Press.

Moreno-Ruiz, N. L., L. Borgatta, S. Yanow, N. Kapp, E. R. Wiebe, and B. Winikoff. 2007. "Alternatives to Mifepristone for Early Medical Abortion." *International Journal of Gynecology and Obstetrics* 96 (3): 212–18.

Morgan, Lynn M. 2009. *Icons of Life: A Cultural History of Human Embryos.* Berkeley: University of California Press.

Morgan, Lynn M. 2015. "Reproductive Rights or Reproductive Justice? Lessons from Argentina." *Health and Human Rights Journal* 17 (1): 136–47.

Morgan, Lynn M. 2019. "Miss Mexico's Dress: The Struggle over Reproductive Governance in Jalisco, Mexico." *Journal of Latin American and Caribbean Anthropology* 24 (2): 536–54.

Morgan, Lynn M., and Meredith Michaels. 1999. *Fetal Subjects, Feminist Positions.* Philadelphia: University of Pennsylvania Press.

Morgan, Lynn M., and Elizabeth F. S. Roberts. 2012. "Reproductive Governance in Latin America." *Anthropology and Medicine* 19 (2): 241–54.

Morris, Stephen. 1999. "Reforming the Nation: Mexican Nationalism in Context." *Latin American Studies* 31 (2): 363–97.

Moyn, Samuel. 2010. *The Last Utopia: Human Rights in History.* Cambridge, MA: Belknap Press of Harvard University Press.

Mulcahy, Caitlin M., Dian C. Perry, and Tory D. Glover. 2010. "The 'Patient Patient': The Trauma of Waiting and the Power of Resistance for People Living with Cancer." *Qualitative Health Research* 20 (8): 1062–75.

Muñoz García, Graciela Beatriz, and Lina Rosa Berrio Palomo. 2020. "Violencias más allá del espacio clínico y rutas de la inconformidad: La violencia obstétrica e institucional en la vida de mujeres urbanas e indígenas en México." In *Violencia obstétrica en América Latina: Conceptualización, experiencias, medición y estrategias*, edited by Patrizia Quattrocchi and Natalia Magone, 103–30. Buenos Aires: EDUNla Cooperativa.

Murillo, Lina-Maria. 2016. "Birth Control on the Border: Race, Gender, Religion, and Class in the Making of the Birth Control Movement, El Paso, Texas, 1936–1973." PhD diss., University of Texas, El Paso. https://scholarworks.utep.edu/dissertations/AAI10247744.

Murphy, Michelle. 2015. "Unsettling Care: Troubling Transnational Itineraries of Care in Feminist Health Practices." *Social Studies of Science* 45 (5): 665–90.

Nahman, Michal R. 2016. "Reproductive Tourism: Through the Anthropological 'Reproscope.'" *Annual Review of Anthropology* 45 (1): 417–32.

Napolitano, Valentina. 2009. "The Virgin of Guadalupe: A Nexus of Affect." *Journal of the Royal Anthropological Institute* 15 (1): 96–112.

Nehring, Daniel, Rosario Esteinou, and Emmanuel Alvarado. 2016. *Intimacies and Cultural Change: Perspective on Contemporary Mexico*. New York: Routledge Taylor and Francis Group.

Nelson, Jennifer. 2019. "Abortion Rights and Human Rights in Mexico." In *Reproductive Justice and Sexual Rights: Transnational Perspectives*, edited by Tanya Saroj-Bakhru, chap. 6. New York: Routledge Press.

Nesvig, Martin Austin. 2006. *Local Religion in Colonial Mexico*. Albuquerque: University of New Mexico Press.

Noonan, John T. 1967. "Abortion and the Catholic Church: A Summary History." *Natural Law Forum* 12 (85): 85–131.

Oaks, Laury. 2000. "Smoke-Filled Wombs and Fragile Fetuses: The Social Politics of Fetal Representation." *Signs* 26 (1): 63–108.

Oaks, Laury. 2003. "The Politics of Health Risk Warnings: Social Movements and Controversy over the Link between Abortion and Breast Cancer." In *Risk, Cultural and Health Inequality: Shifting Perceptions of Danger and Blame*, edited by Barbara Herr Harthorn and Laury Oaks, 79–101. Westport, CT: Greenwood.

Ojeda, Norma. 2006. "Abortion in a Transborder Context." In *Women and Change at the U.S.-Mexico Border: Mobility, Labor, and Activism*, edited by Doreen J. Mattingly and Ellen R. Hansen, 53–69. Tucson: University of Arizona Press.

Olson, Madeleine. 2020. "Blurring the Division between Church and State in AMLO's Mexico." NACLA, February 10. https://nacla.org/news/2020/02/10/Church-and-State-AMLO-Mexico.

Ortiz-Millán, Gustavo. 2018. "Abortion and Conscientious Objection: Rethinking Conflicting Rights in the Mexican Context." *Global Bioethics* 29 (1): 1–15.

Ortiz-Millán, Gustavo, and Frances Kissling. 2020. "Bioethics Training in Reproductive Health in Mexico." *International Journal of Gynecology and Obstetrics* 151 (2): 308–13.

Ortiz-Ortega, Adriana. 2005. "The Politics of Abortion in Mexico." In *Where Human Rights Begin: Health, Sexuality, and Women in the New Millennium*, edited by Wendy Chavkin and Ellen Chelsier, 154–79. New Brunswick, NJ: Rutgers University Press.

Ostrach, Bayla. 2017. *Health Policy in a Time of Crisis: Abortion, Austerity, and Access*. New York: Routledge.

Paine, J., R. T. Noriega, and A. L. Beltrán y Puga. 2014. "Using Litigation to Defend Women Prosecuted for Abortion in Mexico: Challenging State Laws and the Implications of Recent Court Judgements." *Reproductive Health Matters* 22 (44): 61–69.

Panella, Cristiana, and Kedron Thomas. 2015. "Ethics, Evaluation, and Economies of Value amidst Illegal Practices." *Critique of Anthropology* 35 (1): 3–12.

Paxman, John, Alberto Rizo, Laura Brown, and Janie Benson. 1993. "The Clandestine Epidemic: The Practice of Unsafe Abortion in Latin America." *Studies in Family Planning* 24 (4): 205–26.

Paxson, Heather. 2002. "Rationalizing Sex: Family Planning and the Making of Modern Lovers in Urban Greece." *American Ethnologist* 29 (2): 307–34.

Peeters, Rik, Humberto Trujillo Jiménez, Elizabeth O'Connor, Pascual Ograrrio Rojas, Michele González Galindo, and Daniela Morales Tenorio. 2018. "Low-Trust Bureaucracy: Understanding the Mexican Bureaucratic Experience." *Public Administration and Development* 38:65–74.

Pennings, Guido. 2002. "Reproductive Tourism as Moral Pluralism in Motion." *Journal of Medical Ethics* 28 (6): 337–41.

Petchesky, Rosalind P. 1995. "From Population Control to Reproductive Rights: Feminist Fault Lines." *Reproductive Health Matters* 3 (6): 152–61.

Peterson, Jeanette F. 1992. "The Virgin of Guadalupe: Symbol of Conquest or Liberation?" *Art Journal* 51 (4): 39–47.

Petryna, Adriana. 2008. "Ethical Variability: Drug Development and Globalizing Clinical Trials." *American Ethnologist* 32 (2): 183–97.

Petryna, Adriana. 2013. *Life Exposed: Biological Citizens after Chernobyl*. Princeton, NJ: Princeton University Press.

Petryna, Adriana, and Karolina Follis. 2015. "Risks of Citizenship and Fault Lines of Survival." *Annual Review of Anthropology* 44:401–17.

Pew Research Center. 2013. "The Global Catholic Population." February 13. https://www.pewforum.org/2013/02/13/the-global-catholic-population/.

Pew Research Center. 2014. "Religion and Morality in Latin America." November 13. https://www.pewforum.org/interactives/latin-america-morality-by-religion/.

Poole, Stafford. 2017. *Our Lady of Guadalupe: The Origins and Sources of a Mexican National Symbol, 1531–1797*. Tucson: University of Arizona Press.

Pou Jiménez, Francisca. 2009. "El aborto en México: El debate en la Suprema Corte sobre la normativa del Distrito Federal." *Annuario de Derechos Humanos* 5:137–52.

Povoledo, Elisabetta, and Liam Stack. 2016. "Pope Francis Extends Priests' Ability to Forgive Abortion." *New York Times*, November 21. https://www.nytimes.com/2016/11/21/world/europe/pope-francis-abortion-priests.html.

Price, Kimala. 2010. "What Is Reproductive Justice? How Women of Color Activists Are Redefining the Pro-choice Paradigm." *Meridians* 10 (2): 42–65.

Price, Kimala. 2011. "It's Not Just about Abortion: Incorporating Intersectionality in Research about Women of Color and Reproduction." *Women's Health Issues* 21 (3): 55–57.

Puig, Andrea, José A. Pagán, and Rebecca Wong. 2009. "Assessing Quality across Health Care Subsystems in Mexico." *Journal of Ambulatory Care Management* 32 (2): 123–31.

Quattrocchi, Patrizia, and Natalia Magnone, eds. *Violencia obstétrica en América Latina*. Buenos Aires: Universidad Nacional de Lanús.

Rabinow, Paul, and Nikolas Rose. 2006. "Biopower Today." *Biosocieties* 1:195–217.

Rapp, Rayna. 1999. *Testing Women, Testing the Fetus: The Social Impact of Amniocentesis in America*. New York: Routledge.

Rapp, Rayna. 2001. "Gender, Body, Biomedicine: How Some Feminist Concerns Dragged Reproduction to the Center of Social Theory." *Medical Anthropology Quarterly* 15 (4): 466–77.

Raymond, Elizabeth G., and David A. Grimes. 2012. "The Comparative Safety of Legal Induced Abortion and Childbirth in the United States." *Obstetrics and Gynecology* 119 (2): 215–19.

Reagan, Leslie J. 1997. *When Abortion Was a Crime: Women, Medicine, and Law in the United States, 1967–1973*. Berkeley: University of California Press.

Reich, Michael R. 2020. "Restructuring Health Reform, Mexican Style." *Health Systems and Reforms* 6 (1): e1763114.

Rivkin-Fish, Michelle. 2005. *Women's Health in Post-Soviet Russia: The Politics of Intervention*. Bloomington: Indiana University Press.

Roberts, Elizabeth F. S. 2006. "God's Laboratory: Religious Rationalities and Modernity in Ecuadorian in Vitro Fertilization." *Culture, Medicine and Psychiatry* 30 (4): 507–36.

Roberts, Elizabeth, F. S. 2012. *God's Laboratory: Assisted Reproduction in the Andes*. Berkeley: University of California Press.

Rocca, Corinne H., Goleen Samari, Diana G. Foster, Heather Gould, and Katrina Kimport. 2020. "Emotions and Decision Rightness over Five Years following an Abortion: An Examination of Decision Difficulty and Abortion Stigma." *Social Science and Medicine* 248:1–8.

Rose, Nicholas. 2000. "Government and Control." *British Journal of Criminology* 40:321–39.

Roseneil, Sarah, Isabel Crowhurst, Ana Cristina Santos, and Mariya Stoilova. 2013. Introduction to "Reproduction and Citizenship / Reproducing Citizens," edited by Sarah Roseneil, Isabel Crowhurst, Ana Cristina Santos, and Mariya Stoilova. Special issue, *Citizenship Studies* 17 (8): 901–11.

Ross, John. 2009. *El Monstruo: Dread and Redemption in Mexico City*. New York: Nation Books.

Ross, Loretta. 2017. "Reproductive Justice as Intersectional Feminist Activism." *A Critical Journal of Black Politics, Culture, and Society* 19 (3): 286–314.

Ross, Loretta, and Rickie Solinger. 2017. *Reproductive Justice: An Introduction*. Oakland: University of California Press.

Ruhl, Lealle. 2002. "Dilemmas of the Will: Uncertainty, Reproduction, and the Rhetoric of Control." *Signs* 27 (3): 614–63.

Sánchez, Carlos Alberto. 2011. "On Documents and Subjectivity: The Formation and Deformation of the Immigrant Identity." *Radical Philosophy Review* 14 (2): 197–205.

Sánchez Fuentes, María Luisa, Jennifer Paine, and Brook Elliott-Buettner. 2008. "The Decriminalisation of Abortion in Mexico City: How Did Abortion Rights Become a Political Priority?" *Gender and Development* 16 (2): 345–60.

Sanders, Nichole. 2009. "Mothering Mexico: The Historiography of Mothers and Motherhood in 20th Century Mexico." *History Compass* 7:1542–53.

Sandoval Cervantes, Iván. 2017. "Uncertain Futures: The Unfinished Homes of Undocumented Migrants in Oaxaca, Mexico." *American Anthropologist* 119 (2): 209–22.

San Martín, Inés. 2020. "Pope Francis Weighs In on Argentina's Abortion Debate." *Crux: Taking the Catholic Pulse*, November 26. https://cruxnow.com/church-in-the-americas/2020/11/pope-francis-weighs-in-on-argentinas-abortion-debate/.

Sargent, Carolyn. 2006. "Reproductive Strategies and Islamic Discourse." *Medical Anthropology Quarterly* 20 (1): 31–49.

Sargent, Carolyn, and Carolyn Smith-Morris. 2006. "Questioning Our Principles: Anthropological Contributions to Ethical Dilemmas in Clinical Practice." *Cambridge Quarterly of Healthcare Ethics* 15:123–34.

Schell, Patience. 2004. "Nationalizing Children through Schools and Hygiene: Porfirian and Revolutionary Mexico City." *The Americas* 60:559–87.

Scheper-Hughes, Nancy. 1992. *Death without Weeping: The Violence of Everyday Life in Brazil.* Berkeley: University of California Press.

Schiavon, Raffaela, and Erika Troncoso. 2020. "Inequalities in Access to and Quality of Abortion Services in Mexico: Can Task-Sharing Be an Opportunity to Increase Legal and Safe Abortion Care?" *Gynecology and Obstetrics* 150 (1): 25–33.

Schiavon, Raffaela, Erika Troncoso, and Gerardo Polo. 2012. "Analysis of Maternal and Abortion-Related Mortality in Mexico over the Last Two Decades, 1990–2008." *International Journal of Gynecology and Obstetrics* 118 (2): S78–S86.

Semple, Kirk, Paulina Villegas, and Natalie Kitroeff. 2020. "Years after 43 Mexican Students Vanished, a Victim's Remains Are Found." *New York Times*, July 7. https://www.nytimes.com/2020/07/07/world/americas/mexico-43-missing-students-remains.html.

Sesia, Paula. 2020a. "Naming, Framing and Shaming through Obstetric Violence: A Critical Approach to the Judicialization of Maternal Health Rights Violations in Mexico." In *Critical Medical Anthropology: Perspectives in and from Latin America*, edited by Jennie Gamlin, Sahra Gibbon, Paola M. Sesia, and Lina Berrio, 222–47. London: UCL Press.

Sesia, Paula. 2020b. "Violencia obstétrica en México: La consolidación disputada de un nuevo paradigma." In *Violencia obstétrica en América Latina*, edited by Patrizia Quattrocchi and Natalia Magnone, 2–29. Buenos Aires: Universidad Nacional de Lanús.

Sethna, C., and G. Davis. 2019. *Abortion across Borders: Transnational Travel and Access to Abortion Services.* Baltimore: Johns Hopkins University Press.

Sethna, C., and M. Doull. 2012. "Accidental Tourists: Canadian Women, Abortion Tourism, and Travel." *Women's Studies: An Inter-disciplinary Journal* 41 (4): 457–75.

Sethna, C., and M. Doull. 2013. "Spatial Disparities and Travel to Freestanding Abortion Clinics in Canada." *Women's Studies International Forum* 38:52–62.

Shakir, Fevzi, and Yasser Diab. 2013. "The Perforated Uterus." *Obstetrician and Gynecologist* 15 (4): 256–61.

Shepard, B. 2000. "The 'Double Discourse' on Sexual and Reproductive Rights in Latin America: The Chasm between Public Discourse and Private Actions." *Health and Human Rights Journal* 4 (2): 110–43.

Shweder, Richard A. 2000. "What about 'Female Genital Mutilation'? And Why Understanding Culture Matters in the First Place." *Daedalus* 129 (4): 209–32.

Singer, Elyse Ona. 2016. "From Reproductive Rights to Responsibilization: Fashioning Liberal Subjects in Mexico City's New Public Abortion Program." *Medical Anthropology Quarterly* 31 (4): 445–63.

Singer, Elyse Ona, and Bayla Ostrach. 2017. "The End of Feminist Abortion Counseling? Examining Threats to Women's Health." In *Transcending Borders: Abortion in the Past and Present*, edited by Shannon Stettner, Katrina Ackerman, Kristin Burnett, and Travis Hay, 255–70. London: Palgrave Macmillan.

Singer, Merrill C. 1989. "The Coming of Age of Critical Medical Anthropology." *Social Science and Medicine* 28 (11): 1193–1203.

Singer, Merrill C., Freddie Valentín, Hans Baer, and Zhongke Jia. 2010. "Why Does Juan García Have a Drinking Problem? The Perspective of Critical Medical Anthropology." *Medical Anthropology: Cross-cultural Studies in Health and Illness* 14 (1): 77–108.

Smith-Oka, Vania. 2012. "Bodies of Risk: Constructing Motherhood in a Mexican Public Hospital." *Social Science and Medicine* 75:2275–82.

Smith-Oka, Vania. 2013a. "Managing Labor and Delivery among Impoverished Populations in Mexico: Cervical Examinations as Bureaucratic Practice." *American Anthropologist* 115 (4): 595–607.

Smith-Oka, Vania. 2013b. *Shaping the Motherhood of Indigenous Mexico*. Nashville, TN: Vanderbilt University Press.

Smith-Oka, Vania. 2015. "Microaggressions and the Reproduction of Social Inequalities in Medical Encounters in Mexico." *Social Science and Medicine* 143:9–16.

Solheim, I. H., K. M. Moland, C. Kahabuka, A. B. Pembe, and A. Bystad. 2020. "Beyond the Law: Misoprostol and Medical Abortion in Dar es Salaam, Tanzania." *Social Science and Medicine* 245:1–8.

Solís González, José Luis. 2013. "Neoliberalismo y crimen organizado en México: El surgimiento del Estado Narco." *Frontera Norte* 25 (50): 7–34.

Sorhaindo, Annik. M., C. Juárez-Ramírez, C. Díaz Olavarrieta, E. Aldaz, M. C. Mejía Piñeros, and S. Garcia. 2014. "Qualitative Evidence on Abortion Stigma from Mexico City and Five States in Mexico." *Women and Health* 54 (7): 622–40.

Soto Laveaga, Gabriela. 2007. "'Let's Become Fewer': Soap Operas, Contraception, and Nationalizing the Mexican Family in an Overpopulated World." *Sexuality Research and Social Policy* 4 (19): 19–33.

Soto Laveaga, Gabriela. 2009. *Jungle Laboratories: Mexican Peasants, National Projects, and the Making of the Pill*. Durham, NC: Duke University Press.

Soto Laveaga, Gabriela. 2016. "Building the Nation of the Future, One Waiting Room at a Time: Hospital Murals in the Making of Modern Mexico." *History and Technology: An International Journal* 31 (3): 275–94.

Sousa, Angelica, Rafael Loano, and Emmanuela Gakidou. 2010. "Exploring the Determinants of Unsafe Abortion: Improving the Evidence Base in Mexico." *Health Policy and Planning* 25 (4): 300–310.

Spade, Dean. 2013. "Intersectional Resistance and Law Reform." *Signs* 38 (4): 1031–55.

Speed, Shannon. 2006. "At the Crossroads of Human Rights and Anthropology: Toward a Critically Engaged Activist Research." *American Anthropologist* 108 (1): 66–76.

Speed, Shannon. 2008. *Rights in Rebellion: Indigenous Struggle and Human Rights in Chiapas.* Stanford, CA: Stanford University Press.

Stepan, Nancy. 1991. *"The Hour of Eugenics": Race, Gender, and Nation in Latin America.* Ithaca, NY: Cornell University Press.

Stern, Alexandra Minna. 1999. "Responsible Mothers and Normal Children: Eugenics, Nationalism, and Welfare in Post-revolutionary Mexico, 1920–1940." *Journal of Historical Sociology* 12 (4): 369–97.

Stevenson, Lisa. 2012. "The Psychic Life of Biopolitics: Survival, Cooperation, and Inuit Community." *American Ethnologist* 39 (3): 592–613.

Strong, Adrienne E. 2020. *Documenting Death: Maternal Mortality and the Ethics of Care in Tanzania.* Oakland: University of California Press.

Sufrin, Carolyn. 2017. *Jailcare: Finding the Safety Net for Women behind Bars.* Oakland: University of California Press.

Suh, Siri. 2019. "Metrics of Survival: Post-abortion Care and Reproductive Rights in Senegal." *Medical Anthropology: Cross-cultural Studies in Health and Illness* 38 (2): 152–66.

Suh, Siri. 2020. "What Post-abortion Care Indicators Don't Measure: Global Abortion Politics and Obstetric Practice in Senegal." *Social Science and Medicine* 254:1–9.

Suh, Siri. 2021. *Dying to Count: Post-abortion Care and Global Reproductive Health Politics in Senegal.* New Brunswick, NJ: Rutgers University Press.

Taracena, Rosario. 2002. "Social Actors and Discourse on Abortion in the Mexican Press: The Paulina Case." *Reproductive Health Matters* 10 (19): 103–10.

Taylor, William B. 1987. "The Virgin of Guadalupe in New Spain: An Inquiry into the Social History of Marian Devotion." *American Ethnologist* 14 (1): 9–33.

Thomas, Kedron, and Rebecca Galemba. 2013. "Illegal Anthropology: An Introduction." *Political and Legal Anthropology Review* 36 (2): 211–14.

Thompson, Charis. 2006. "God Is in the Details: Comparative Perspectives on the Intertwining of Religion and Assisted Reproductive Technologies." *Culture, Medicine and Psychiatry* 30 (4): 557–61.

Totenberg, Nina. 2021. "Challenge to Roe, Supreme Court to Review Mississippi Abortion Law." National Public Radio, May 17. https://www.npr.org/2021/05/17/997478374/supreme-court-to-review-mississippi-abortion-ban.

Tuckman, Jo. 2012. *Mexico: Democracy Interrupted.* New Haven, CT: Yale University Press.

Turner, Terence. 1997. "Human Rights, Human Difference: Anthropology's Contribution to an Emancipatory Cultural Politics." *Journal of Anthropological Research* 53 (3): 273–91.

Ubaldi Garcete, Norma. 2008. *El proceso de despenalización del aborto en laCiudad de México.* Mexico City: Grupo de Información en Reproducción Elegida.

Unnithan, Maya, and Silvia De Zordo. 2018. "Re-situating Abortion: Bio-Politics, Global Health and Rights in Neo-liberal Times." *Global Public Health* 13 (6): 657–61.

Urías Horcasitas, Beatriz. 2003. "Eugenesia y aborto en México (1920–1940)." *Debate Feminista* 27:305–23.

US National Security Council. 1974. "National Security Memorandum: Implications of Worldwide Population Growth for U.S. Security and Overseas Interests." December 10. https://pdf.usaid.gov/pdf_docs/PCAAB500.pdf.

Vasconcelos, José. 1997. *The Cosmic Race.* Translated by Didier T. Jaén. Afterword by Joseba Gabilondo. Baltimore: Johns Hopkins University Press.

Villoro, Juan. 2021. *Horizontal Vertigo: A City Called Mexico.* Translated by Alfred MacAdam. New York: Pantheon Books.

Voekel, Pamela. 2002. *Alone before God: The Religious Origins of Modernity in Mexico.* Durham, NC: Duke University Press.

Wentzell, Emily. 2013. *Maturing Masculinities: Aging, Chronic Illness, and Viagra in Mexico.* Durham, NC: Duke University Press.

Wentzell, Emily. 2015. "Medical Research Participation as Citizenship: Modeling Modern Masculinity and Marriage in a Mexican Sexual Health Study." *American Anthropologist* 117 (4): 652–64.

Wentzell, Emily. 2021. *Collective Biologies: Healing Social Ills through Sexual Health Research in Mexico.* Durham, NC: Duke University Press.

Whittaker, A., and A. Speier. 2010. "'Cycling Overseas': Care, Commodification, and Stratification in Cross-border Reproductive Travel." *Medical Anthropology* 29 (4): 363–83.

Willen, Sarah S. 2007. "Toward a Critical Phenomenology of 'Illegality': State Power, Criminalization, and Abjectivity among Undocumented Migrant Workers in Tel Aviv, Israel." *International Migration* 45 (3): 8–38.

Willen, Sarah S. 2011. "Do 'Illegal' Im/migrants Have a Right to Health? Engaging Ethical Theory as Social Practice at a Tel Aviv Open Clinic." *Medical Anthropology Quarterly* 25:303–30.

Willen, Sarah S. 2012. "How Is Health-Related 'Deservingness' Reckoned? Perspectives from Unauthorized Im/Migrants in Tel-Aviv." *Social Science and Medicine* 74 (6): 812–21.

Willen, Sarah S. 2019. *Fighting for Dignity: Migrant Lives at Israel's Margins.* Philadelphia: University of Pennsylvania Press.

Williamson, Eliza K. 2020. "Interventive Care: Uncertainty, Distributed Agency, and Cesarean Section in a Zika Virus Epidemic." *Medical Anthropology Quarterly*, prepublished November 11. https://doi.org/10.1111/maq.12620.

Wilson, Richard Ashby. 2006. Afterword to "Anthropology and Human Rights in a New Key," edited by Mark Goodale. Special issue, *American Anthropologist* 108 (1): 77–83.

Wolf, Eric R. 1958. "The Virgin of Guadalupe: A Mexican National Symbol." *Journal of American Folklore* 71 (279): 34–39.

World Health Organization. 2018. *Medical Management of Abortion.* Geneva: World Health Organization.

Wright, Melissa W. 2011. "Necropolitics, Narcopolitics, and Femicide: Gendered Violence on the Mexico-U.S. Border." *Signs* 36 (3): 707–31.

Zampas, Christina, and Jaime M. Gher. 2008. "Abortion as a Human Right—International and Regional Standards." *Human Rights Law Review* 8 (2): 249–94.

Zavella, Patricia. 2016. "Contesting Structural Vulnerability through Reproductive Justice Activism with Latina Immigrants in California." *North American Dialogue* 19 (1): 36–45.

Zavella, Patricia. 2020. *The Movement for Reproductive Justice: Empowering Women of Color through Social Activism.* New York: New York University Press.

Zetterman, Eva. 2010. "Frida Kahlo's Abortions: With Reflections from a Gender Perspective on Sexual Education in Mexico." *Journal of Art History* 75 (4): 230–43.

INDEX